LEGENDARY LOCALS

OF

KEARNY

NEW JERSEY

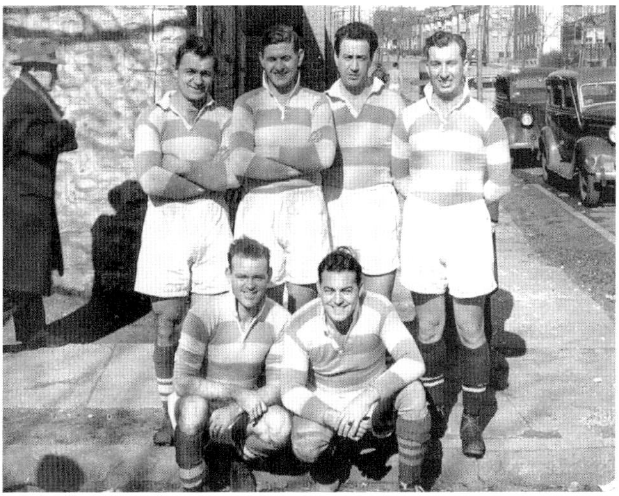

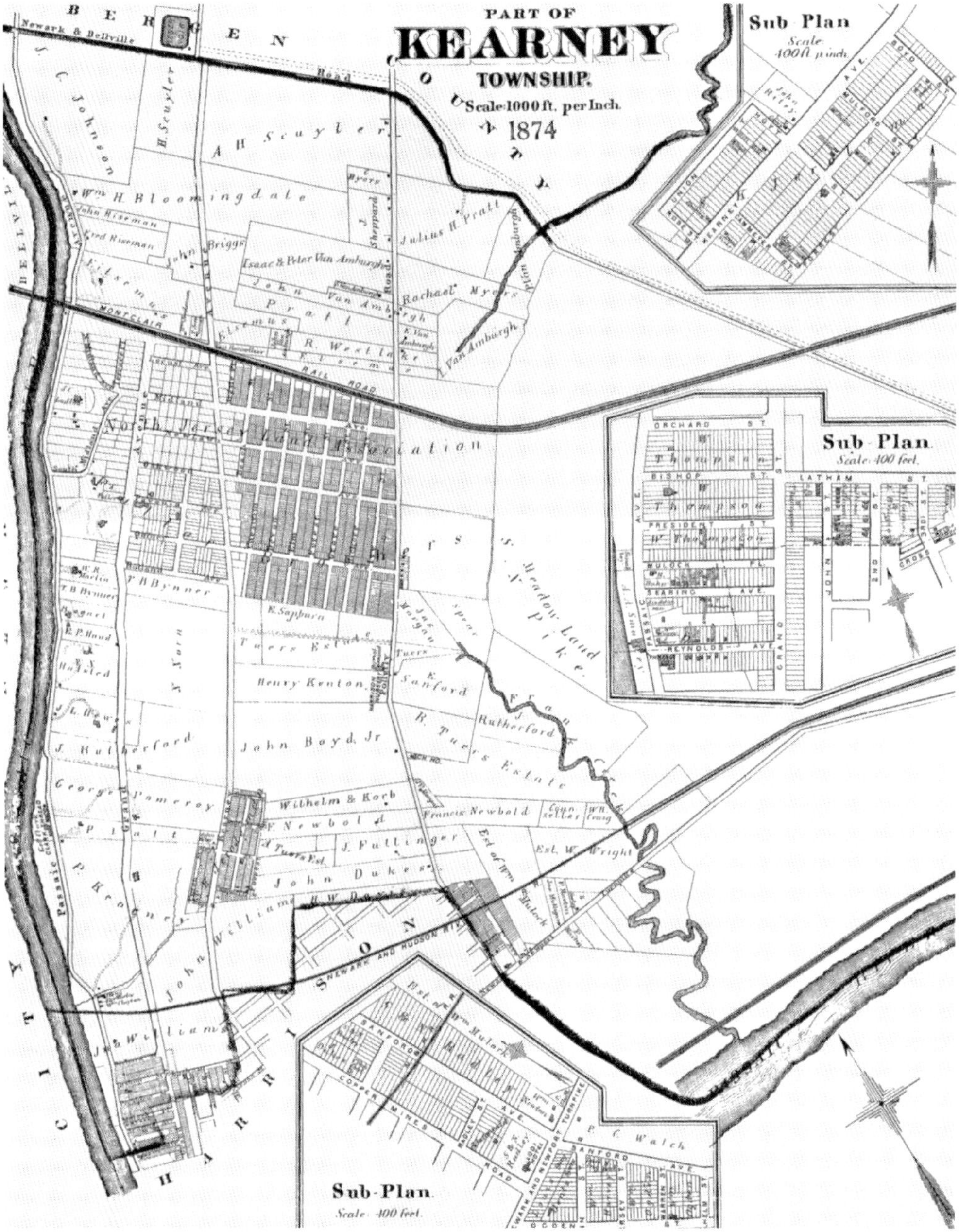

The Township of Kearny, 1874

The now urban town of more than 40,000 people was once made up of large tracts of land owned as estates. In 1880, Kearny had 777 people. (Courtesy of Kearny Museum.)

Page 1: **Soccer Town, USA**

Kearny has long been known as a birthplace of American soccer. It has produced an inordinate share of National Soccer Hall of Fame players. Shown here is the Scots American team in 1946. (Courtesy of Kearny Museum.)

LEGENDARY LOCALS

OF

KEARNY

NEW JERSEY

BARBARA KRASNER

LEGENDARY LOCALS

ISBN 978-1-4671-0224-7

Legendary Locals is an imprint of Arcadia Publishing
Charleston, South Carolina

Printed in the United States of America

Library of Congress Control Number: 2015937655

For all general information, please contact Arcadia Publishing:
Telephone 843-853-2070
Fax 843-853-0044
E-mail sales@arcadiapublishing.com
For customer service and orders:
Toll-Free 1-888-313-2665

Visit us on the Internet at www.arcadiapublishing.com

Dedication
To the people of Kearny—past, present, and future, and to my parents, Milton Krasner and Lillian Perlman Krasner, who are legendary locals to me

On the Front Cover: Clockwise from top left:
Dave Morrell, Beatlemaniac (Courtesy of Dave Morrell; see page 91), Peg Bixler, enduring elementary school teacher (Courtesy of Kearny UEZ; see page 57), Joseph Healey, Kearny's longtime mayor (Courtesy of Tom Healey; see page 13), Frank Monaco, Lincoln School principal (Courtesy of Denise Viscuso Monaco; see page 51), Edward Strong, realtor (Courtesy of the Bixler family; see page 18), Tony Mottola, jazz guitarist (Courtesy of Tony Mottola Jr.; see page 88), Bill Gordon, part owner of Argyle Fish & Chips (Courtesy of Kearny UEZ; see page 24), Ed Karolasz, Iraq War casualty (Courtesy of Krystyna Karolasz; see page 44), and Louis Lindblom, real estate developer (Courtesy of Rich Wall; see page 12).

On the Back Cover: From left to right:
Lady Liberty Barbara Toczko (Courtesy of Barbara Toczko; see page 46) and Gabriela Salvador, restorer of historical costumes (Photograph by the author; see page 98).

CONTENTS

ACKNOWLEDGMENTS

This book would not have been possible without the generosity and nostalgia of the nearly 8,000 members of the "You Know You're from Kearny If . . ." Facebook page. When I asked for nominations of legendary locals, they poured in. The caveats of inclusion in this book, however, included the availability of photos and biographical information. Therefore, unfortunately, many legendary locals could not be represented here.

I would like to express my gratitude to the Kearny Museum Committee, especially Carol Jean Doyle, Sandra McCleaster, Barbara Toczko, and Josh Humphrey for their help and guidance; John Peneda and the Kearny UEZ; St. Stephen's Church and Maureen at St. Cecelia's Church; Walter Tomasheski of the American Legion, Joseph Edwin Frobisher Jr. Post No. 99; Felicia Wivchar at the US House of Representatives; Mary Ann Matlock at the College of St. Elizabeth; Annie Pratt at USA Today Sports; Doug Oxenhorn at the New Jersey Historical Society; Joanne Nestor of the New Jersey State Archives; Jill Hershorin at the Jewish Historical Society of New Jersey; and Tom Healey.

It took a village to bring this book to fruition. Many of the photos and background information come from current and former Kearny residents. Therefore, I'd also like to thank the following people for their help: Bartner family; Ed and Peg Bixler; Bixler family; Bob Blackwell; Sharyne Blevins; Nancy Branin Waller; Donna Caputo Shandle; Lyla DeCastro; John R. DeVincenzo; Bernadette Dolan Jerry; James Fitzsimmons; Herbert Flavell; Friend family; Cilla Gillespie Nagy; Fred Gillespie; Lynn Gillespie Chater; Ellen Goodlad; Michele Gordon; Michael Gray; Barbara Hagan; Jim Hague; Susan Harsley; Fred Hartley; Carol Hearn Manley; David Hoffman; Hilary Hoffman Fandel; Christine Jablonski; Sanford Kahn; Krystyna Karolasz; Wendy Kessler; Cyndie King; Jeff Klepacki; Michelle Kraus; Lisa Krulik; Lorry Kuhrt Fitzgerald; Gail Landi; Joe McGonigal; Carole Leahy Miller; Dave Morrell; Diane Morrell; Tony Mottola, Jr.; Ron Leir; Susan Lignowski; Karen McCloud; Vicki Lerner Megna; Hugh O'Neill; Arlene Onnembo; Diane Onnembo Barone; Lou Pandolfi; Mary Lynn Pettigrew; Tom Reese; Evelyn Rocha Carson; Eileen Rogers McDonald; Norman Rutan; Ryan children; Gabriela Salvador; Chris Sands; Lawrence Sansone; Ron Schmidt; Maria Shymko; Sally Sprague; Richard Tully; Walt Whimpenny; Denise Viscuso Liptak; Lisa Wagner; Rich Wall; Mark Webster; Laura Williams; and Yamaguchi family.

INTRODUCTION

As the Town of Kearny approaches its 150th anniversary in 2017, an opportunity arises to look at the town's past, present, and future. In 1967, Mayor Joseph Healey and the town council engaged many of Kearny's civic and business leaders to commemorate the town's 100th anniversary. Town historian Jessie Hipp visited the schools where children were given assignments to write about Kearny's history or future. Items were placed in a time capsule that is now within the grounds of Memorial Park along Kearny Avenue near Quincy Avenue.

History, however, cannot be kept in a capsule. Much of what we see around town is the result of the people who came before us—the leaders who helped to develop the community economically and culturally; the soldiers who fought bravely for their loved ones and represented Kearny on the battlefield; the educators who nurtured the minds of our young and introduced them to the challenges that lay beyond our borders; the sports heroes, who often followed in their fathers' traditions to distinguish themselves on the soccer, baseball, and football fields; the healers, who selflessly gave of themselves; the musicians, artists, and writers who brought the Town of Kearny to greater heights; and, of course, our neighbors, the core of our everyday lives and those men and women who lent a helping hand.

Kearny has changed a great deal since its beginnings as the Lenni-Lenape settlement of Mighgeticock. Chief Tantaqua sold the land in 1668 to Capt. William Sandford in trust for his friend, Maj. Nathaniel Kingsland, in Barbadoes. This land, now dubbed New Barbadoes Neck, occupied an advantageous position between the Pasawack (Passaic) and Hackensack Rivers and encompassed present-day Rutherford, Lyndhurst, North Arlington, Kearny, East Newark, and Harrison. In 1671, Kingsland, who never came to America, sold the southern sections to Sandford and kept Rutherford and Lyndhurst. When Kingsland died, one-third of his land passed to his nephew, Isaac. New York trader Arent Schuyler purchased the Kingsland Plantation from Isaac Kingsland in 1710. He selected an area for his own estate, Fairlawn Manor, just below the ridge and extending to the Passaic River.

The land of New Barbadoes Neck changed to Lodi and, in 1840, to Harrison in honor of then-president William Henry Harrison. Due to Gen. Nathanael Halstead's persistent efforts in a meeting at the Lodi Hotel on Harrison Turnpike, the part of Harrison Turnpike north of Johnston Avenue adopted the name of an area resident and one of his friends, late Maj. Gen. Philip Kearny, in 1867.

With the development of thread mills and linoleum manufacturing, many Scottish and Irish workers came to Kearny. They brought along their love of soccer, and Kearny developed a reputation as the home of American soccer, yielding a disproportionate number of National Soccer Hall of Fame inductees.

The northern section of town took the name Arlington, a borough developed by the Arlington Homestead Association. It formed in 1867 and, in 1876, advertised "cheap and rural homes" on land previously held for farming "and is consequently cheaper than any other within an equal distance from New York. The property has been laid out in lots with broad avenues, handsomely graded streets, and plank walks. Here is the site of a great future city, we have one mail out and one mail in per day." Arlington was named for Arlington Heights, Virginia, because of its elevation. Arlington stretched from the Newark-Belleville Road (now the Belleville Turnpike) to Grove Street between Passaic Avenue and Pollyfly Road (now Schuyler Avenue).

We owe a debt of gratitude to those founders and shapers of the town's identity. Challenges on the national and international levels brought change to the town. Brothers, sons, and husbands were called into service. A home guard protected the community during World War I. Street names like Berlin Street changed to Liberty Street. In World War II, war bonds, victory gardens, and rallies kept spirits up and supported our loved ones.

Commerce and industry rose to meet wartime needs head-on. Several companies received the Army-Navy "E" for excellence, including Federal Shipbuilding and Dry Dock Company, Western Electric Company, and Standard Tool & Manufacturing Company. Pollack Manufacturing gave many young men their start in the workforce and generously participated in the war effort. Despite the many changes, Kearny's residents and businesses maintain a commitment to the town. The Urban Enterprise Zone (UEZ) helps local commerce thrive. New roads accommodate convenience and traffic patterns.

While celebrities have passed through Kearny—from movie stars such as Paulette Goddard and William Gargan in the 1940s and Sean Connery in the 1970s to television stars like James Gandolfini in *The Sopranos*—we have generated our own enviable roster of legendary locals of past and present. We should give thanks to them for making and keeping Kearny a diverse, adaptive, and vibrant community that keeps pace with the times.

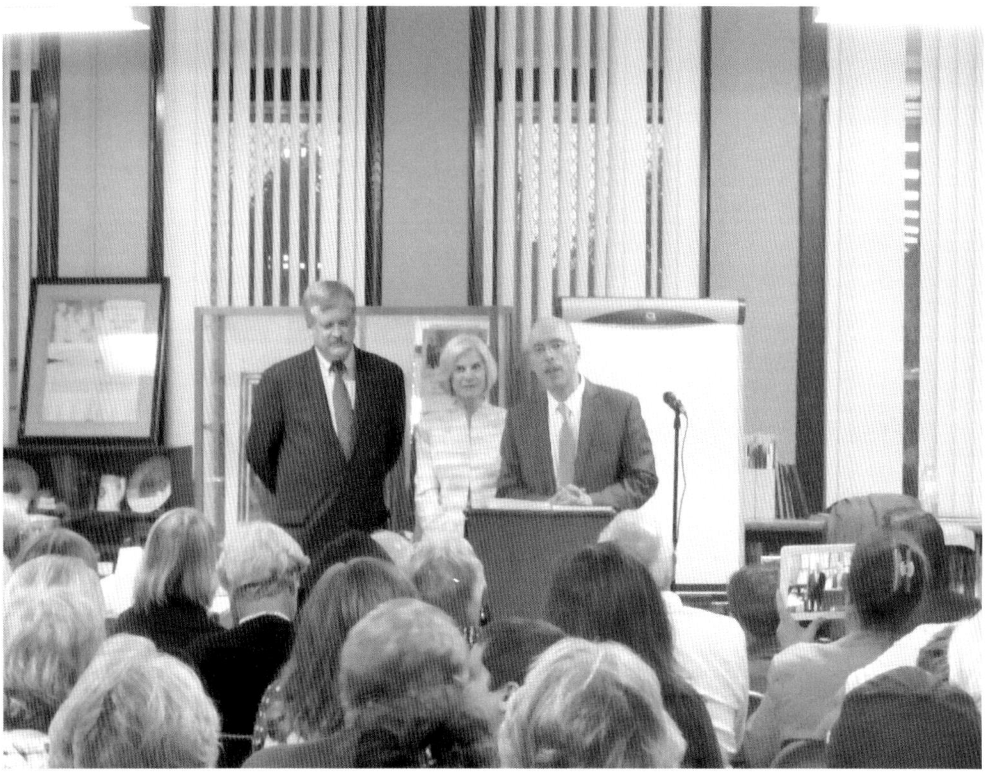

Phil Kearny's 200th Birthday Celebration

Past and present "Kearnians" came together on June 1, 2015, to celebrate Maj. Gen. Philip Kearny's 200th birthday. After a few words from Councilwoman Carol Jean Doyle, keynote speaker William Styple began a riveting narrative of Kearny's life and unfortunate death. Mayor Santos wrapped up the program with a few words of thanks and a heads-up about the Town of Kearny's upcoming 150th anniversary. (Photograph by the author.)

CHAPTER ONE

Civic and Business Leaders

Local commerce has always been an integral element of the Kearny community. Before the advent of high-speed trains and luxury buses, the local "dinky" delivered patrons to the many businesses along Van Emburgh (later named Kearny Avenue) and Midland Avenues, Elm Street, and other commercial sections.

Kearny was also home to larger industry, beginning perhaps with the arrival of thread and linen companies in the late 1800s. In 1875, Clark Thread Mills of Scotland opened two mills in Kearny. It added two more in 1890. In 1883, Marshall's Flax Spinning Company of England opened. In 1888, Sir Michael Nairn established Nairn Linoleum. Thousands of skilled Scots, Irish, and English came directly to Kearny to work in these factories. Nairn Linoleum merged with Congoleum of Philadelphia in 1924 and kept its home as a combined company in Kearny on land of the former Philip Kearny estate. The town's easy access to waterways and industrial cities like Newark and New York City made it an attractive location. Large companies found a home in the southern section of Kearny. These included Federal Shipbuilding and Dry Dock and Western Electric, both of which provided plenty of employment to Kearny's residents.

Business leaders became actively involved in the town's civic affairs. They became members of town councils and board of education committees as well as directors of real estate and banking concerns. This powerful group included real estate developers Ed Strong, Edmund Bixler, and Louis Lindblom. Gerrish Newell, general superintendent of celluloid manufacturer Arlington Company (later a subsidiary of E.I. du Pont de Nemours Company), assumed several leadership roles in the town.

The tradition of community service founded by Gen. Nathanael Halstead, Alfred King, and others of their day and improved by longtime mayor Joseph Healey and the Doyle family, continues today. Local business owners, from real estate moguls to restaurant entrepreneurs, continue a dedication to the community and the welfare of the town. Working together with municipal government, Kearny businesses celebrate success.

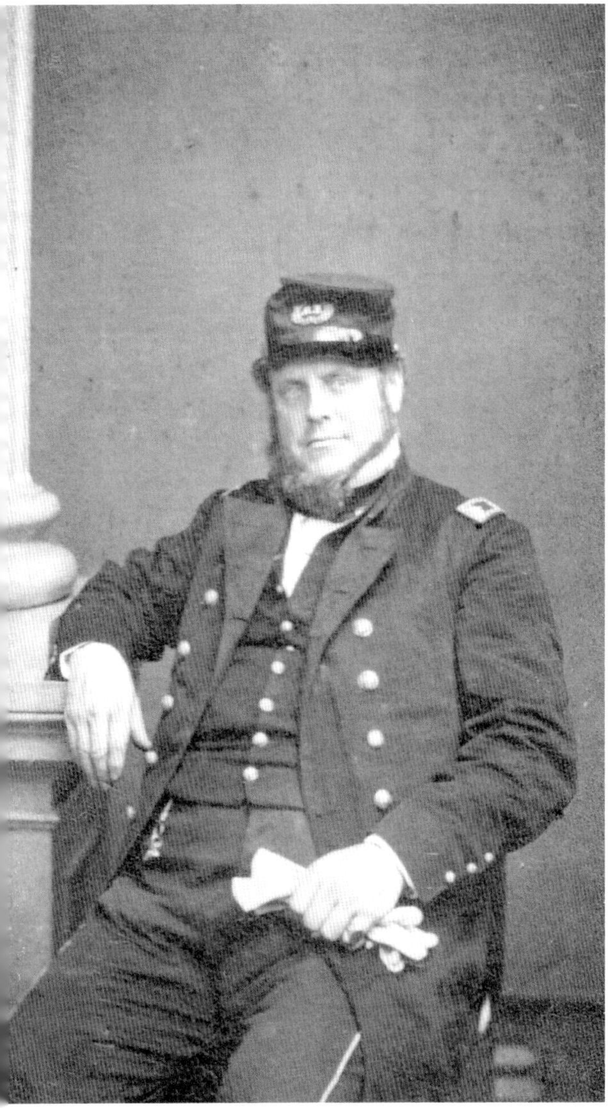

All-Around Leader and Philanthropist Nathanael Halstead

New Jersey, and especially Kearny, benefitted from the tireless leadership and philanthropic efforts of Gen. Nathanael Halstead. Born in Elizabeth in 1816, he attended a boys' seminar in Woodbridge and graduated from the College of New Jersey, now Princeton. He joined his uncle's dry goods business, where he worked his way up to partner by the age of 29. He amassed a fortune and retired in 1855. In 1860, his 40-acre Harrison estate along Passaic Avenue, "Hillside," was valued at $160,000 and would be worth nearly $5 million today. The home was built in 1853, and the property extended from the river's edge to beyond the ridge, enclosed by a wall of stonemasonry, a piece of which is still evident today on the east side of Passaic Avenue, north of Hoyt Street. Many structures comprised the estate, including a porter's lodge, a group of barns, henhouses, a corncrib, stables with a repair shop, and farmhand homes. A confidante of President Lincoln, Halstead received an appointment in the early years of the Civil War as lieutenant colonel on the New Jersey governor's staff. He was then placed in command of militia training camps in Trenton as a brigadier general. After the war, Halstead turned his attention to other matters. The town's first chairman of the board in 1867, he led efforts for incorporation and to rename the town after his friend, the late Maj. Gen. Philip Kearny. Despite appearances, such as running his household with four servants in 1870, Halstead gave generously of his money and time. Through an ample endowment, an astronomical observatory at Princeton University bore his name until 1932, when it was razed. He was first president of the New Jersey Agricultural Society and was lauded as a benefactor by the New Jersey Historical Society. He donated the land for Knox Presbyterian Church. Halstead is also known as a developer of a hand-propelled submarine, the *Intelligent Whale*, built during the Civil War. Halstead took his family for rides on the Passaic River in the submarine, but it failed Navy tests. He was a founder of the Washington Association of New Jersey, with the mission of preserving George Washington's Morristown headquarters as a public historical site. The retired merchant-turned-farmer met an untimely death when the ex-boyfriend of his mistress shot and killed him in Newark in 1884. Halstead Street is named for him. (Courtesy of New Jersey Historical Society.)

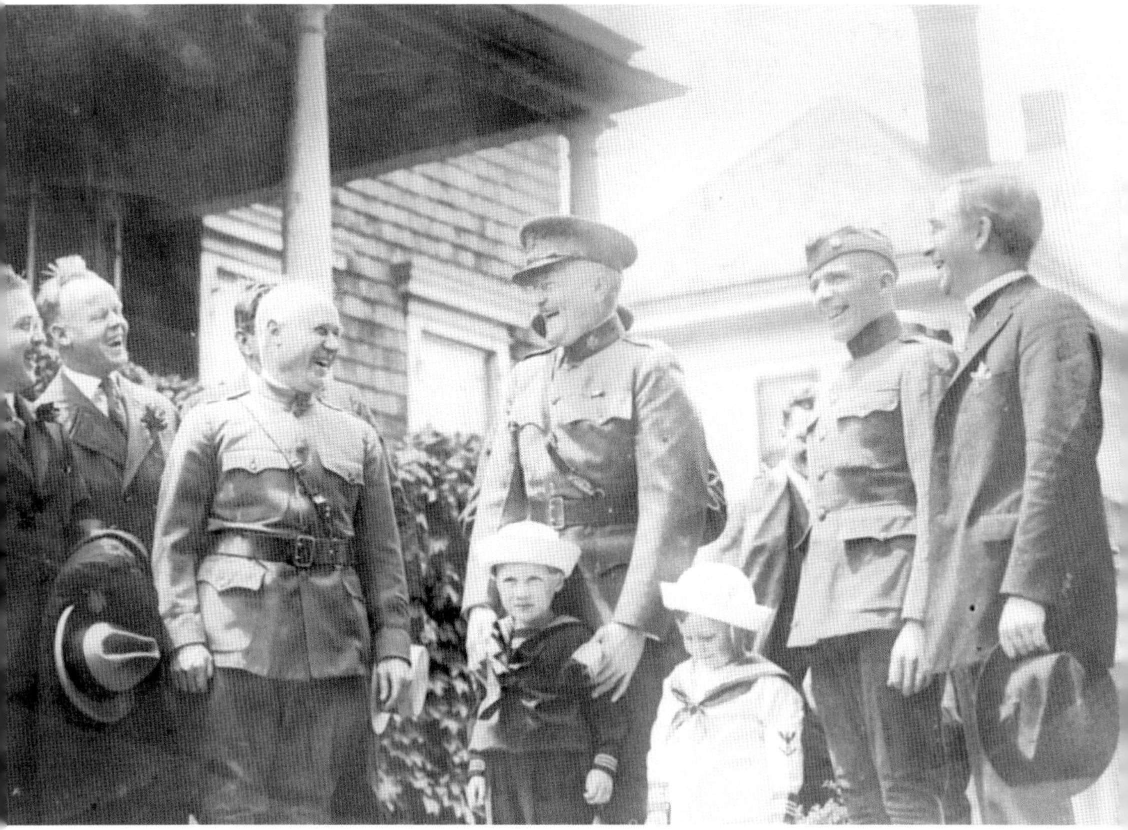

Maj. Gerrish Newell, Well-Connected Manufacturer
Gerrish Newell was born in Connecticut in 1873. After graduating from Harvard in the class of 1898, he entered the business of celluloid manufacturing. That brought him to the Arlington Company in Kearny. He rose up the corporate chain to become the company's general superintendent. The position gave him cachet, and he became a director of the First National Bank of Arlington and of the Arlington Building and Loan Association. When the United States entered World War I in 1917, he was called into service as captain of the 1st New Jersey Infantry. After his engagement in the 1918 Argonne Offensive, he was promoted to major. He played a significant role in getting Gen. John J. Pershing to Kearny, as shown here at Newell's Seeley Avenue home, for the dedication of the World War I memorial in 1922. He died in 1941. (Courtesy of the Kearny Museum.)

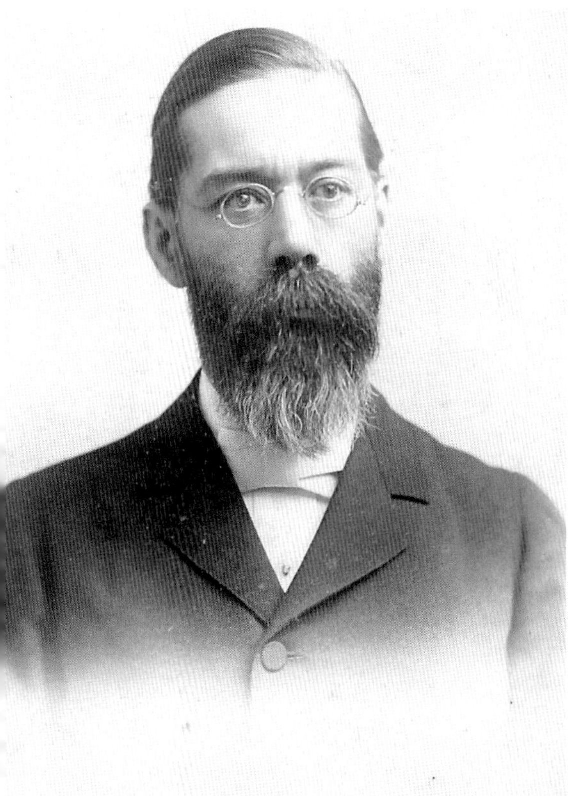

The "Swedish King," Louis W. Lindblom

A member of Kearny's Swedish community, Louis W. Lindblom was a founder of the First National Bank and the Building and Loan Association and a member of the committee that established the Kearny Public Library. Lindblom was a prominent Midland Avenue real estate developer, building up Kearny's Arlington section from the Erie Lackawanna Railroad cut to Oakwood Avenue. Born in Lindesberg, Sweden, in 1850, he came to America in 1870. (Courtesy of Rich Wall.)

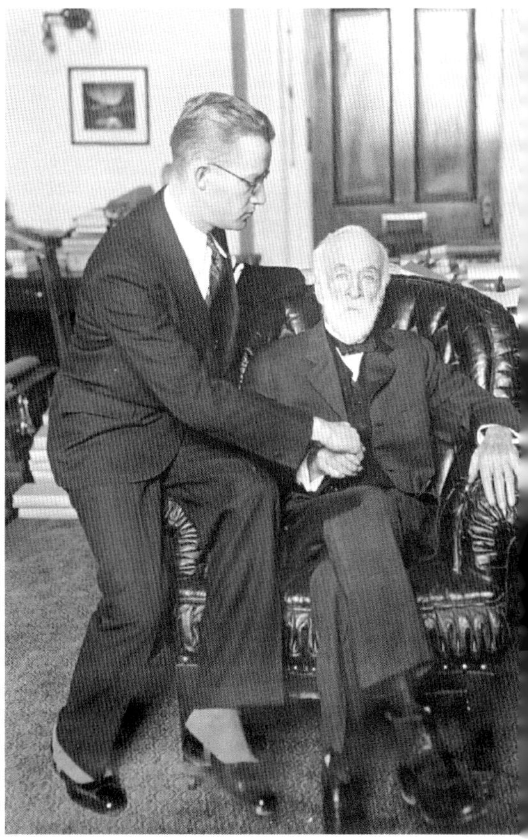

Congressman Fred Allan Hartley Jr.

Cocreator of the Taft-Hartley Act of 1947, Fred Allan Hartley Jr. of Livingston Avenue was elected Kearny library commissioner in 1923 and 1924. He served as police and fire commissioner from 1924 to 1928. Then, he was elected to Congress and served from 1929 to 1949. The youngest member of Congress in 1930, here he sits on the lap of the eldest member of Congress, Civil War veteran Charles Stedman. (Courtesy of the Collection of the US House of Representatives.)

Kearny's Longtime Mayor, Joseph M. Healey Sr.

Joe Healey served as Kearny's mayor from 1950 to 1969, and his history parallels Kearny itself. Born at 173 Johnston Street in 1910, he was the first surviving son of Irish immigrants Michael and Winifred Gannon Healey. Joe attended Kearny High School. But when his father sustained a burn injury at Clark Thread and his drinking worsened, Joe had to drop out after his sophomore year to support his family. "Kearny Castle," town namesake Philip Kearny's chateau-like home, was on Joe's newspaper route. He witnessed the landmark's demolition and according to his family, announced to his friends that if he had been mayor, he would have stopped it. In 1932, during the Great Depression, he was out of work and ran for town tax collector. While he lost the overall election, he won for the Second Ward, where he lived. With that kind of support, Joe ran for the Second Ward seat on the town council the following year and won. He served on the town council from 1934 to 1949. When he confided in friends and family that he wanted to run for mayor, his mother-in-law and members of the Catholic and Irish American communities advised against it. Joe was the first-ever Catholic mayoral candidate in Kearny and would face a tough race. He vowed to knock on every door in town. Although he won, his campaign efforts physically weakened him. As mayor, Joe's focus was on building the community, not political organizations, in this new postwar era. He appointed a school board comprised not of cronies but of people who cared about education, including the first Jewish member, Saul J. Abraham; the first female member, Belle Theobald; and the first African American member, Edwina Gwynn. He founded community organizations, including the Friends of Erin, and held leadership positions such as trustee of St. Cecilia Church. He focused on public safety, recreation, and economic health. The highlight of his administration was the 1967 town centennial, celebrated with a yearlong gala. He decided not to run for reelection in 1969 due to illness. Instead, he sought and won election to the New Jersey Assembly and served for two years. He died in 1973 from an illness linked to issues he suffered during his initial mayoral campaign. The photograph here shows Joe kissing his wife, possibly after his 1949 election. (Courtesy of Tom Healey.)

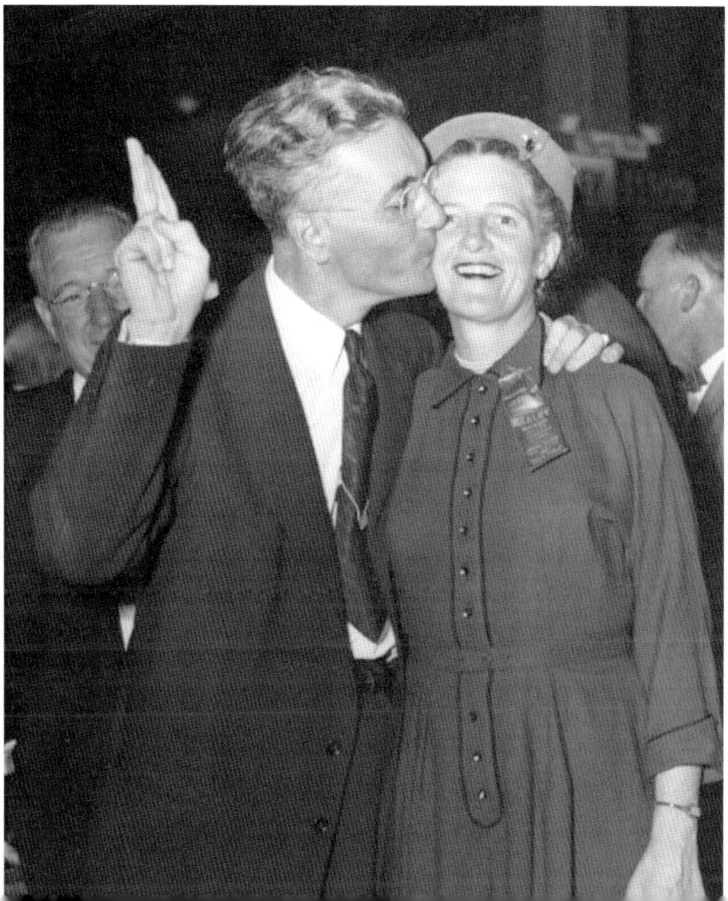

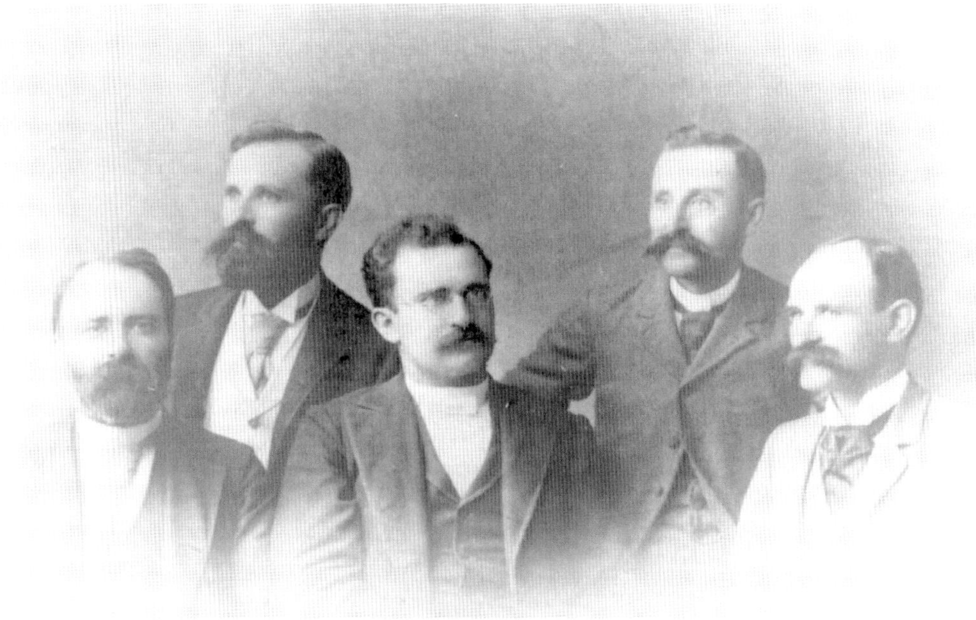

"Remember the Maine" Alfred King

In 1898, the USS *Maine* exploded in Cuba's Havana harbor, sparking the Spanish-American War. Born in Nova Scotia, Canada, in 1842, Civil War veteran Alfred Erling King successfully waged a campaign in 1912 to raise the USS *Maine* and honor its remains and crew with dignity. Pres. William Taft presented the Town of Kearny with a 500-pound shell from the ship. The shell and one of the ship's cannons stand in Town Hall Park. When King died in 1927, flags were lowered all over town. King Street may possibly be named for him. He is shown here, to the far left, with his brothers. (Courtesy of Cyndie King and the Kearny Museum.)

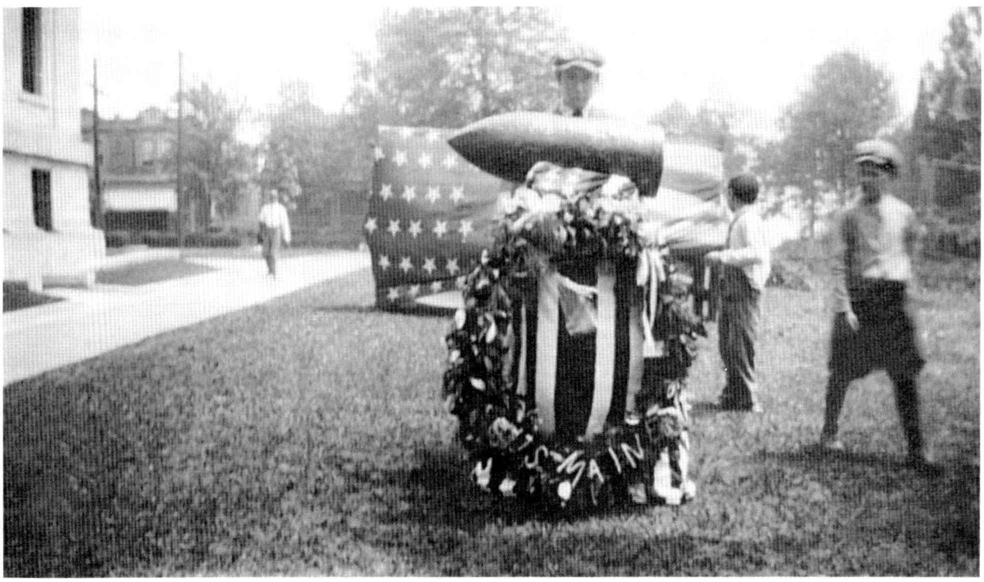

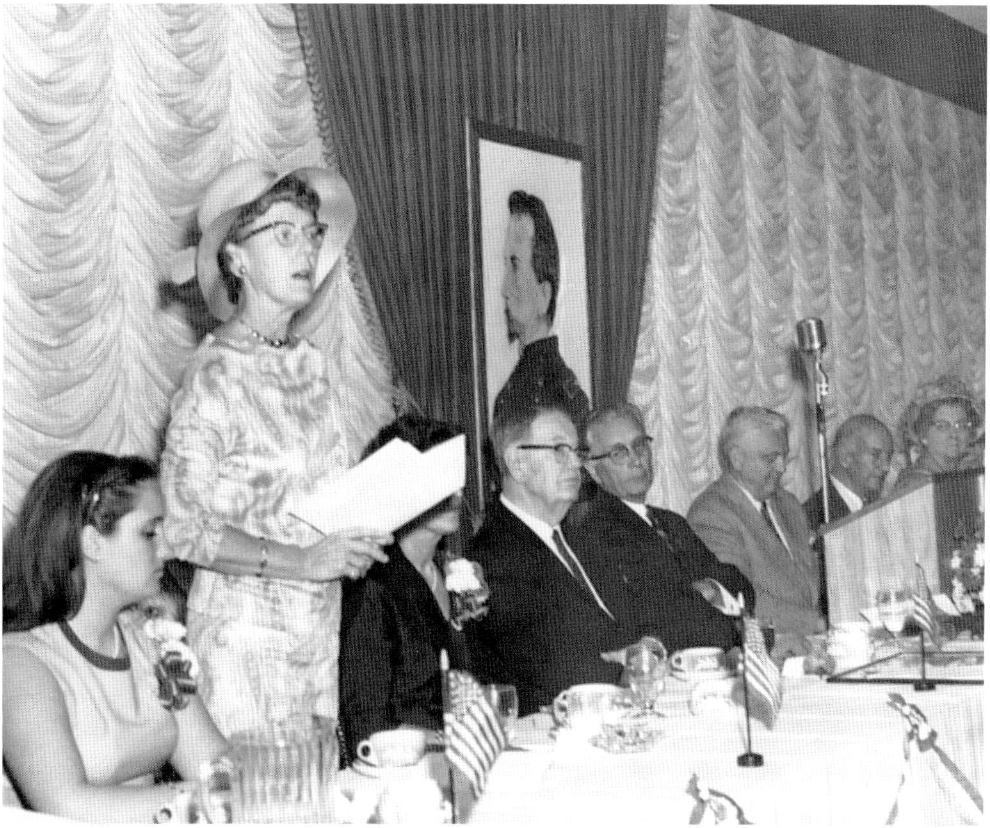

Kearny's First Town Historian, Jessie Hipp

Born in 1909, Jessie Goodison Hipp was instrumental in documenting Kearny's town history, including walking tours and proposals for historic landmark preservation. During Kearny's 1967 centennial year, she visited the elementary schools and talked about the town history, among her many duties. She was a founder of the Kearny Museum. Without her pioneering efforts, much of Kearny's history would have been lost. (Courtesy of the Kearny Museum.)

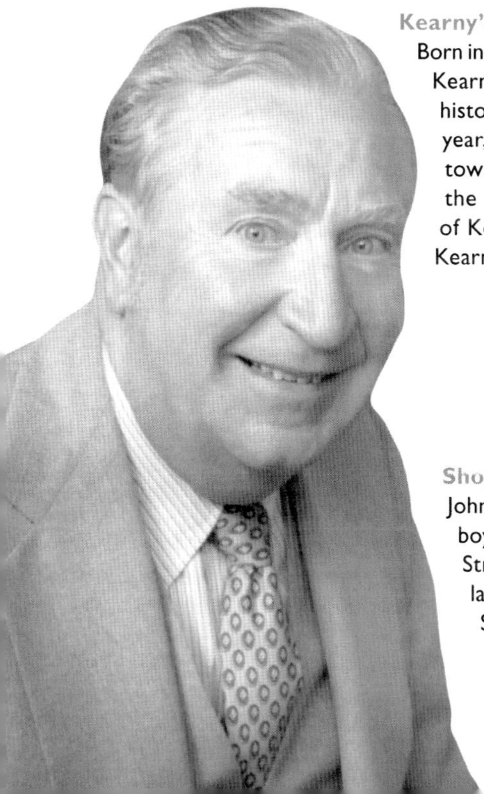

Shop-Rite Founder John Tully

John Tully's career in the grocery business began as a delivery boy in 1928 at age 14. He opened Tully's Market on Beech Street between Stewart and Magnolia Avenues in 1937 and later helped to found Wakefern Food Corporation and Shop-Rite. In 1966, he opened the Shop-Rite on Passaic Avenue, one of the area's largest supermarkets of that time. (Courtesy of Richard Tully.)

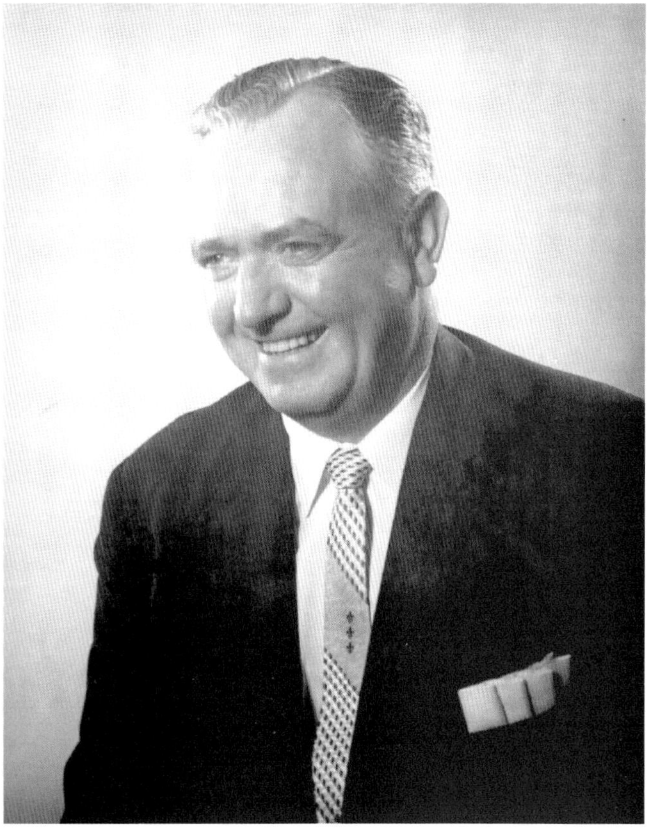

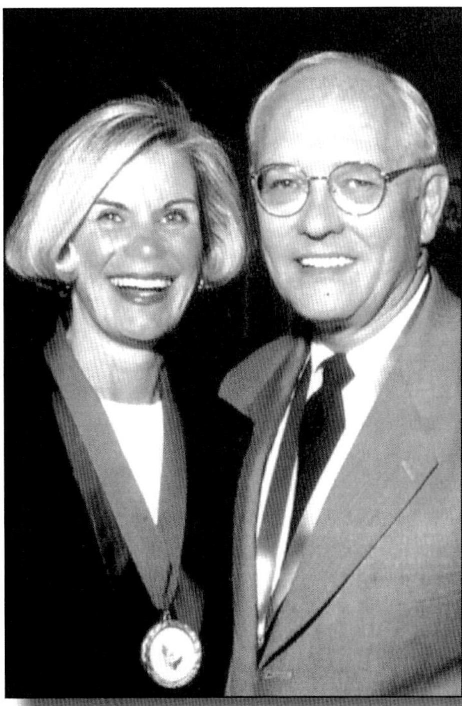

The Doyle Family, Committed to Community Service

Norman Doyle Sr. founded the family's public service pedigree. He served as councilman for the First Ward for many years. His constituents remember his kindness and willingness to help in any way he could. A pavilion in Riverside Park is named for him. His son, Norman Doyle Jr., served as the town attorney, general legal adviser to the mayor, and town council member for many years. His wife, Carol Jean, has volunteered in Kearny for nearly 50 years. She has represented the Third Ward on the town council since 1998. She has served on many committees, including as president of the Woman's Club of Arlington, the American Legion Auxiliary Unit No. 99, and the Hudson County American Cancer Society. She chairs the Passaic River Clean-Up, Senior Picnic, Memorial Day Parade, and the Christmas Giving Tree events annually. (Above, courtesy of the Kearny Museum; below and opposite page below, courtesy of Carol Jean Doyle; opposite page above, photograph by the author.)

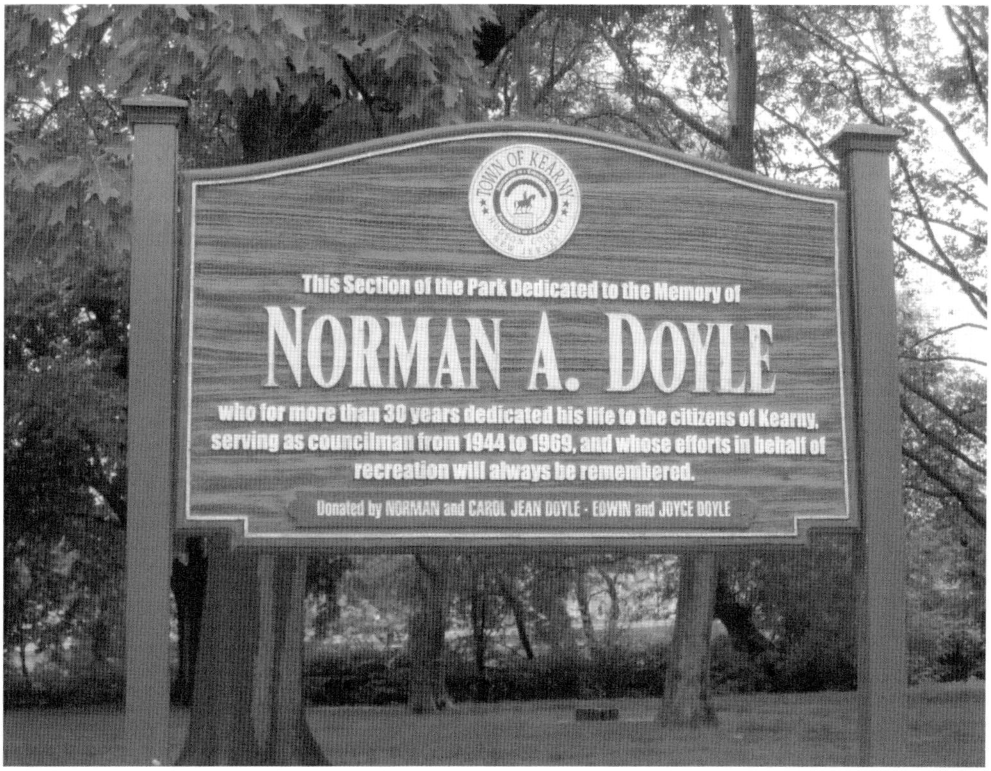
TOWN OF KEARNY
This Section of the Park Dedicated to the Memory of
NORMAN A. DOYLE
who for more than 30 years dedicated his life to the citizens of Kearny,
serving as councilman from 1944 to 1969, and whose efforts in behalf of
recreation will always be remembered.
Donated by NORMAN and CAROL JEAN DOYLE - EDWIN and JOYCE DOYLE

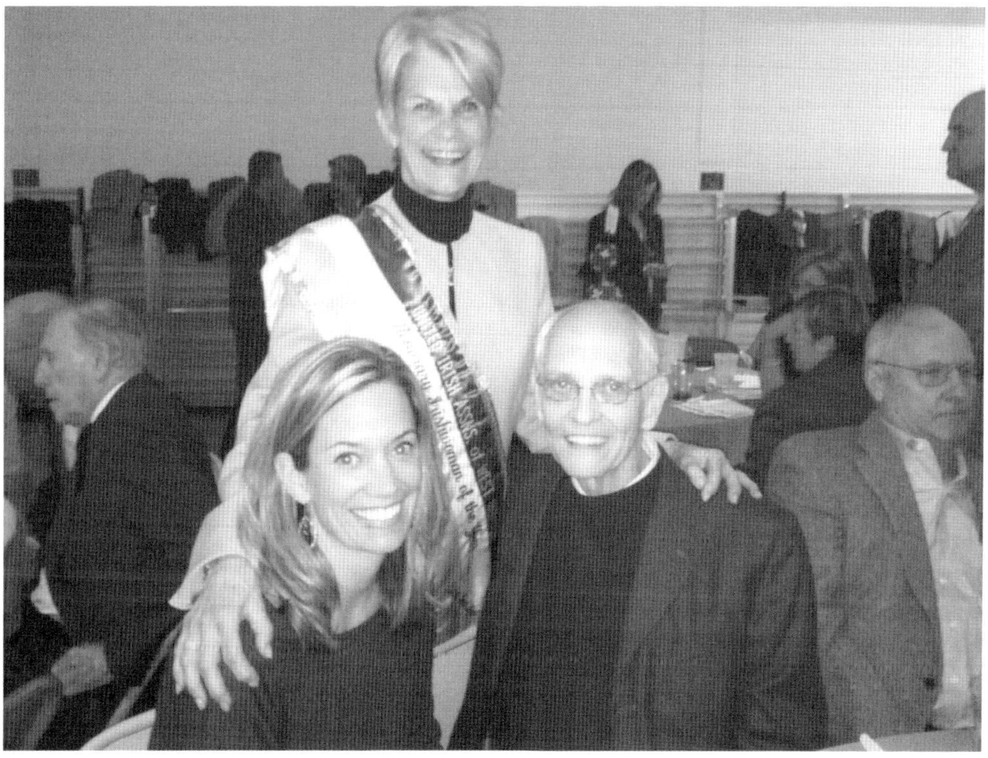

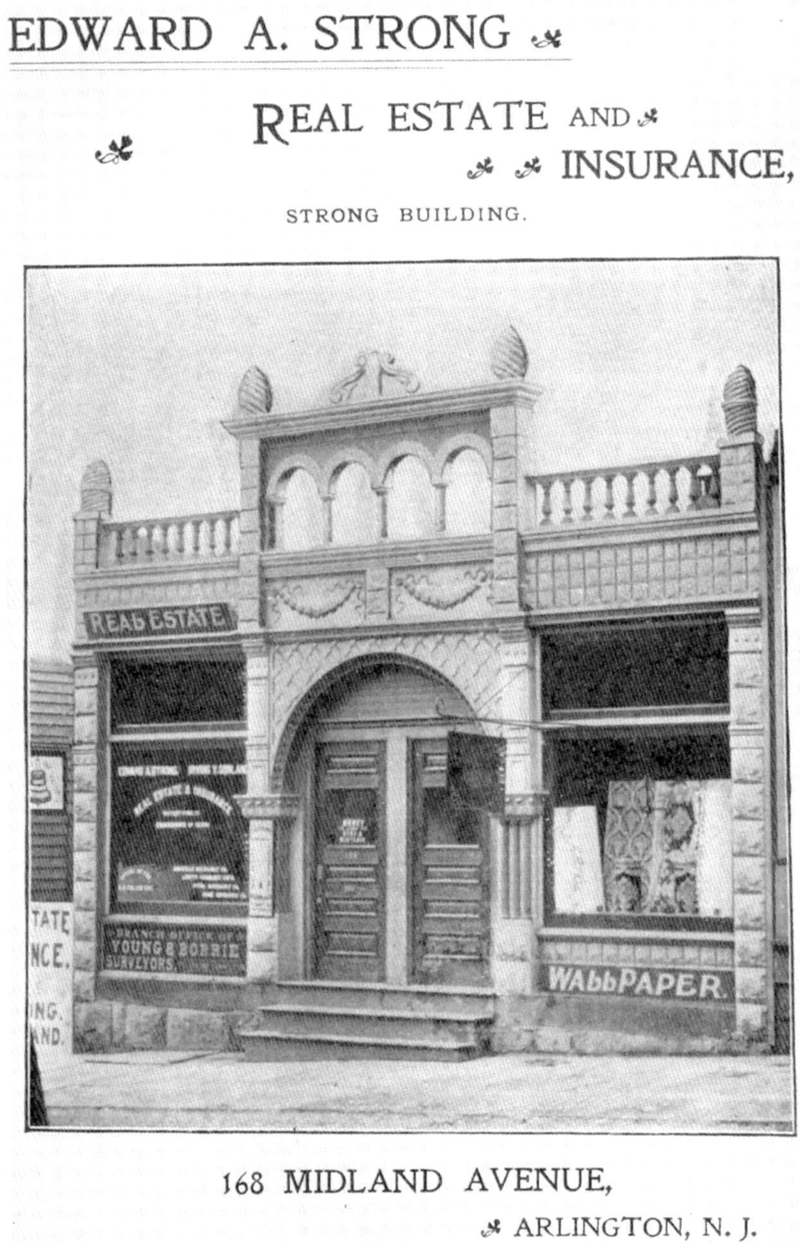

Edward A. Strong, Founder of a Real Estate and Community Tradition

In 1891, Edward A. Strong opened a real estate and insurance business on Midland Avenue, founding the Bixler Group LLC. Strong moved to Kearny from New York City in 1882 at age 20. He became a leader in the town and continued in community service for many decades. He served as a volunteer fireman, was a charter member of the Kearny Elks Lodge, helped organize the Arlington Country Club, and served as president of the Arlington Choral Society. Furthermore, he was one of the organizers and founders of the First Presbyterian Church of Arlington, the First National Bank and Trust Company of Kearny, and the Kearny Federal Savings and Loan Association. He was instrumental in developing the Fairlawn Manor section of Kearny. (Courtesy of the Kearny Museum.)

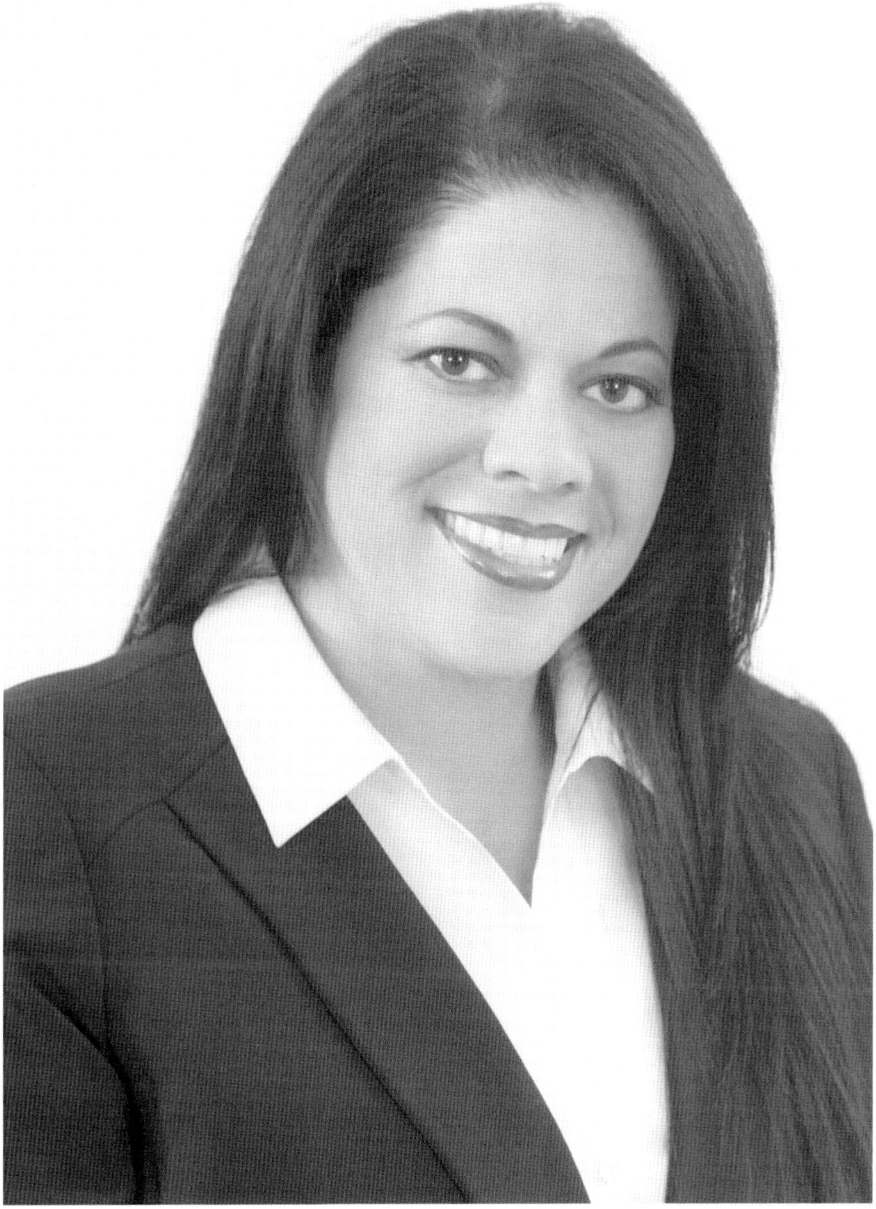

First Ward Councilwoman Marytrine de Castro
A New Jersey/New York registered nurse, Marytrine de Castro works as an occupational health nurse in Jersey City. She attended Franklin School, Kearny High School, and the Kearny Portuguese School (Escola de Lingua e Cultura Portuguesas de Kearny). She has lived in Kearny for 41 years and in the First Ward for the past 19 years. She serves the town in a variety of ways, including membership in the Portuguese Cultural Association of Kearny and the Board of Health. She has also volunteered in the Passaic River Clean-up, March of Dimes, Breast Cancer Walk for the Cure, and the Lupus Walk. (Photograph by Jenifer Studio, courtesy of Marytrine de Castro.)

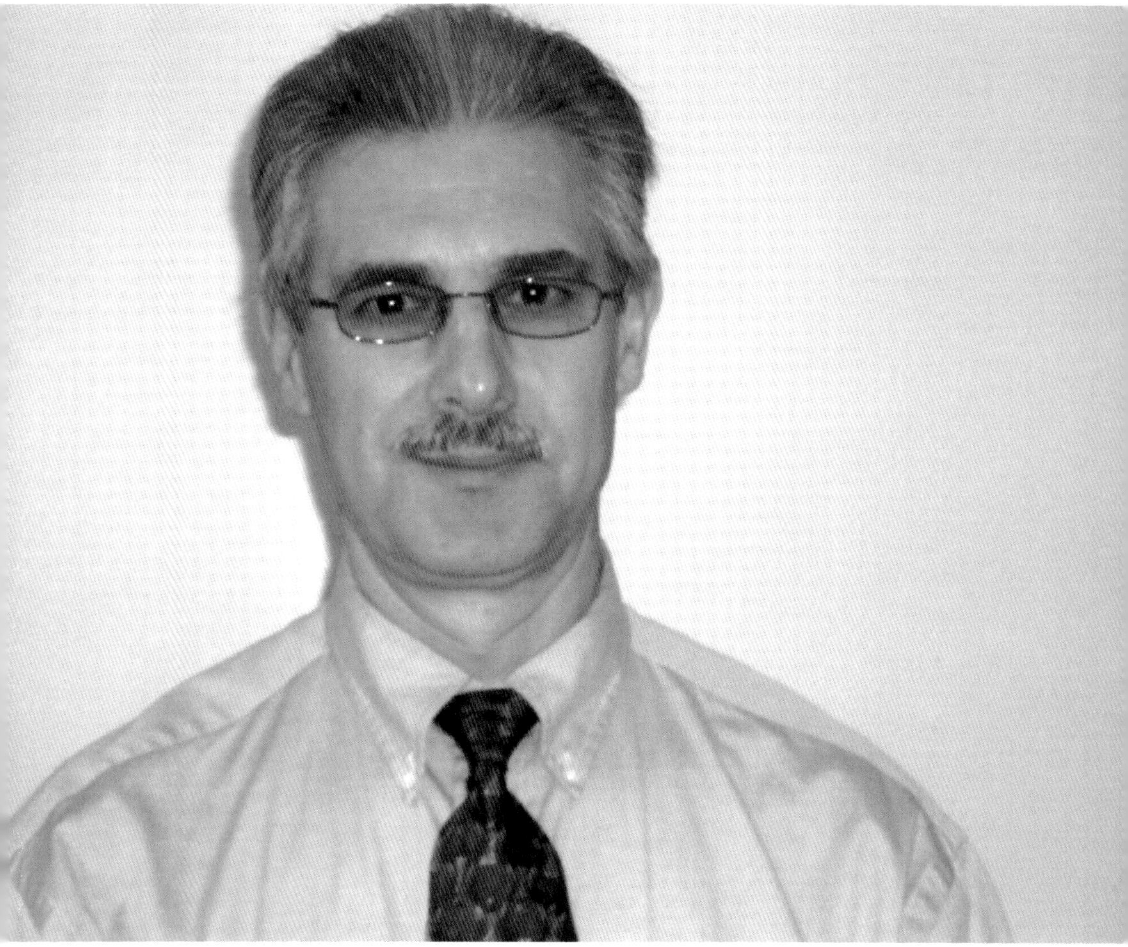

First Ward Councilman Albino Cardoso
Born in Portugal and raised in a Portuguese colony in Angola, Albino Cardoso came to the United States in 1981. He has lived in the First Ward for 28 years. Once he became a US citizen in 1988, he began serving the Town of Kearny in voluntary and civic organizations. Aside from representing First Ward interests, Cardoso has served as a commissioner for eight years and vice-chair for five years on Kearny's Zoning Board of Adjustment. He was a major advocate for a monument to honor the contributions of the town's Portuguese community, which was unveiled in June 2014 at Riverbank Park. He is a member of the Parish Council at St. Cecilia Church as serves as president of the Portuguese Holy Family Association. He belongs to the Portuguese Cultural Association of Kearny. (Courtesy of Albino Cardoso.)

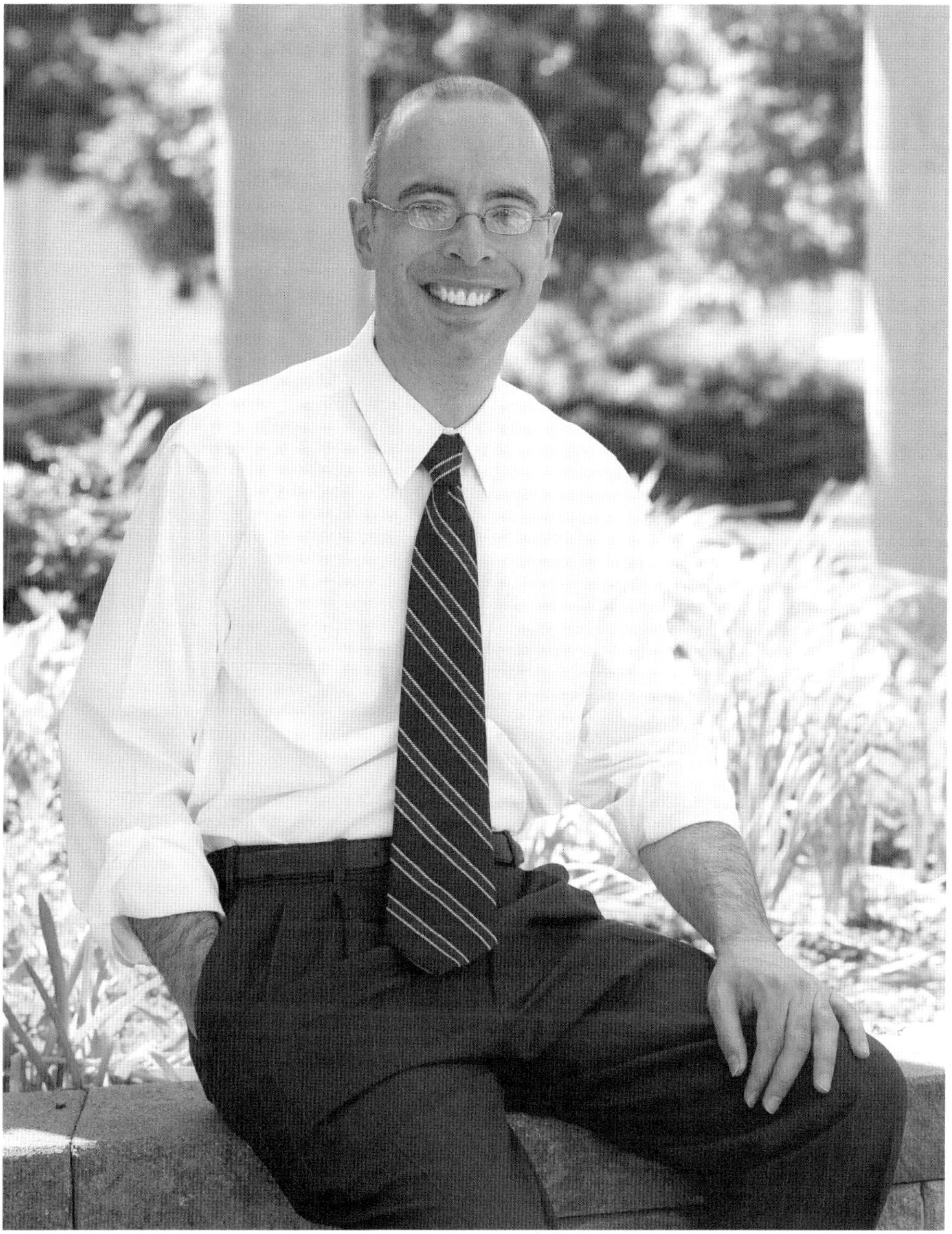

Alberto Santos, Mayor for the New Millennium
Born in Venezuela in 1965 to Portuguese parents, Domingos Santos and Doralice Craco, Alberto Santos immigrated to the United States in 1970 and settled in Kearny in 1979. Mayor Santos received his bachelor's degree from Georgetown University's Edmund A. Walsh School of Foreign Service and his Juris Doctor and LLM in Tax Law from New York University. He worked as an associate in New York City and Newark law offices and served as councilman for the Second Ward one year prior to his mayoral election. He has served as Kearny's mayor since 2000 and was most recently elected to a four-year term in 2013. (Courtesy of Kearny UEZ.)

Mayor Daniel T. Sansone, "Man of the People"

Daniel Sansone, born in 1927 to Italian immigrants, served as Kearny's mayor from 1988 to 1991. He is memorialized with a Riverbank Park plaque, testifying to his community leadership. He served on the town council from 1978 to 1985. He is perhaps best remembered for reintroducing holiday celebrations, such as the Halloween parade and Fourth of July fireworks, that had disappeared through budget cuts. Sansone passed away in 1992. (Courtesy of Lawrence Sansone.)

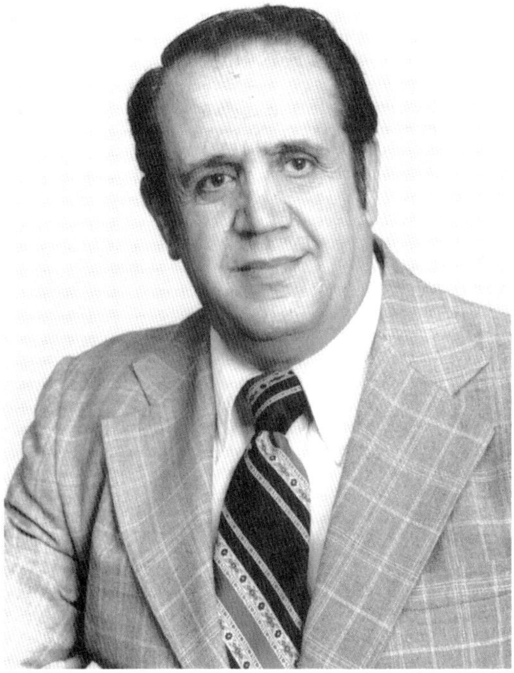

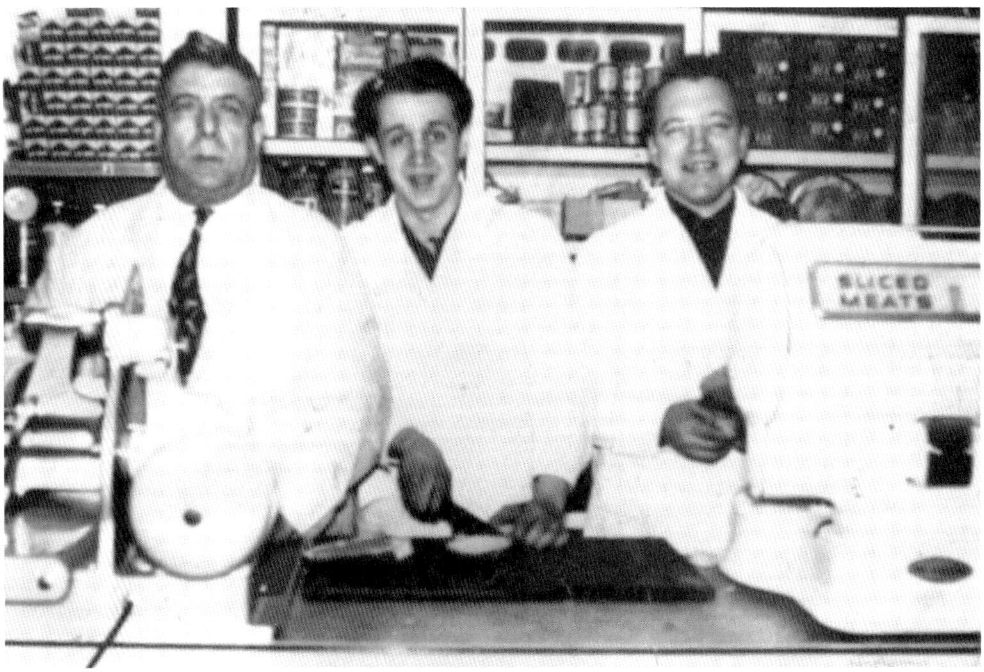

The Sansone Family Business Gave Hope in Hard Times

Working with their father, Joe, Danny and Tony manned the counter at Sansone's Market at 461–463 Elm Street. The well-known Italian grocery store operated for more than 60 years. Joe's generosity helped many people through hard times. (Courtesy of Lawrence Sansone.)

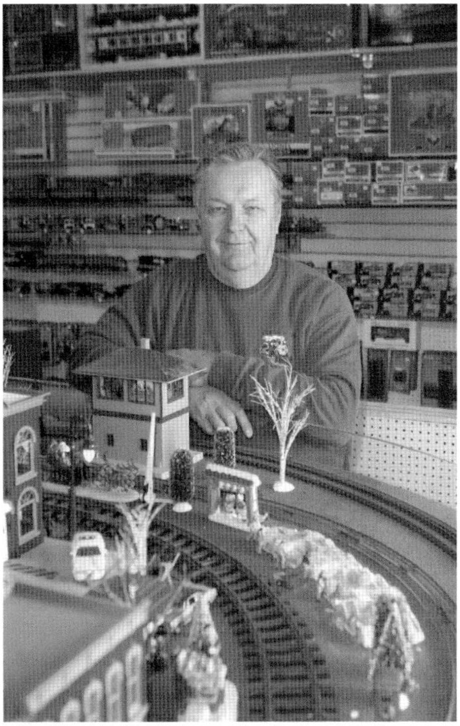

Gene Pakulniewicz and Kearny's Grand Central Station
Gene Pakulniewicz owned gas stations in Jersey City for 25 years. He sold trains from the front office as a hobby—a hobby that refused to let go. Years later, he turned his hobby into a full-time business when he opened Grand Central Station on the Belleville Turnpike, southeast of the Kearny Avenue and Ridge Road intersection. (Courtesy of Kearny UEZ.)

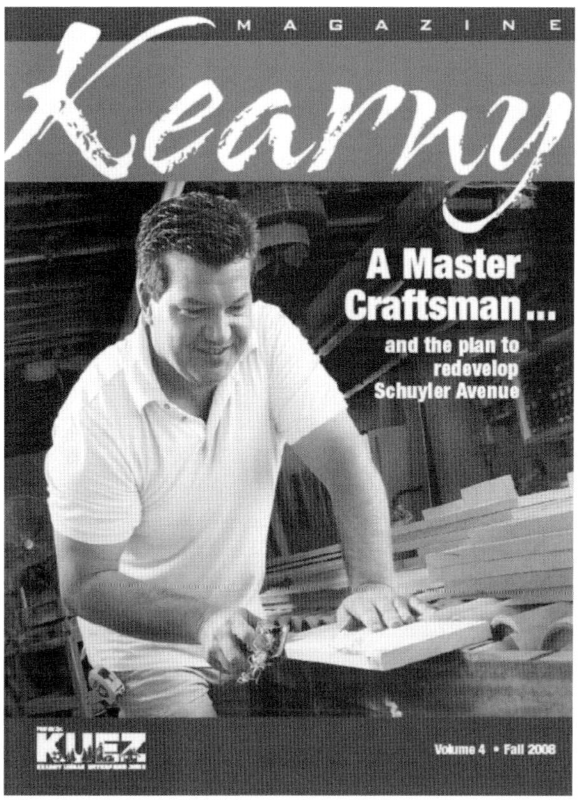

Master Craftsman, Second Ward Councilman Jon Giordano
The name Giordano in Kearny has come to be synonymous with high-quality woodworking. Jon Giordano, owner of West Hudson Lumber & Millwork, is the third generation Giordano to be in the cabinet-manufacturing business. He is also the president of Josam Realty, managing more than three acres and seven industrial complex warehouses. He has served as a councilman for the Second Ward since 2014. (Courtesy of Kearny UEZ.)

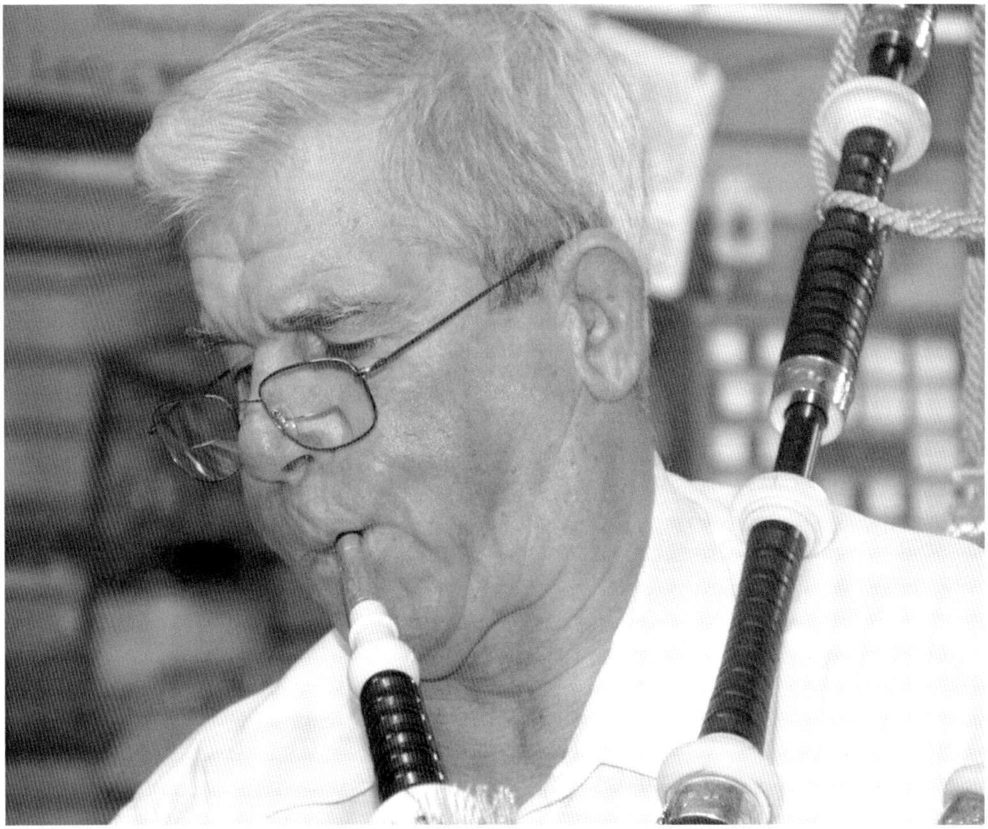

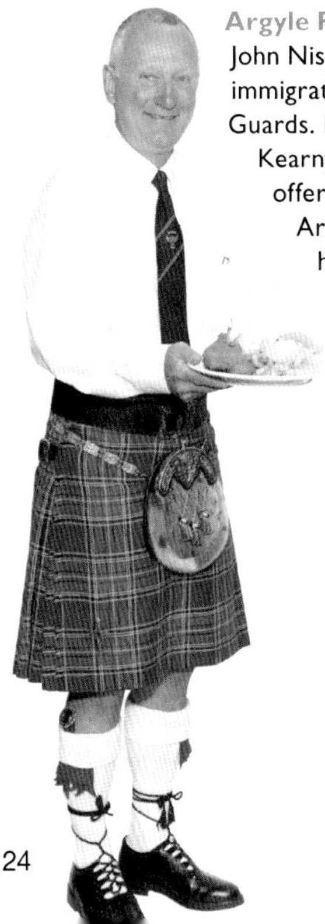

Argyle Fish & Chips John "Jock" Nisbet and Bill Gordon

John Nisbet was born in Scotland and has deep roots in the piping community. He immigrated to America in 1962 after serving in the British Army and the Scotch Guards. He lived in Brooklyn and was a tool and die maker. Then, he heard about Kearny's Scottish community. He is a champion piper, and with his son, Colin, offers piping for hire. Bill Gordon, born and raised in Kearny, worked at the Argyle part-time in 1971 while still attending Montclair State College. He and his wife, Michele, became part owners with Nisbet and his Northern Irish wife, Joan, in 1983. Many fans attend the annual birthday celebration of poet Robert Burns at the Argyle and witness the "addressing the haggis" ceremony. Since 1982, the Nisbets have owned The Piper's Cove, the adjoining store that celebrates Scottish and Irish heritage. (Above, courtesy of Michele Gordon; left, courtesy of Kearny UEZ.)

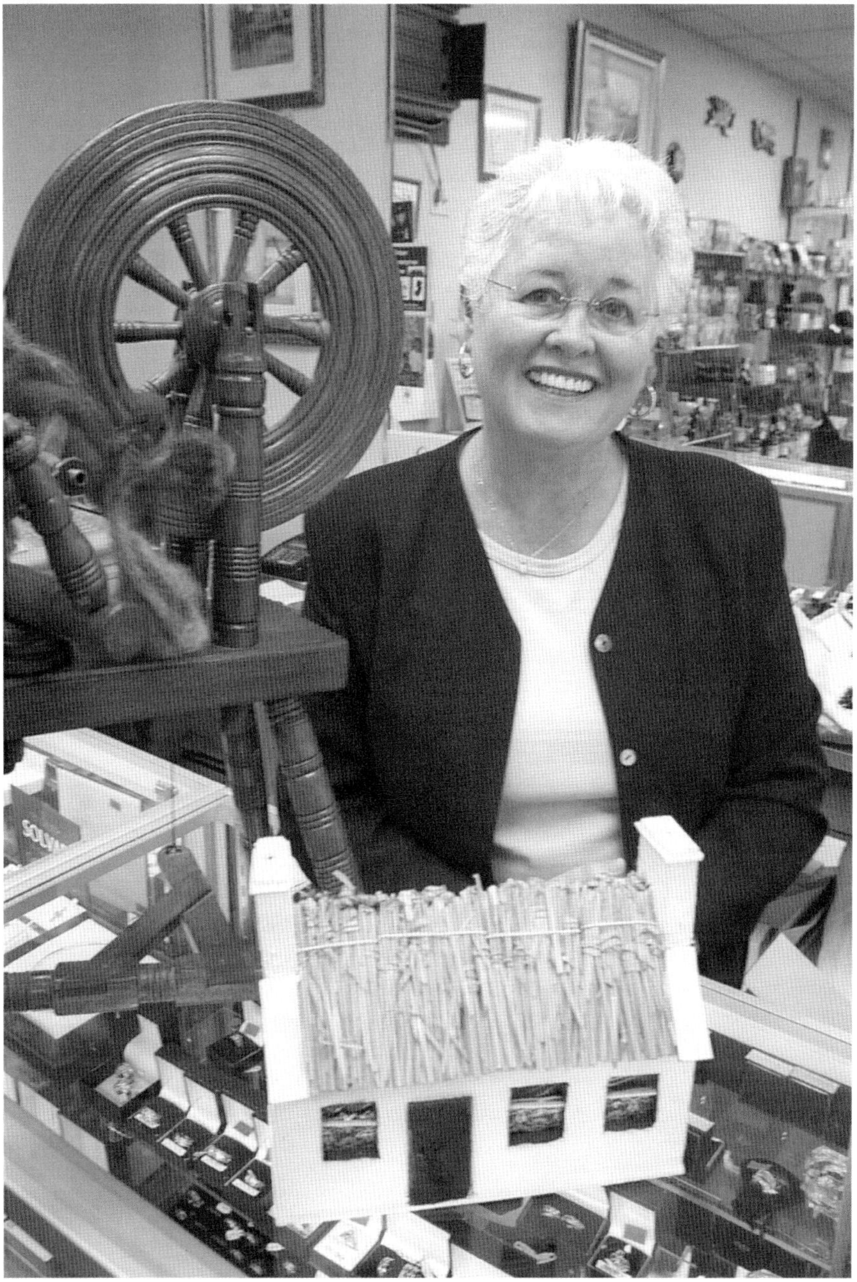

Maggie Millar and the Luck of the Irish

Eighteen-year-old Maggie Millar immigrated to the United States from County Donegal, Ireland, in 1962. Living among her sister and aunts and uncles in Brooklyn, she worked first for a New York City bank and then a brokerage firm. When she married her husband, Peter, she moved to Kearny in 1969 to start a family. Once her two children grew older, Millar took a part-time position at the Irish Quality Shop, then owned by Peter Murphy. She worked there nearly 20 years. Murphy offered her the business in 2004 when he wanted to retire. She accepted and moved the shop to 465 Kearny Avenue, formerly a tailor shop. As luck would have it, the new location even had a green awning. (Courtesy of Kearny UEZ.)

Lawyer Fred "Fritz" Gillespie

Frederick "Fritz" Gillespie was born in Kearny in 1916 and graduated from Kearny High School in 1933. Upon graduation from Gettysburg College, he received his commission as second lieutenant of the US Army Reserve. At the same time, he earned his law degree from the New Jersey School of Law. In 1941, he entered active duty and, in 1942, became the youngest full colonel commissioned at that time; he was 27. He was associated with Gillespie, Gillespie & Jablonski Law Offices for 68 years. He served as counsel for various churches, banks, and the Kearny Arlington Board of Realtors. A lifelong supporter of scouting, he served as counsel for the West Hudson Girl Scout Council. He chaired fundraising activities for the American Red Cross and served on the board of directors of the Salvation Army Kearny Corps and of Clara Maas Hospital for 25 years. (Courtesy of Lynn Gillespie Chater.)

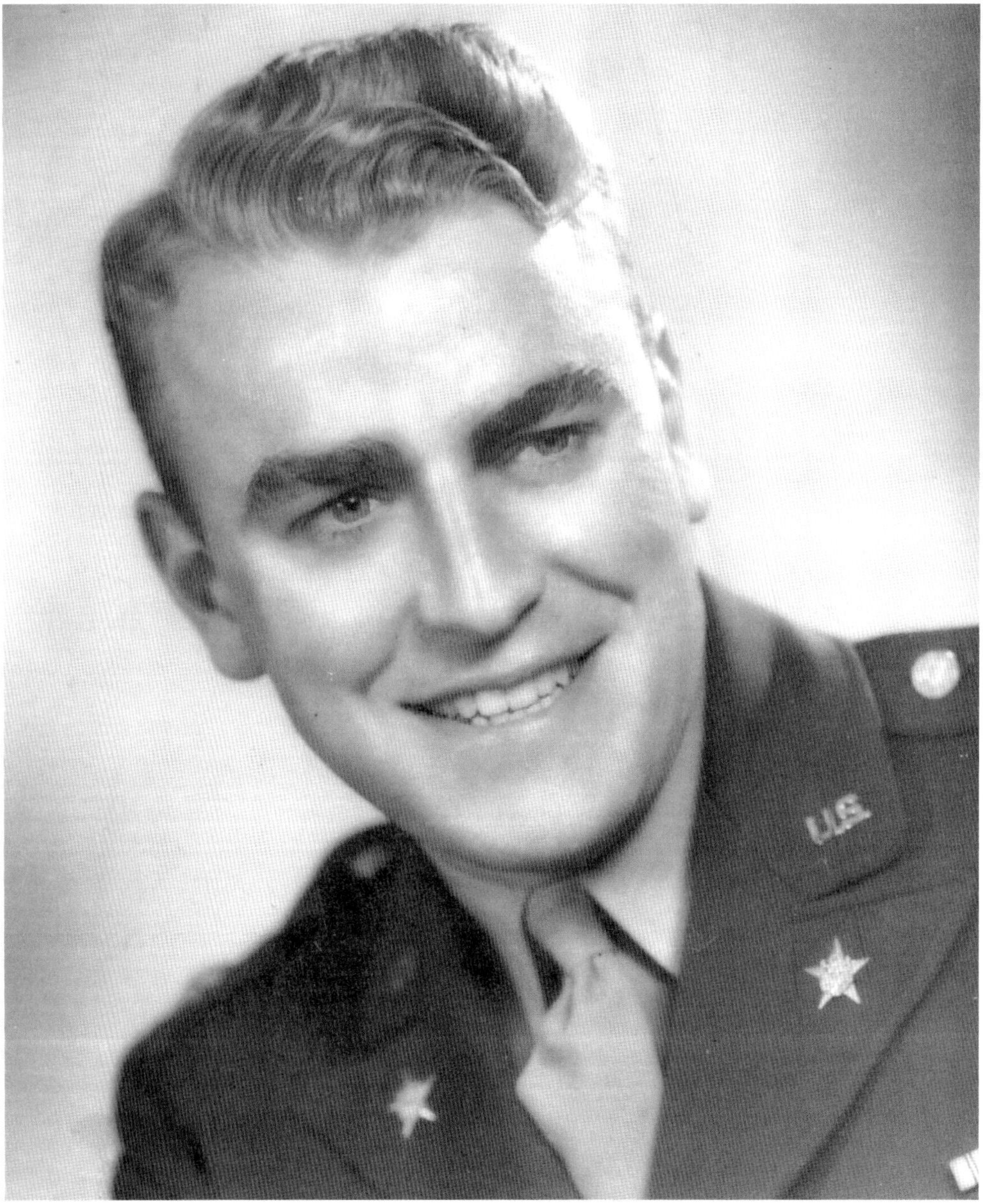

CHAPTER TWO

Soldiers

Kearny has always had a special place in its heart and memory for war veterans. In 1887, the state set aside $225,000 to build and furnish the New Jersey Home for Disabled Soldiers in Kearny. The site selected was a portion of Joseph Huge's estate, 15 acres overlooking the Passaic River along Belgrove Drive. Veterans from the Civil War, Spanish-American War, Mexican-American War, and World War I lived at this facility. They participated in town events, celebrations, and elections. On Memorial Day, instituted in 1868, they would decorate the graves of their comrades in Arlington (New Jersey) Cemetery. The home, which came to be known colloquially as the Old Soldiers' Home, closed in July 1932. Its remaining 55 veterans were bused to Menlo Park. They ranged in age from 85 to 93.

The first veterans' association in town was chartered in May 1888. Any citizen who served with honor during the Civil War was eligible for membership in this Phil Sheridan Veterans' Association. Forty-three veterans joined the organization.

Other associations sprang up in Kearny, including the Joseph E. Frobisher Post 99 of the American Legion, Post 1302 of the Veterans of Foreign Wars and their Ladies Auxiliaries, and the Marine Corps League. It is no surprise that they are situated on Belgrove Drive between Bergen and Afton Avenues, across from where the Old Soldiers' Home used to be (now Veterans Field). Eligible Kearny residents were also members of the Sanford L. Kahn Post 538 of Jewish War Veterans.

Memorials to honor Kearny veterans stand in the town hall foyer and in Memorial Park at the convergence of Beech Street and Kearny Avenue near Quincy Avenue. These honor rolls pay homage to fallen soldiers of World War I (56), World War II (178), the Korean War (11), the Vietnam War (11), and the War in Afghanistan and Iraq War (Edward Karolasz). The park memorial dedication was commemorated with much fanfare in May 1922. A 5,000-person parade along Kearny Avenue attracted some 25,000 people. Town hall's Wall Memorial Hall was dedicated in November 2008.

Around town, street names and parks also memorialize Kearny's fallen. These include Peden Terrace, Washington Avenue, Father Washington Way, and Gunnell Oval. The section of Riverbank Park known as Veterans Memorial Park is dedicated to all veterans.

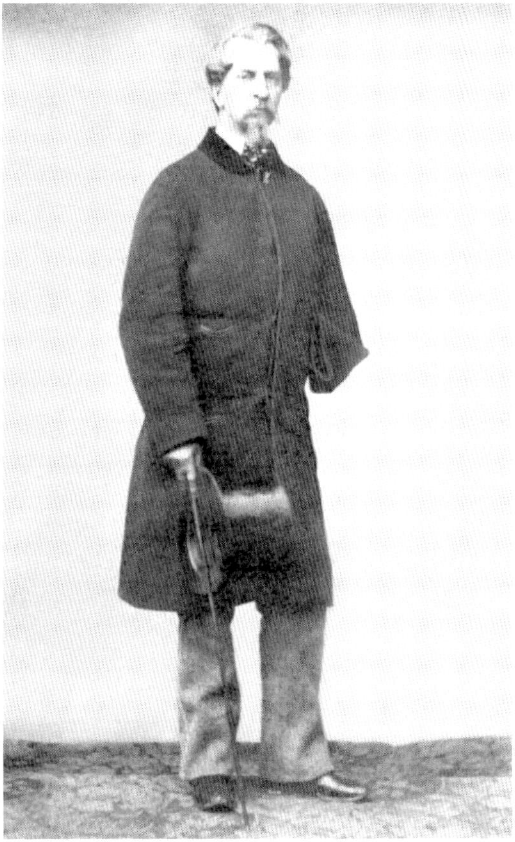

Fighting Phil Kearny

The town's namesake, Maj. Gen. Philip Kearny, was born in New York City in 1815 into a prominent and wealthy family. His father was a founder of the New York Stock Exchange, and Kearny inherited the family fortune, including whole blocks of New York City real estate. Although his economic status presented him with a life of leisure, Kearny instead chose a life of combat. On the battlefield, the soldier earned the respect of his men. He lost his left arm in the Mexican-American War in 1847; a cannonball blasted through bone.

Scandal broke when he took up with Agnes Maxwell while in Paris, still married to Diana Bullitt of Kentucky. He asked for a divorce, which was eventually granted, but the stipulations of his divorce mandated he never remarry. Kearny bypassed the issue by moving from New York to New Jersey. He married Maxwell in 1858 in Jersey City. By then, he had built his redbrick chateau, Bellegrove, also called the Kearny Castle, on 100 acres of woodland overlooking the Passaic in what is now the town's First Ward. Though the structure was magnificent, he rarely spent time there.

When the Civil War broke out in 1861, Kearny requested a command post with the Union Army from the New York governor. But given his scandalous divorce, New York refused him. Kearny looked to New Jersey and was appointed the commander of its 4,000 troops. He then commanded the US Army of the Potomac during the Civil War. He was just 48 when he was shot by Confederates in Union uniforms at Chantilly, Virginia, on September 1, 1862. His death stunned the nation. A truce was declared, and his friends from before the war, Robert E. Lee and Stonewall Jackson, saw to his funeral. They delivered his body to Northern troops. He was buried first at Trinity Church in Manhattan but moved in 1912 to Arlington National Cemetery in Virginia.

The Kearny Museum has on exhibit some of Phil Kearny's memorabilia, including a sword, a smoking chair, and a Legion of Honour Medal given to him in France. (Courtesy of the Kearny Museum.)

Joseph Edwin Frobisher Jr., Namesake of American Legion Post 99

Joseph Edwin Frobisher Jr. of Belgrove Drive was a young man with a bright future. Following his graduation from Lehigh University with a degree in mechanical engineering, he worked as an assistant engineer in New York City. He registered for the draft in June 1917. Lieutenant Frobisher "helped to carry out the very highest and most important function of a fighting pilot, namely to drive the Huns out of the sky and permit our own observation machines to carry out their all important missions." Although sorely wounded, he managed to land his machine with courage and stamina. He died in France on September 10, 1918, at age 23. American Legion Post 99, founded in Kearny in 1921 as a patriotic veterans organization with a mission of community service, bears his name. (Courtesy of American Legion Joseph Edwin Frobisher Jr. Post 99.)

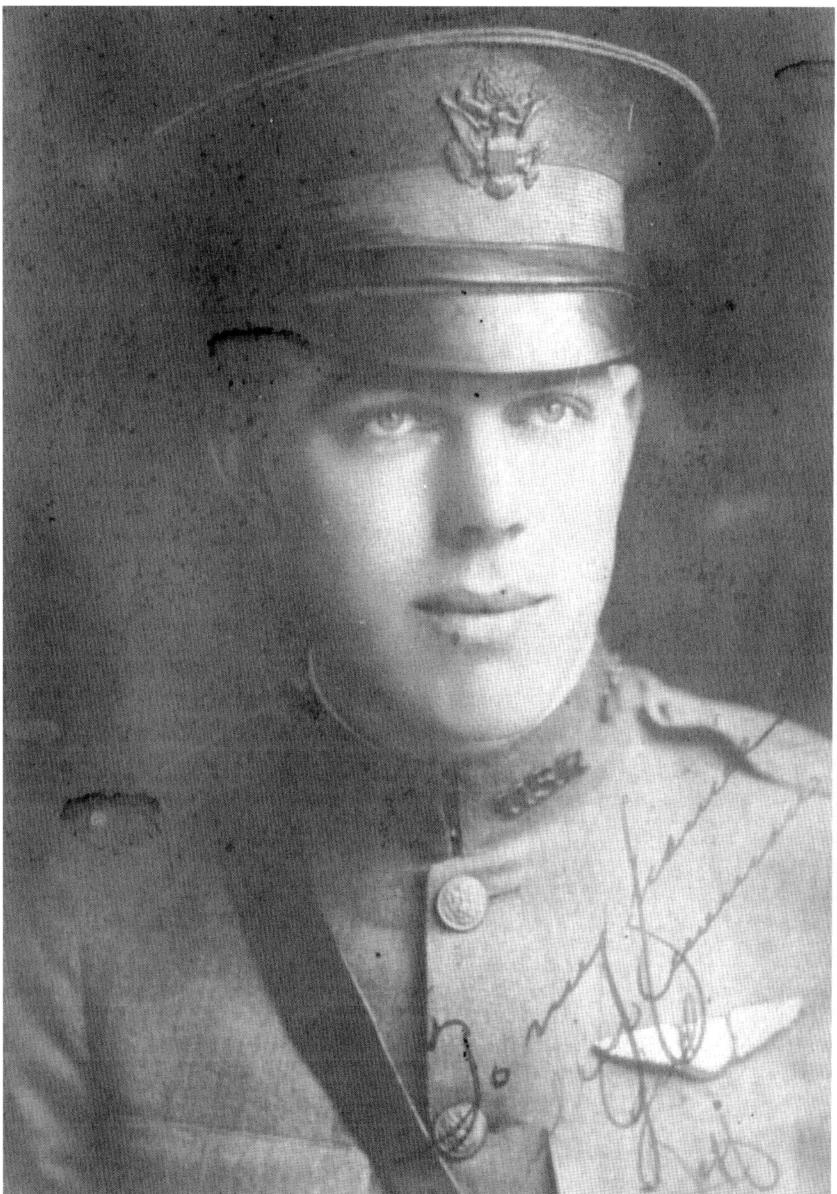

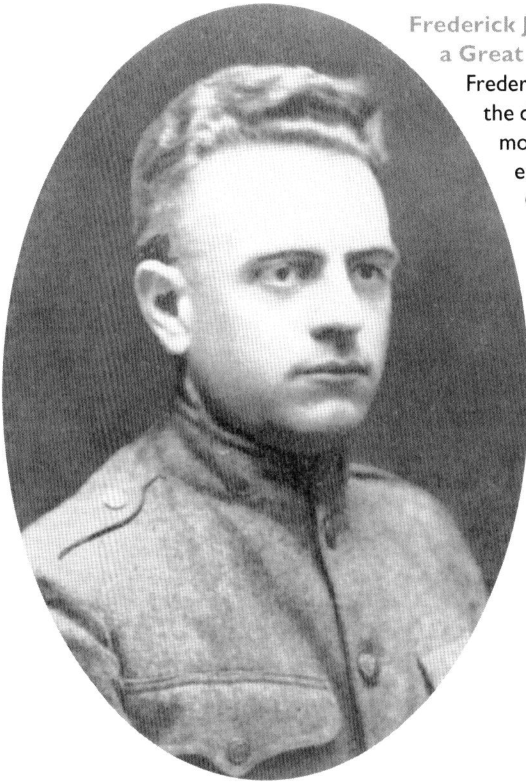

Frederick Jacob Gugelman, a Great War Soldier Forever in Memory

Frederick Jacob Gugelman of Forest Street registered for the draft in 1917 at age 28. He supported his widowed mother, a German immigrant, as a clerk in the foreign exchange department of a Manhattan bank. But Gugelman never made it back home alive. He was killed in action as a private in the 310th Infantry on September 16, 1918. VFW Wilson Gugelman Post 1302 is partially named for him. (Courtesy of the New Jersey State Archives; Department of State.)

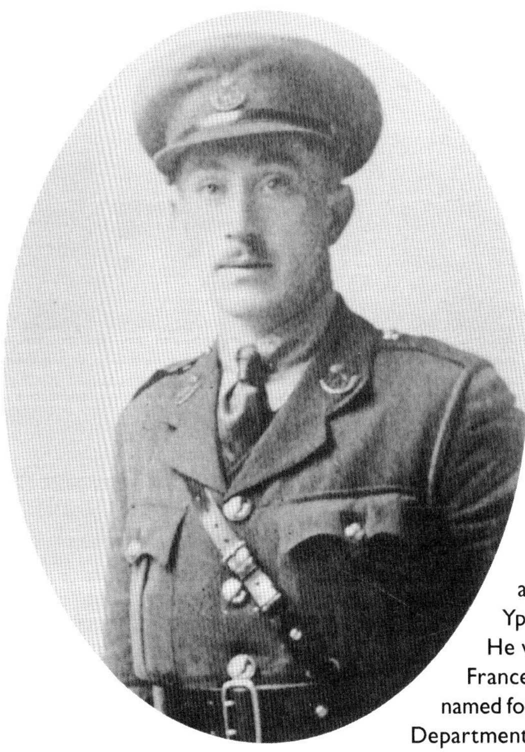

Kearny's William Wilson Enlisted in British Army

Not much is known about William Wilson of Kearny. He enlisted in the British Army at Liverpool, England, on November 20, 1914. He became a second lieutenant in the British Infantry and saw engagements in Neuve Chapelle, Somme, Ypres, and the German Spring Offensive of 1918. He was killed in action on April 12, 1918, at Bailleul, France. VFW Wilson Gugelman Post 1302 is partially named for him. (Courtesy of the New Jersey State Archives; Department of State.)

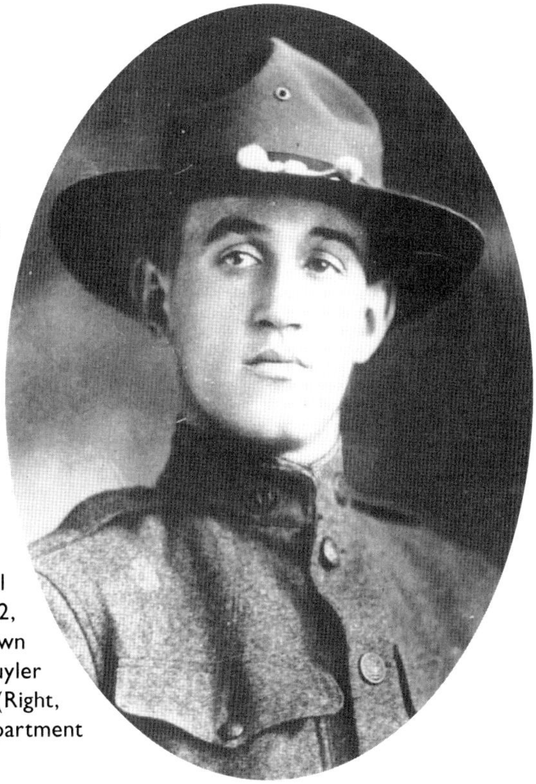

Benjamin Elliott Gunnell, the Oval's Namesake

Benjamin Elliott Gunnell was born around 1896 in Oshkosh, Wisconsin. By 1910, his family lived on Elizabeth Avenue in Arlington. Gunnell enlisted at the 69th Regiment Armory in New York City on April 17, 1917. He began his service overseas on October 26, 1917, as a private in the 165th Infantry, once known as the "Fighting Irish." He was killed on July 28, 1918, during the Battle of Château-Thierry, one of Gen. John J. Pershing's first actions in France and one that decimated the regiment. Gunnell was the first Kearny casualty of US involvement in World War I. He is listed on the World War I Memorial Monument, dedicated by Pershing himself in 1922, and on the World War I Honor Roll on the Town of Kearny Memorial Hall. The "Oval" off Schuyler Avenue near Midland Avenue is named for him. (Right, courtesy of the New Jersey State Archives, Department of State; below, photograph by the author.)

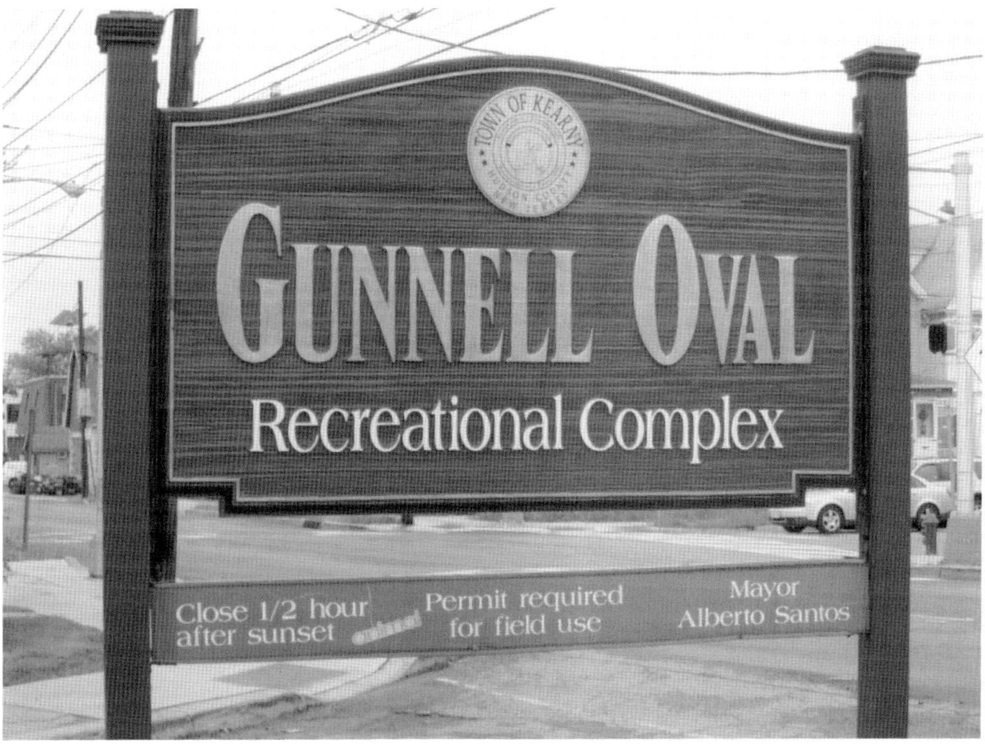

Donald A. Pegg, Distinguished Service Cross

Born in Indiana in 1898 to an Australian father and Irish mother, Donald A. Pegg of Beech Street represented the town in World War I. Private Pegg served in the US Army Medical Department, 12th Machine Gun Battalion, 4th Division. During the Argonne Offensive, he was administering first aid under machine gun fire and voluntarily went to an especially dangerous position to care for a wounded soldier. He himself was killed on September 30, 1918. The posthumous recipient of the Distinguished Service Cross in February 1919 by Commander in Chief John J. Pershing for extraordinary heroism in action, Pegg is buried in the Meuse-Argonne American Cemetery in France. His parents left Kearny and moved to England. (Courtesy of the New Jersey State Archives; Department of State.)

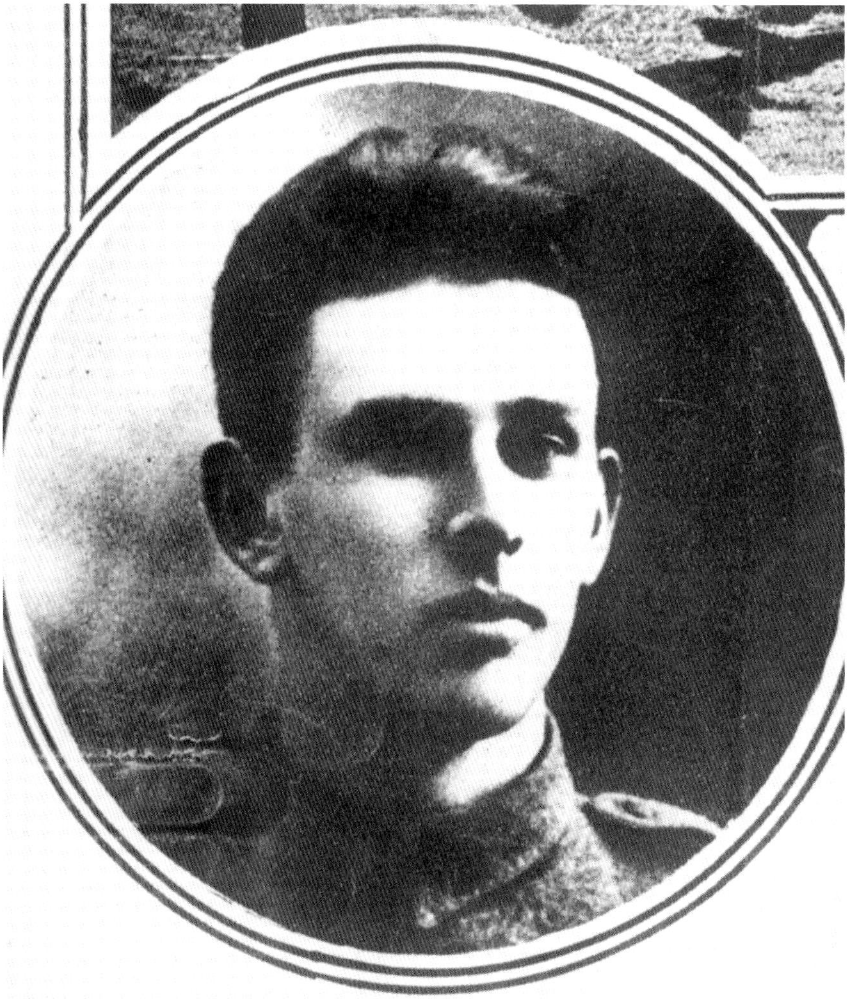

Private Donald A. Pegg, Medical Corps, awarded, posthumously, the Distinguished Service Cross; killed in action October 1 in the Argonne while giving aid to a wounded comrade. His home was at 117 Midland avenue, Arlington.

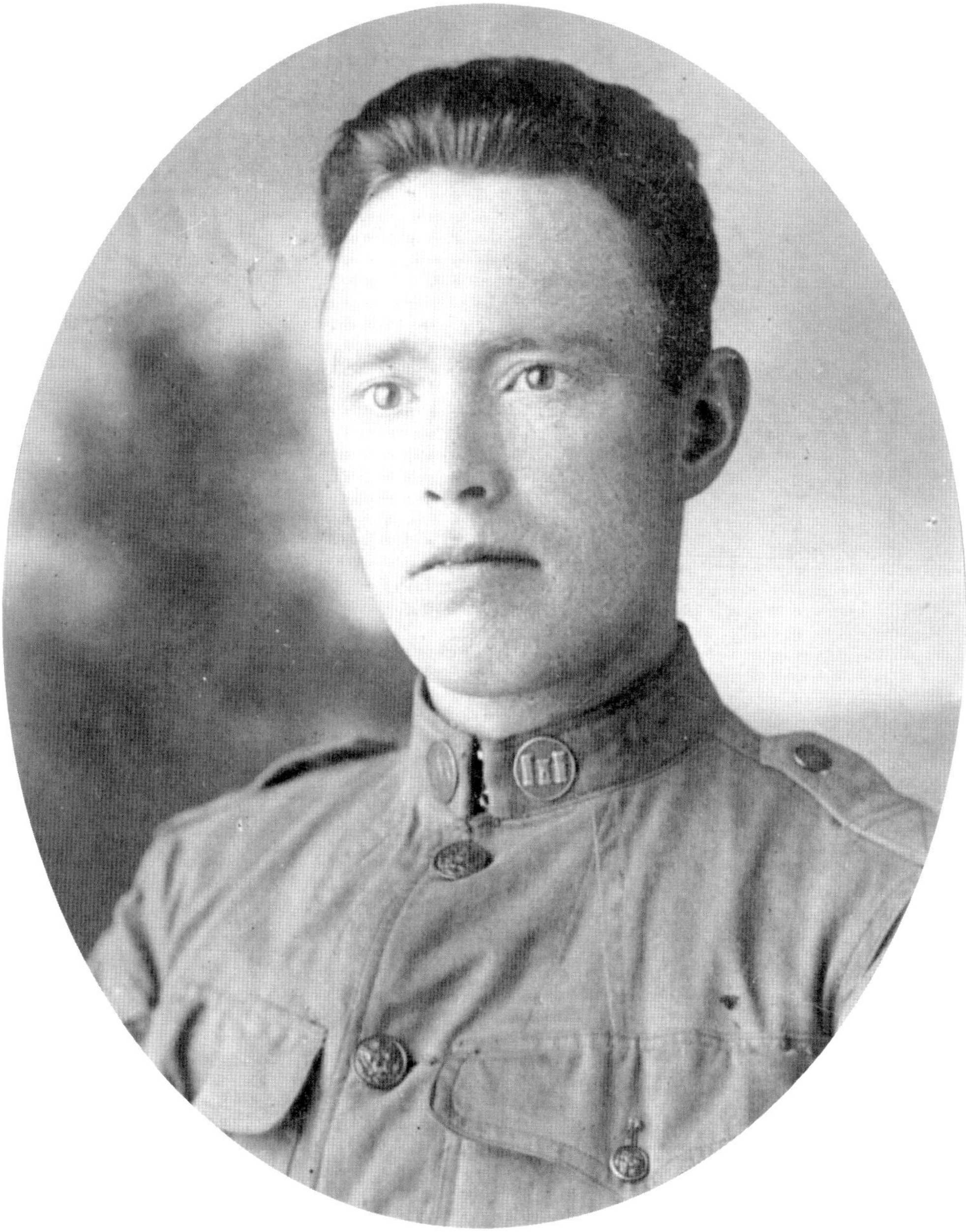

Robert John Flack, a Family Mystery
Robert John Flack followed his brother, Walter, to the United States from County Down, Ireland. Born in 1891, he settled in Kearny and worked as a chauffeur and general mechanic at the New Jersey Home for Disabled Soldiers. He entered the US Army to serve in World War I and was a private first class in the 104th Engineer Regiment, 29th Infantry Division. Walter reported in 1920 that his brother had been wounded and taken as a German prisoner of war. The American government officially declared him as killed in action on August 7, 1918. However, his family now believes he was killed by a land mine just before the Argonne Offensive. He is buried at the Meuse-Argonne American Cemetery in France. (Courtesy of the New Jersey State Archives; Department of State.)

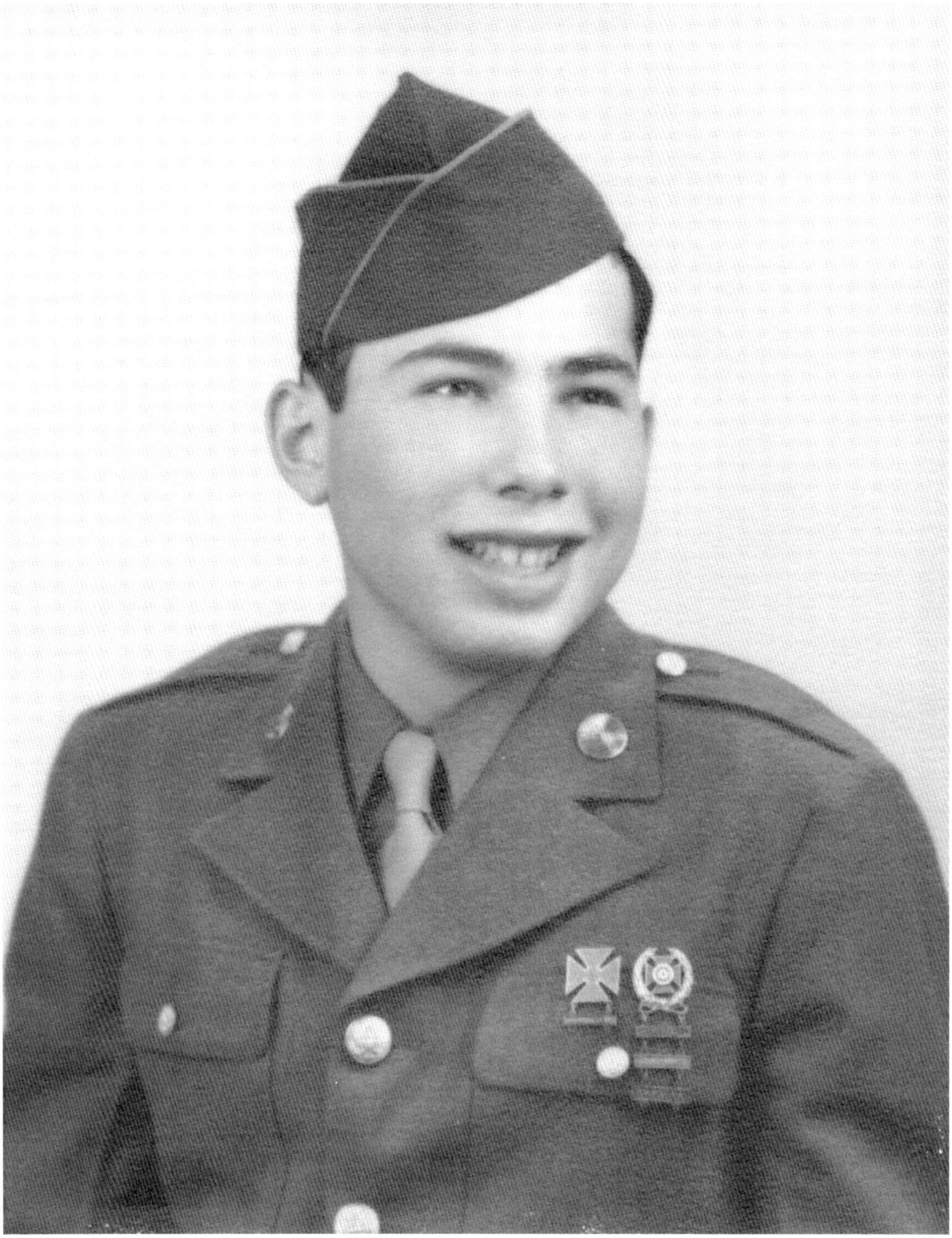

Sanford L. Kahn and His Patriotic Duty

Sandy Kahn of Chestnut Street enlisted in the US Army in June 1943 at age 19. In February 1944, he wrote his family in Kearny: "Don't worry about me. I still have a long time before I hit combat. For all anyone knows, I may miss it." Six months later, his parents received a telegram stating their son was missing in action. Later, they learned a German sniper's bullet instantly killed him during the battle of St. Lo in northern France. Kahn became the first Jewish soldier from town to be killed in World War II. The local post of the Jewish War Veterans bears his name: Sanford L. Kahn Post 538. (Courtesy of Sanford Mallon.)

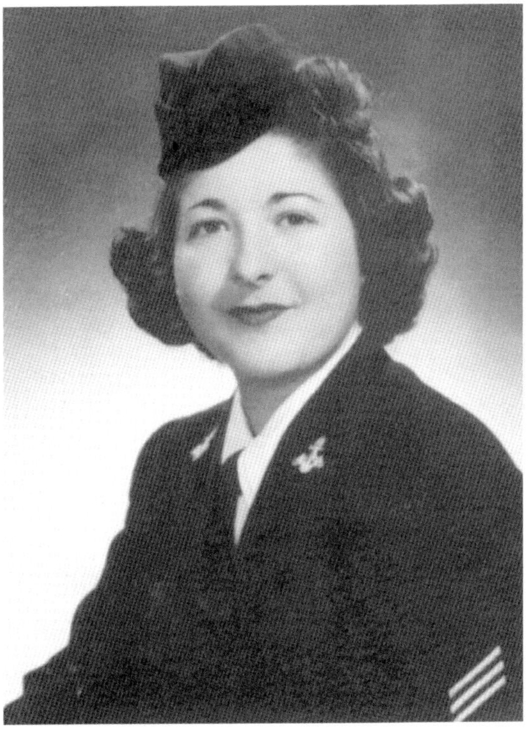

Lenore Gans Bartner, the WAVE
Lenore Gans was the first woman from Kearny's Jewish community to join the US Armed Forces in World War II. She served from 1944 to 1945 as a Women Accepted for Volunteer Emergency Service (WAVE), a division of the US Naval Reserves. She married Milton Bartner, also of Kearny. She was a proud member of the Sanford L. Kahn Jewish War Veterans Post and the American Legion Frobisher Post 99. (Courtesy of the Bartner family.)

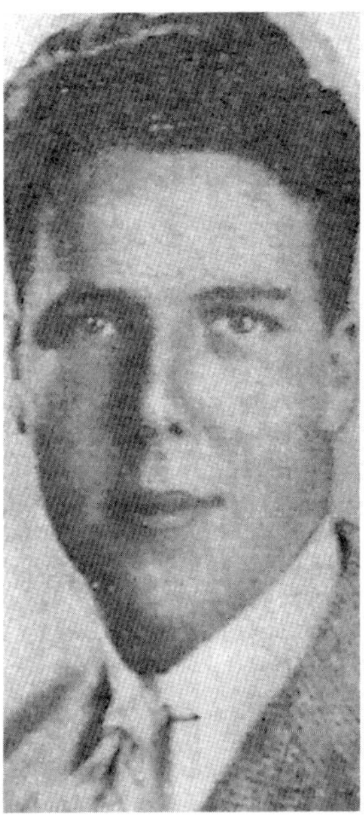

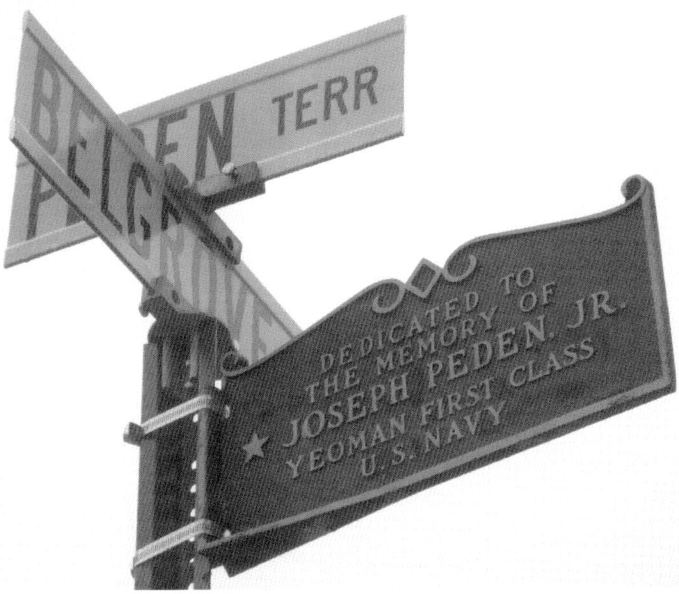

Joseph Peden Jr., Kearny's First World War II Victim
Joseph Peden of Brighton Avenue announced during his senior year at Kearny High School in 1940 that he wanted to enlist in the US Navy. His assignment was airplane mechanic on the USS *Langley*. He was promoted to yeoman and hoped to become a pilot. Unfortunately, the ship was sunk in February 1943. He was the war's first casualty from Kearny. Peden Terrace is named for him. (Left, courtesy of Norman Rutan; right, photograph by the author.)

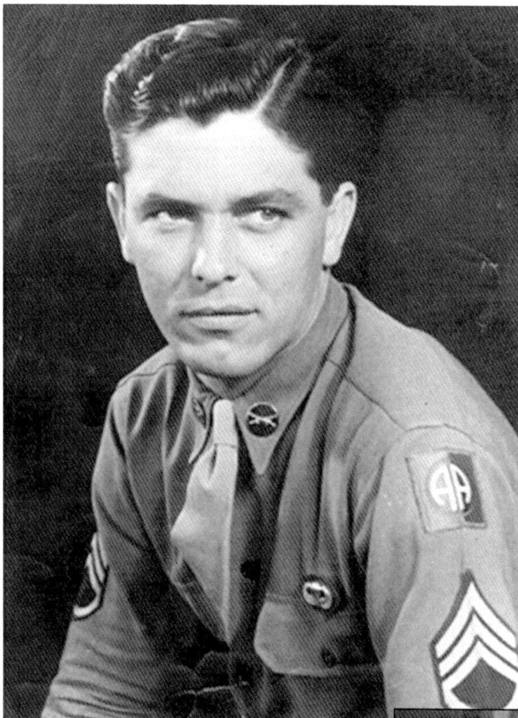

Heroic Paratrooper and Green Beret Joseph J. Ryan

In his youth, Joseph J. Ryan lived at Cooper's Block, an immigrant tenement building at the corner of Johnston and Sheridan Avenues. A graduate of Kearny High School, Ryan enlisted into the U.S. Army in 1942 and joined the famed 82nd Airborne Division. He distinguished himself in the infantry during the D-day invasion at Ste. Mere Eglise. After the war, he returned to Kearny briefly before re-enlisting. He was among the first to wear the reinstated Green Beret in 1953. He entered military intelligence, which took him around the world, and became a polygraph expert. Despite the time away from them, Ryan was devoted to his family. After his retirement from military service, he served as First Ward councilman for two terms. He remained active with the 82nd Airborne for the rest of his life. (Courtesy Ryan children.)

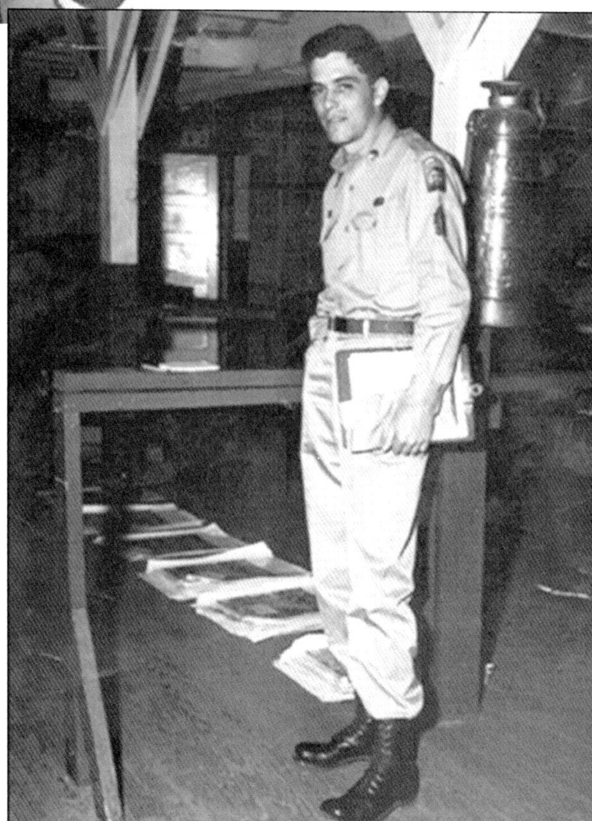

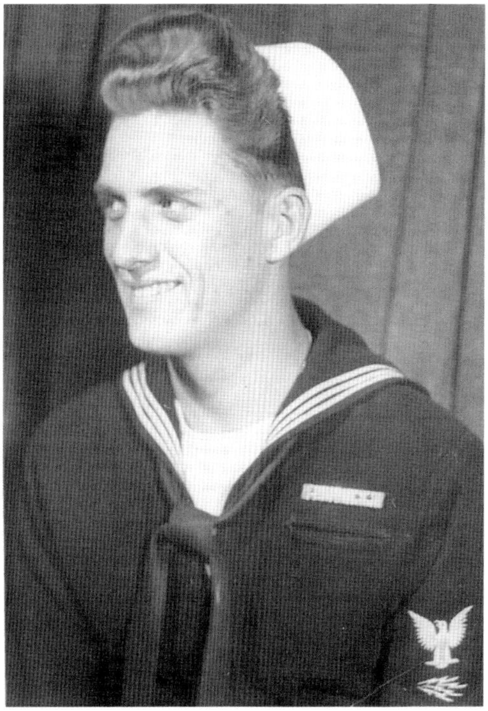

Eugene William Rudomanski, Radio Technician

Born in 1925, Eugene William Rudomanski of Duke Street attended Kearny High School and one semester at Rutgers University. He entered the US Navy and served as petty officer, second class, training as a radio technician. He was killed at sea on July 30, 1945, when enemy torpedoes sank the USS *Indianapolis* in the Philippine Sea. (Courtesy of Terry Petty.)

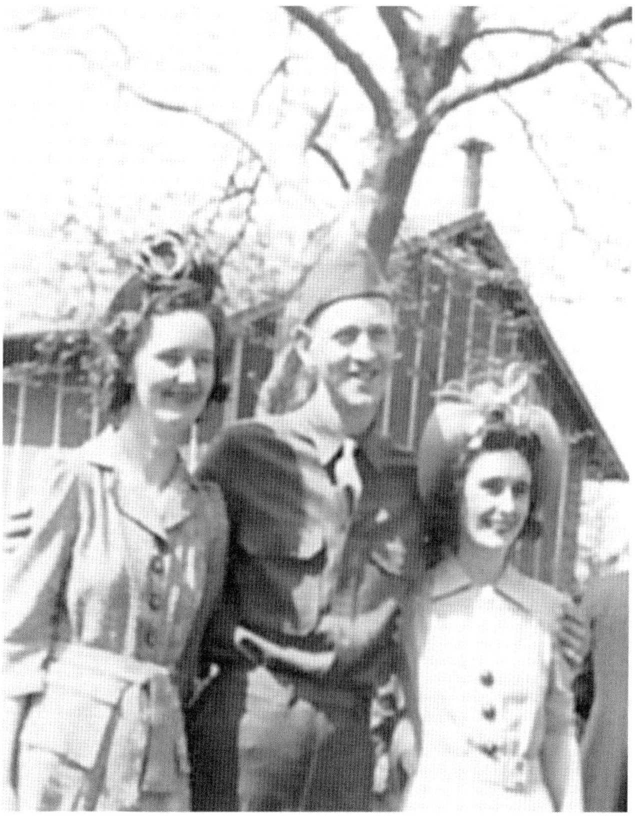

Thomas F. Walsh, Healey Cousin Killed in Action

Pvt. Thomas F. Walsh of Elm Street was killed in action in Italy on November 11, 1943. The former employee of Hyatt Roller Bearings Division of General Motors in Harrison, Walsh was inducted in March of the previous year and was deployed overseas to participate in the Sicily and Italian campaigns. He is shown here with his cousins Loretta and Mae Healey at Fort Dix. (Courtesy of Tom Healey.)

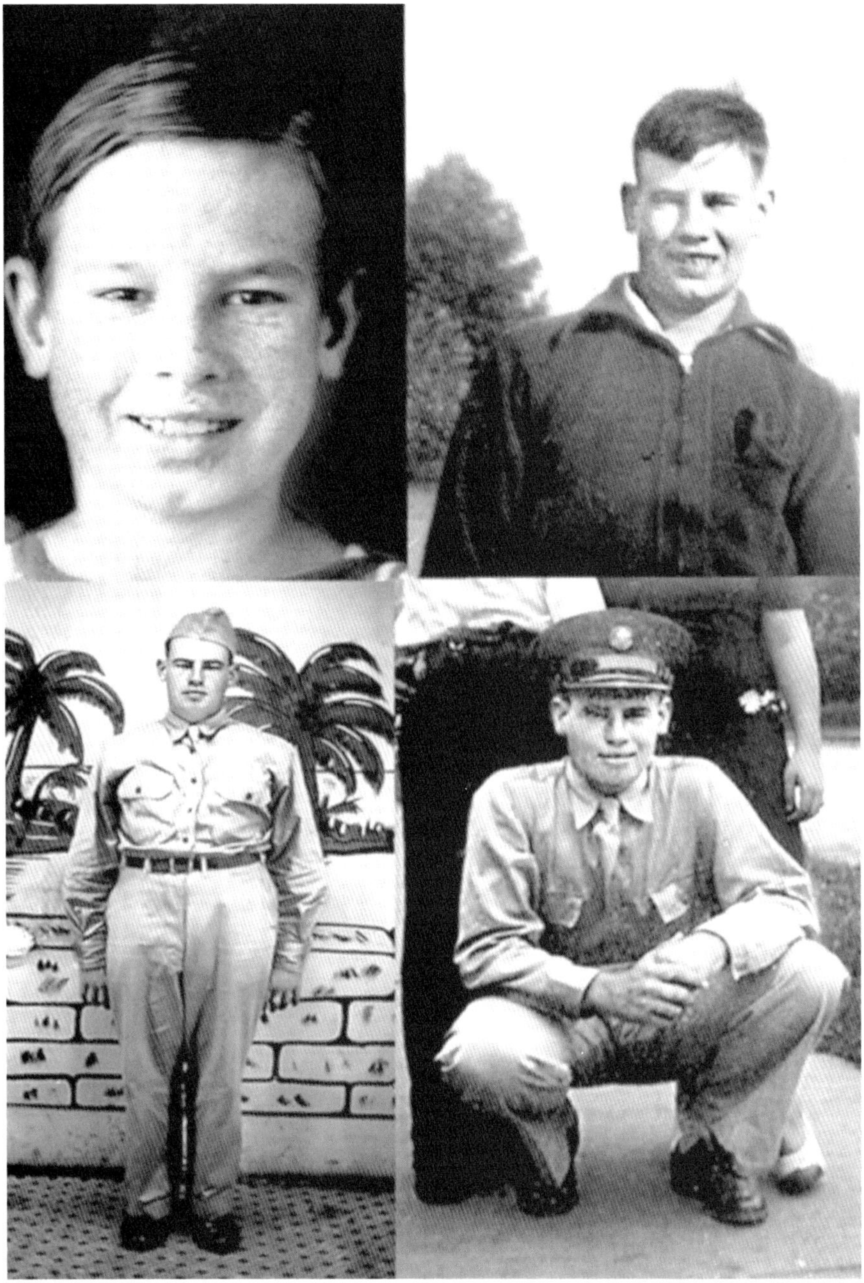

Richard D. Perry, Killed during Allied Invasion of Italy

Richard D. Perry was born and raised in Kearny. He lived at 264 Bergen Avenue and was the second youngest of 16 children. He took part in the Allied invasion of Sicily in July 1943, and at 18, he was killed in action on January 28, 1944, as the Allies advanced north through Italy after the invasion. He is buried in the Sicily-Rome American Cemetery in Italy. In this collage of photographs, he is shown top left, at about 12 or 13 years old, and top right, about 15 or 16. At the bottom left, he is 17 and dressed in his first uniform, and at bottom right, he is pictured during his last home visit before shipping out overseas. (Courtesy of A.J. Perry.)

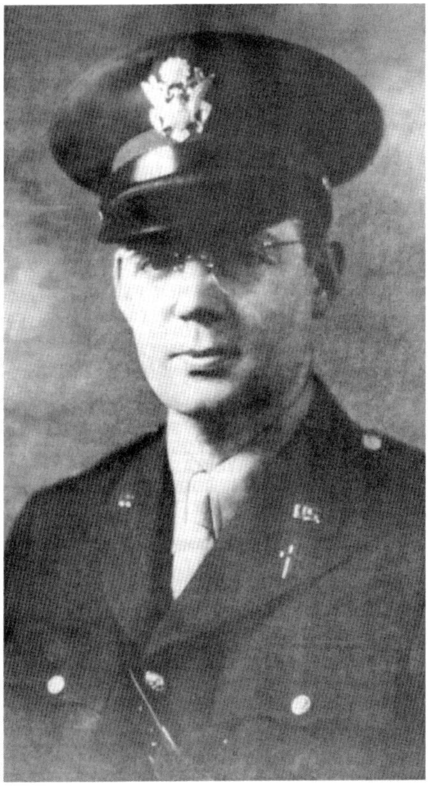

Father Washington, One of the Four Chaplains Who Sacrificed Their Lives
On December 7, 1941, Fr. John P. Washington was on his way back from treating his mother to the movies when he heard the devastating news on his car radio that the Japanese bombed Pearl Harbor. Born in Newark in 1908, Father Washington served as associate pastor at St. Stephen's Church. When he arrived home, he notified the church pastor, Fr. George Murphy, of his desire to enlist. Father Murphy, a World War I veteran, was sure to approve. Despite eye damage sustained in a street fight years before in Newark, Father Washington was accepted into the US Army. He waited impatiently for his overseas duty request to be granted while at Fort George G. Meade in Maryland.

Father Washington joined three other chaplains at Fort Standish in November 1942: Rev. Clark Poling (Dutch Reformed), Rev. George Lansing Fox (Methodist), and Rabbi Alex Goode (Jewish). On January 3, 1943, the four boarded the USAT *Dorchester*, a troopship with 900 passengers and crew, leaving New York harbor as ship 23 in a 64-ship convoy headed toward a destination only known to a few—Greenland.

To get to Greenland, the ship needed to move through U-boat-infested waters. The chaplains sought to calm the nerves of the newly drafted and enlisted men. Father Washington's amiable personality made him popular with the men. But when a German torpedo hit the ship on February 3, all four chaplains sprang into action. Each gave up his life vest to a passenger or crew member. Father Washington had faced a deathly illness earlier in his life, so he considered himself immune to fearing death. Linked in prayer and hymns, he and the three other clergy went down with the ship into the icy depths of the Atlantic.

A stained-glass window at St. Stephen's commemorates the beloved pastor surrounded by saints. Washington Avenue, previously Eilshemius Avenue, memorializes the brave and selfless chaplain. A portion of Washington Avenue has borne the name Father Washington Way. He received several posthumous awards, including the Distinguished Service Cross for extraordinary heroism (the second highest military decoration), the Purple Heart, and a Special Medal for Heroism, authorized by Congress. Father Washington was also featured with his fellow clergy on a 1948 US postage stamp that included the words "These Immortal Chaplains." (Courtesy of St. Stephen's Church.)

Frank R. Pettigrew, Bronze Star Medal for Distinguished Service

Frank Pettigrew of Chestnut Street enlisted in the US Army in 1942. He served as Private First Class in the 305th Infantry, 77th Division, and was part of the Guam initiative. On D-Day, he was assigned to guide troops to assembly areas, exposing himself to enemy and friendly fire in the process. The campaign resulted in the liberation of the strategic Marianas Island. Pettigrew was killed later in action on January 29, 1945, in Leyte, Philippines, leaving behind a wife and twins. He was awarded the Bronze Star Medal for distinguished service and the Combat Infantryman Badge for proving himself in combat. Before the war, he had been employed at the war plant of Crucible Steel. Both he and William Pettigrew were sons of fireman John Pettigrew of Rose Street and brothers of the Kearny recreation commissioner, John Pettigrew Jr. In Frank's honor, Pettigrew Park stands at the corner of Highland and Woodland Avenues. (Photograph by the author.)

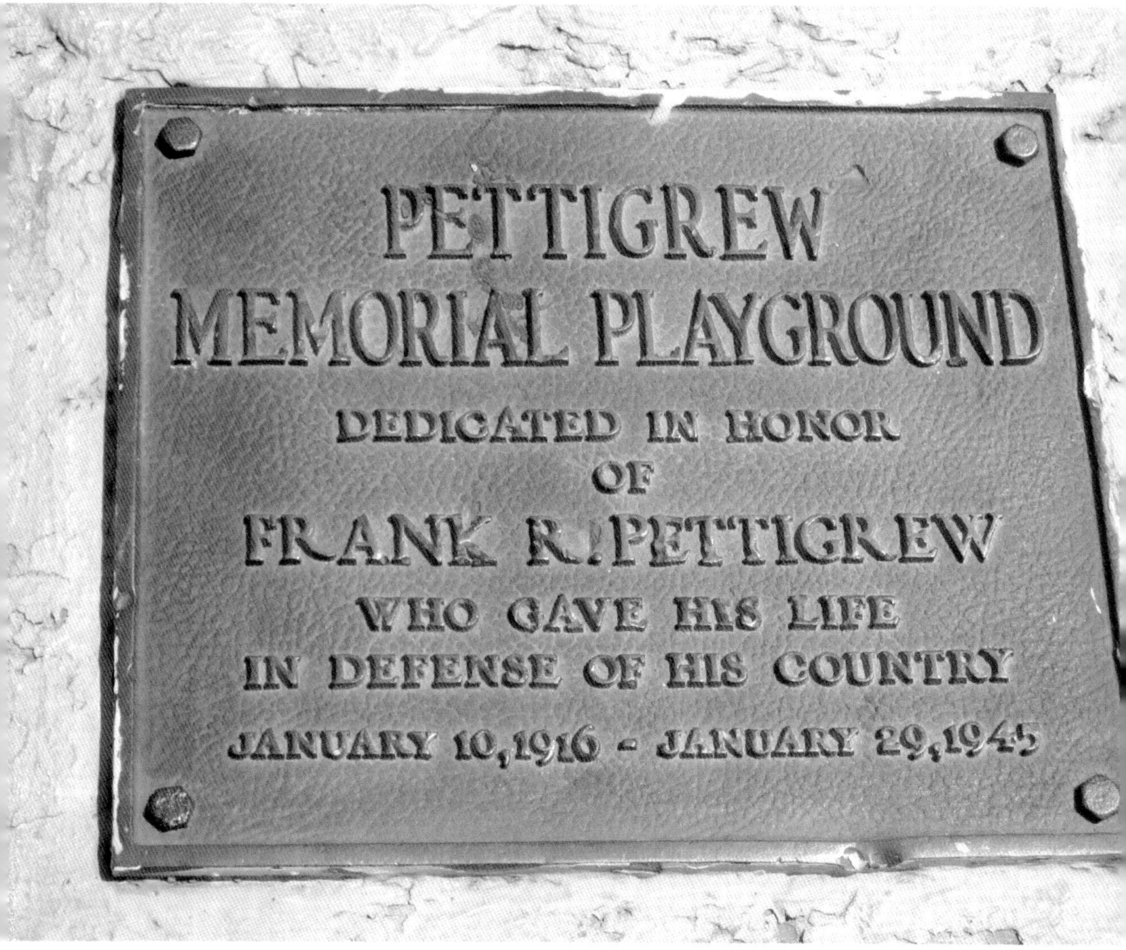

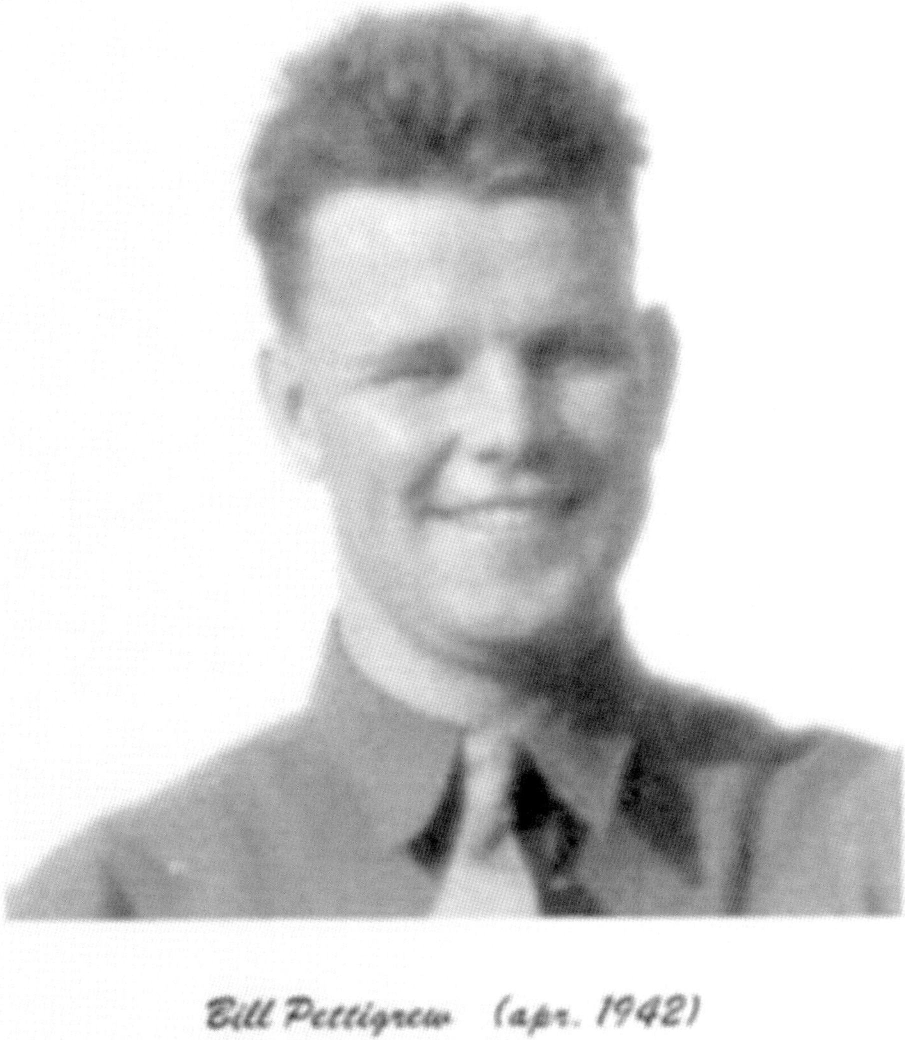

William Pettigrew, Wounded by Sniper

Pfc. William Pettigrew, Frank's brother, served in the same infantry division. On December 28, 1944, the 26-year-old was walking with another solider in Leyte, Philippines, when a sniper fired from a cave and hit the other soldier. Pettigrew killed the sniper but while removing his colleague to safety, was hit in the leg by another sniper. He was sent back to the United States for medical treatment. Pettigrew was a Kearny High School graduate and the captain of its soccer team. Before the war, he played professional soccer with Kearny's Irish American team and worked as a production engineer for Federal Shipbuilding and Dry Dock Company. He survived his wounds and passed away in 1980. (Courtesy of James Fitzsimmons.)

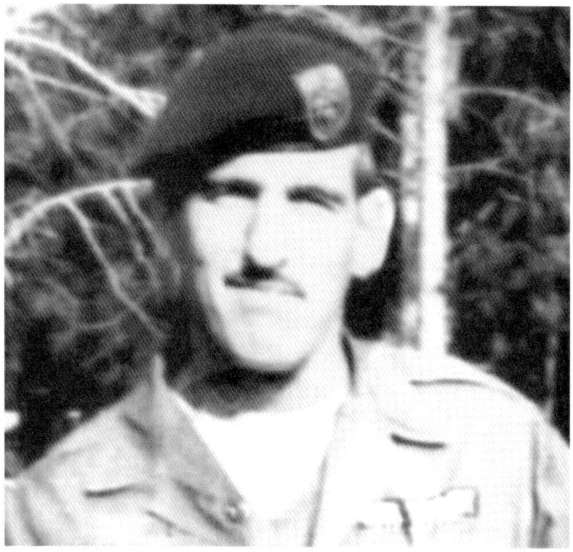

Thomas Welsh, Killed in Action
Born in 1930, Thomas Welsh served in the US Army as sergeant, first class of Special Forces in the Vietnam War. He was killed in action in 1966. He was the recipient of many awards, including the Bronze Star Medal, the Army Green Beret, and the Purple Heart. (Courtesy of Tom Reese.)

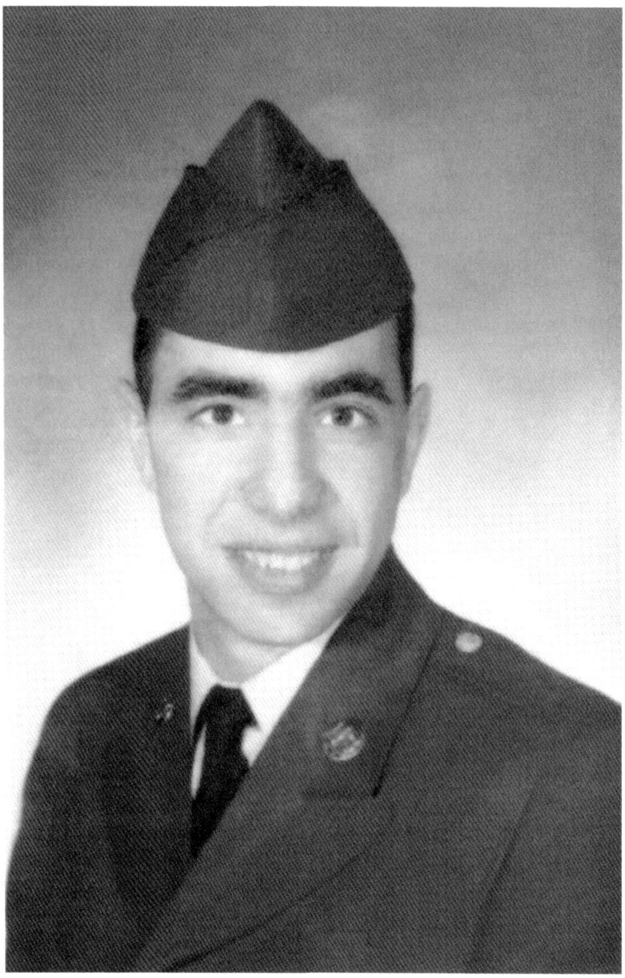

Michael Francis Branin Jr.
Born in 1948, Michael Francis Branin Jr. served in the US Army 4th Infantry Division, having joined through the Selective Service in August 1968. He reached the rank of corporal but was killed in action in Vietnam on November 13, 1968. Among other awards, he received the Purple Heart. (Courtesy of Nancy Branin Waller.)

Michael Sinibaldi Memorialized

In 2010, Mayor Santos, members of the town council, and Fire Chief Stephen Dyl dedicated the fire department's rescue truck in memory of Cpl. Michael W. Sinibaldi, who was killed in action in the Vietnam War. Sinibaldi attended St. Stephen's School, Franklin Junior High School, and Kearny High School. He enlisted in the US Army on his 18th birthday in October 1967. He was killed with two rounds to the chest on August 14, 1968, while 22 miles south of Saigon. He received the Bronze Star, Silver Star, and Purple Heart. He is buried in North Arlington. (Courtesy of Jason Reid.)

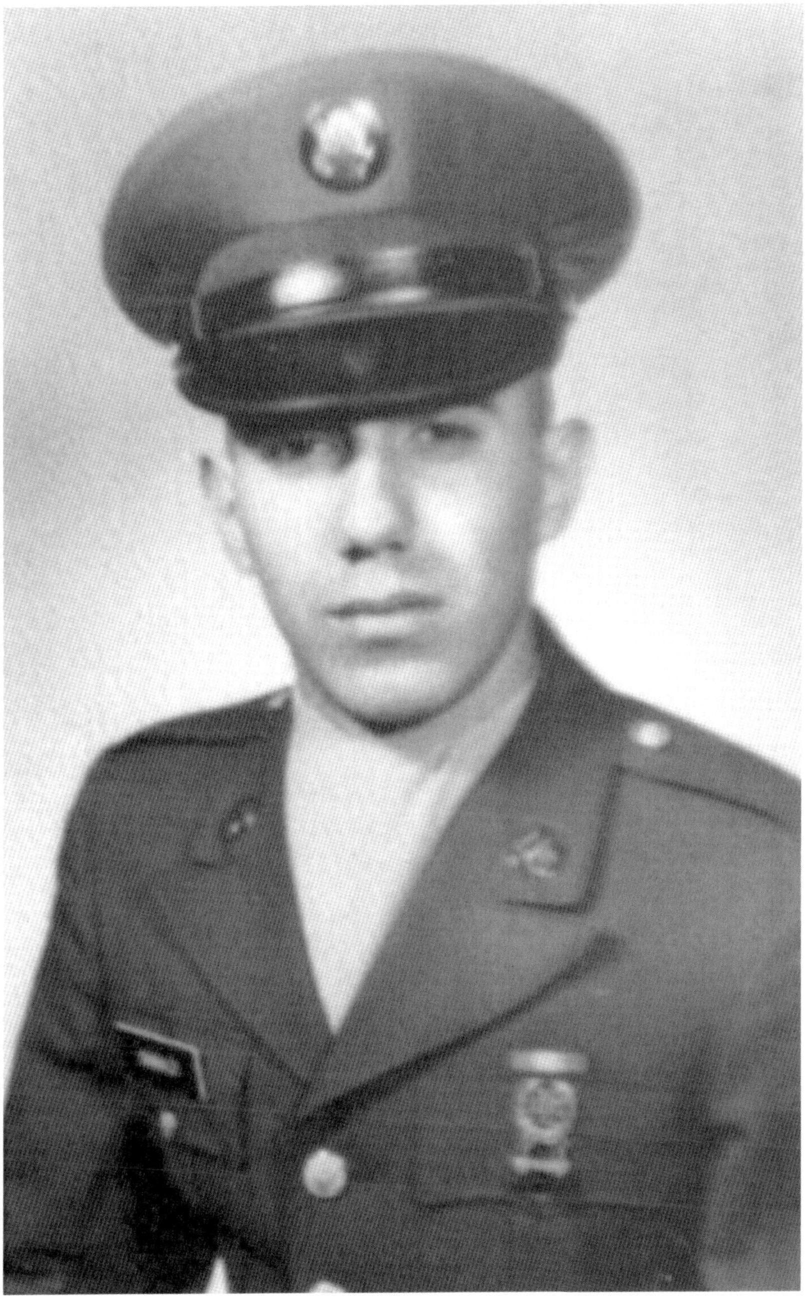

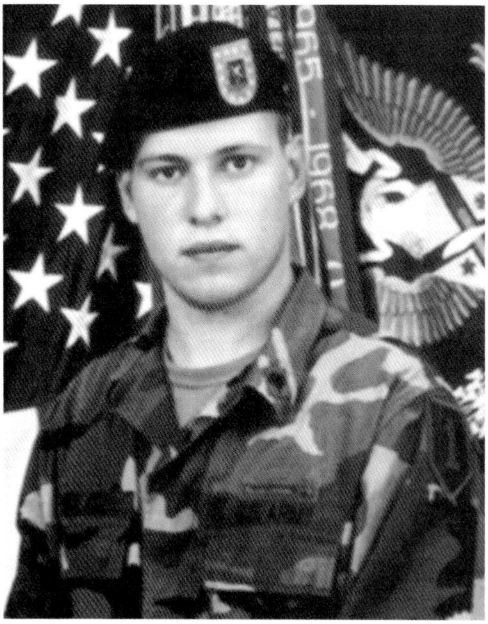

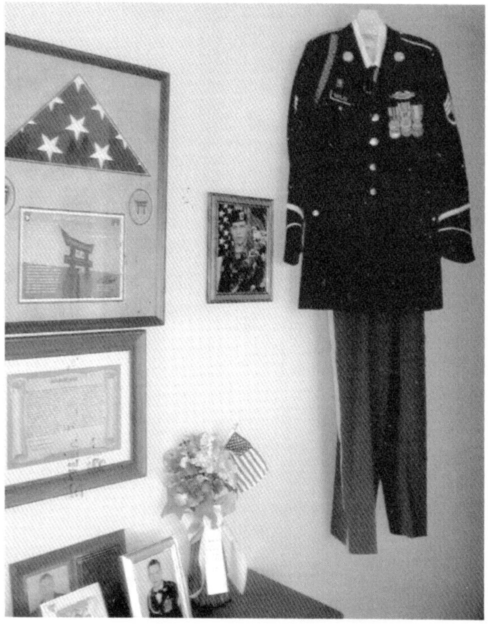

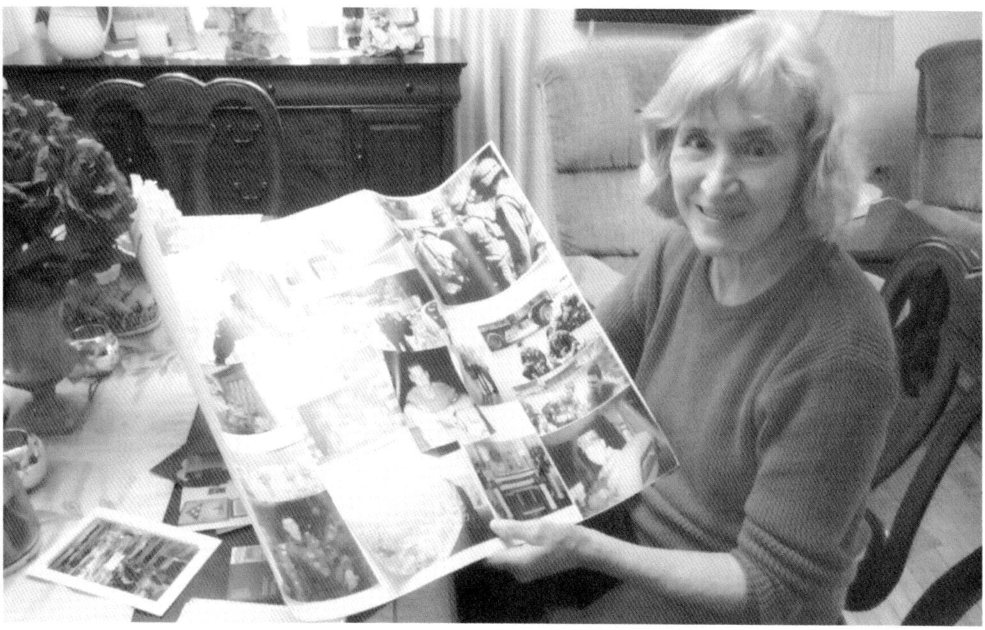

Ed Karolasz, Mourned by Community

Sgt. Edward Karolasz of Chestnut Street was the first Kearny casualty of the Iraq War. Born in 1980 to Polish immigrants, the Kearny High School graduate died during his second tour of duty near Baiji, north of Baghdad, by a roadside bomb on November 19, 2005. He was with the 101st Airborne Division's 3rd Brigade Combat Team. The town gave him a farewell tribute with an outpouring of support in December 2005. The Kearny Museum exhibits his uniform and other memorabilia, and he is listed in the Town of Kearny Memorial Hall and at Memorial Park. The First Annual Motorcycle Race and Pig Roast in his honor was held in July 2015. (Above images, courtesy of Krystyna Karolasz; below, photograph by the author.)

CHAPTER THREE

Educators

The first record of a schoolhouse in Kearny reported it was built from stone on the Sandford estate in 1820. It was ordered abandoned 10 years later. In 1839, a schoolhouse was built from cedar logs along the west side of Coppermine Road (another predecessor of Schuyler Avenue), north of Bergen Avenue. A Mr. Pell was in charge of the first students, who entered in 1840. Pell was quickly replaced, and the woman who followed him fared no better. Armed with his hickory switch, Mr. Kennedy had no problem keeping his students disciplined. He stayed on for 11 years. In 1856, this school building was ordered to be closed. In its stead, a new schoolhouse was erected on the opposite side of Coppermine Road. Trustees of the Meadow District School saw to the proper erection of this one-room school and to the hiring of Alice Morgan, teacher of what would now be known as School No. 1. Morgan received an assistant, Esther A. Kelsey, in 1872, and yet another new school on Coppermine Road was completed in April 1873. It was called Back Road Public School, under the care of Harriet Potter.

Clearly, there had to be a school for children closer to Kearny Avenue. The town bought three city lots on Kearny Avenue from John Williams. School No. 2 opened in 1873, ready for 100 children. Mr. Noble offered to take the $800 a year position but was quickly followed by Mr. Musgrave the next April. New Jersey legislature mandated school attendance in 1874. Kearny's Township Committee responded with the formation of a board of education, effective August 1874.

C.P. Hatch donated a site for a public school at the corner of Midland and Kearny Avenues. In 1879, School No. 3 was ready. To accommodate children working in factories, classes were held on Monday nights.

Some of the schools have fallen by the wayside, deemed no longer necessary. Others continue to thrive. Today, we know the schools as Franklin, Washington, Lincoln, Roosevelt, Garfield, and Schuyler Schools. Kearny High School on Devon Street opened in 1922.

Schools may have been enlarged, torn down, or repurposed, but the dedication of the school district administrators and faculty has remained constant. Peggy Bixler has become legend, a fixture of Roosevelt School for more than 50 years. Barbara Toczko of Washington and Franklin Schools inspired her students with fresh approaches to social studies. Kearny teachers seek to innovate and cultivate, no matter how many years they spend in the system. Many of the legendary locals featured in this compendium owe their education and careers to these unsung heroes.

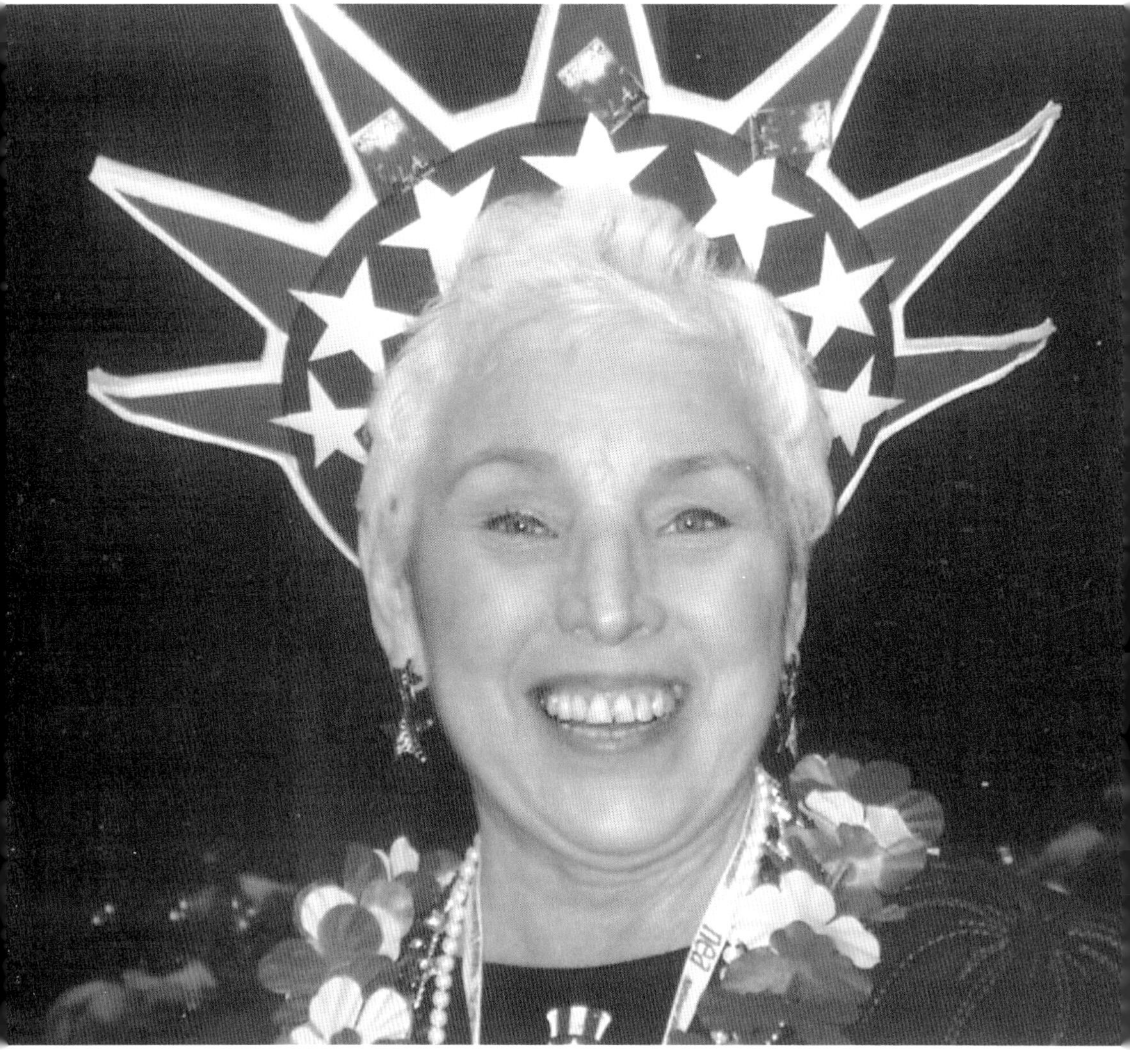

"Lady Liberty" Barbara Toczko

A member of the Kearny Museum Board of Directors and an avid traveler, Barbara Toczko first moved with her family from Harrison to Kearny in 1947. She attended Kearny High School, where she served on student council and the cheerleading squad. She majored in history at Montclair State College and began her career teaching seventh-grade English and then history at Washington School, followed by a long stint teaching eighth-grade American history. She cultivated a classroom environment of current events and debate, instructing her students, "Your opinions matter. You can do anything in the world you want to do. Don't let anyone ever stop you." (Courtesy of Barbara Toczko.)

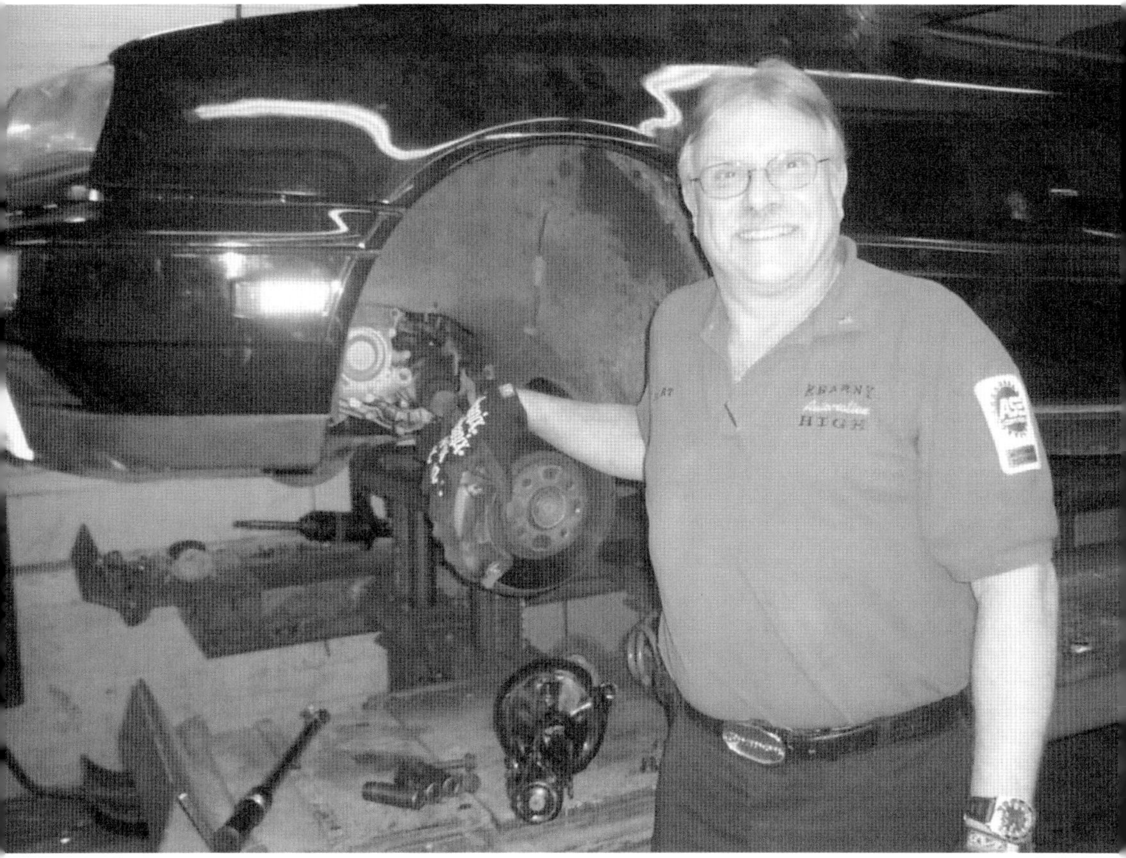

Fred Kuhrt, Coach and Mentor

Fred Kuhrt could fix anything. He taught automotive technology at Kearny High School for 34 years. He died suddenly in January 2014 at the age of 58. He graduated in 1973 from Kearny High School, where he played football and ran track. He worked at an auto garage on Dukes Street before earning his degree in industrial technology from Kean College. He instilled his passion for vehicle maintenance, including that of his beloved 1969 MG, into his students. A former student estimated that at least 50 people gained inspiration to enter the trade from Fred Kuhrt. Another former student said of Kuhrt, "He was a great coach with incredible mentoring skills." The Fred Kuhrt Scholarship was established in his name. (Courtesy of Lorry Kuhrt Fitzgerald.)

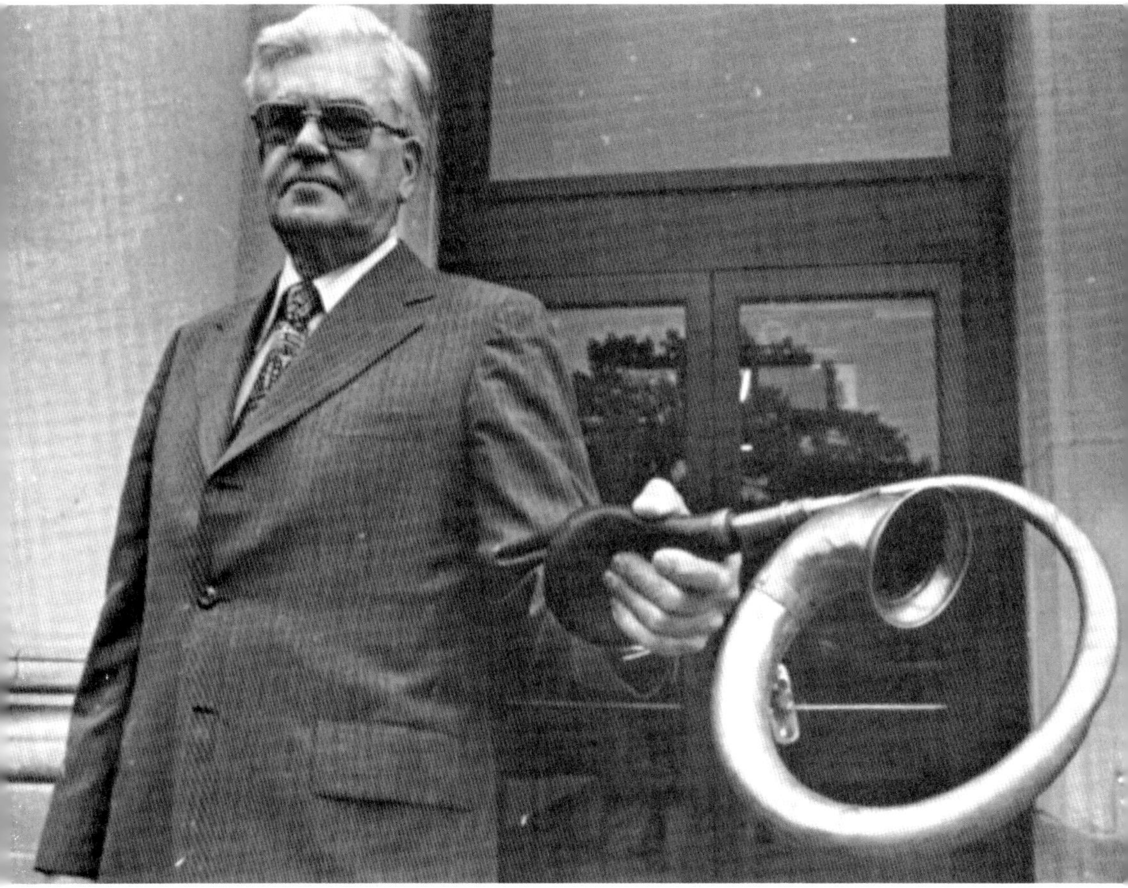

Edward R. Brehm, Kearny High School Principal
"We are the recipients of his investment of time and sacrifice," says the class of 1976 in a tribute to Edward R. Brehm, who retired as principal of Kearny High School on December 31, 1975. He started in the Kearny school system as a substitute math teacher in the 1940–1941 school year. He was hired the following year. In 1956, he was promoted to head of the department, where he remained until his appointment as principal in 1964. He was troubled by miniskirts in the 1960s and 1970s and was known to ask female students to bend down so he could measure the length of the skirt. He was well-respected, though quiet. He passed away in 1998. (Courtesy of Kearny High School.)

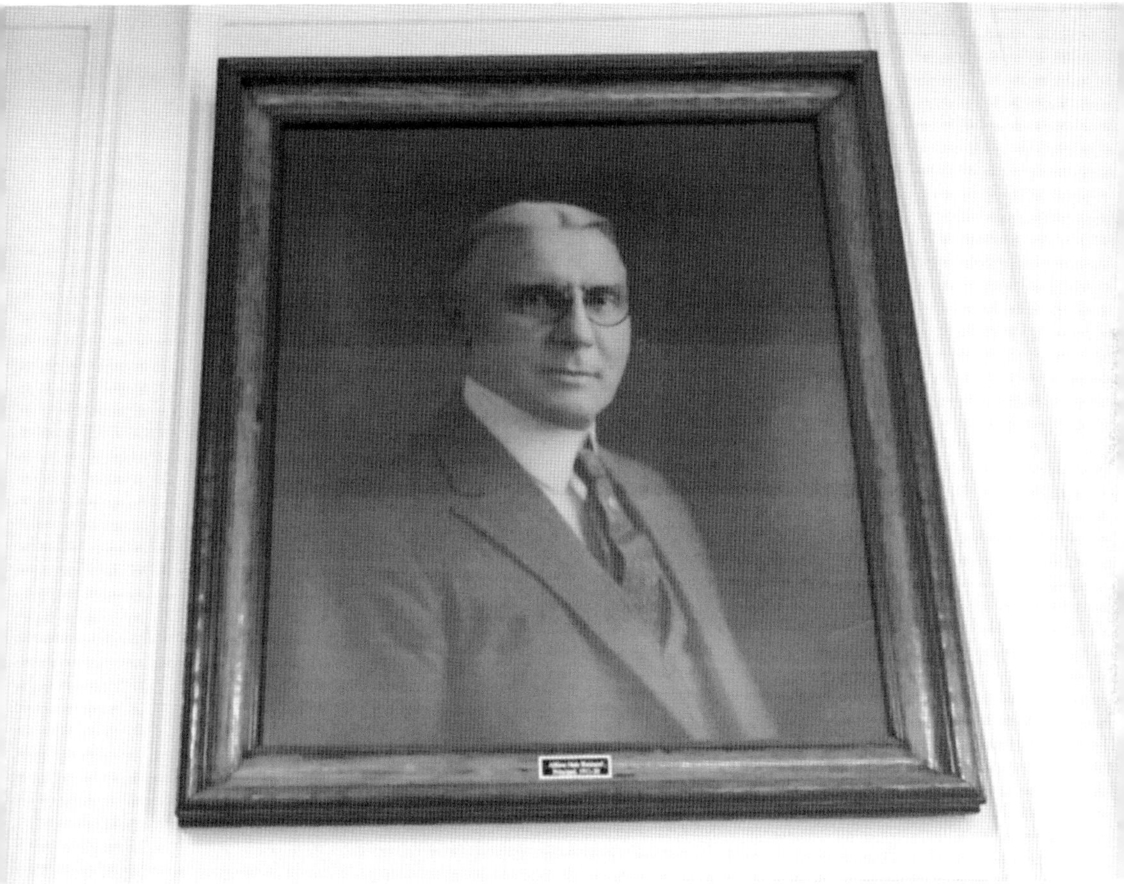

Albion Hale Brainard, Kearny High School's First Principal

Albion Hale Brainard served the Kearny School District as high school principal for 19 years until a sudden heart attack took his life in West Boothbay Harbor, Maine, in 1930. Born in Maine in 1866, he attended Teacher's College in New York and then received his master's degree from Columbia in 1916. He was a member of the Harvard Club of New Jersey. He lived in various places in town, including Eilshemius Avenue and upper Kearny Avenue. A Kearny High School scholarship is named for him, starting in 1934, as is a Lyndhurst High School memorial award established by his Kearny alumni there. This portrait hangs in the Kearny High School Media Center. (Courtesy of Kearny High School.)

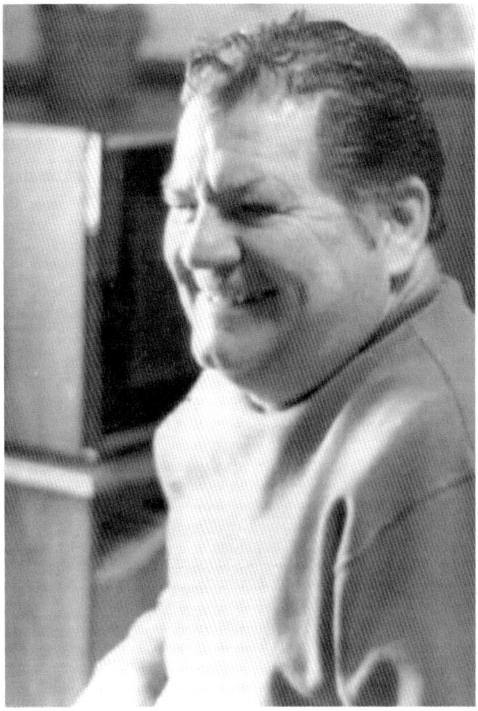

Joseph "Chubby" Gray

Known to Roosevelt and Lincoln School students as a kind-hearted "teddy-bear kind of a guy," Joseph "Chubby" Gray was born in 1928 in Kearny at 142 Dukes Street. He played baseball for Kearny High School and became the head custodian at Roosevelt School, where he played Santa every year. He was also known around town as the Good Humor man, delivering ice cream from his truck. He is now retired. (Courtesy of Michael Gray.)

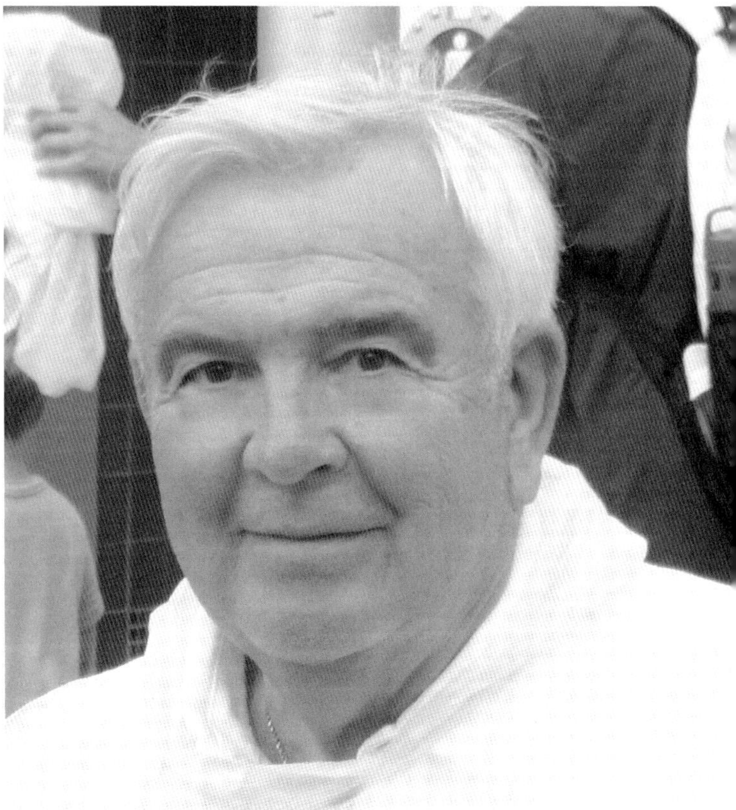

Witty Walter Whimpenny

Walt Whimpenny taught math at Kearny High School for 40 years, retiring in 2006. A native of Kearny, he was born in 1944 and graduated from Kearny High School. He married Kearny High German teacher Marie Horwath. Whimpenny's sharp wit engaged students and made algebra more fun. Although he now lives in Manahawkin, he continues a commitment to Kearny as a member of the Kearny Museum Committee. (Courtesy of Walt Whimpenny.)

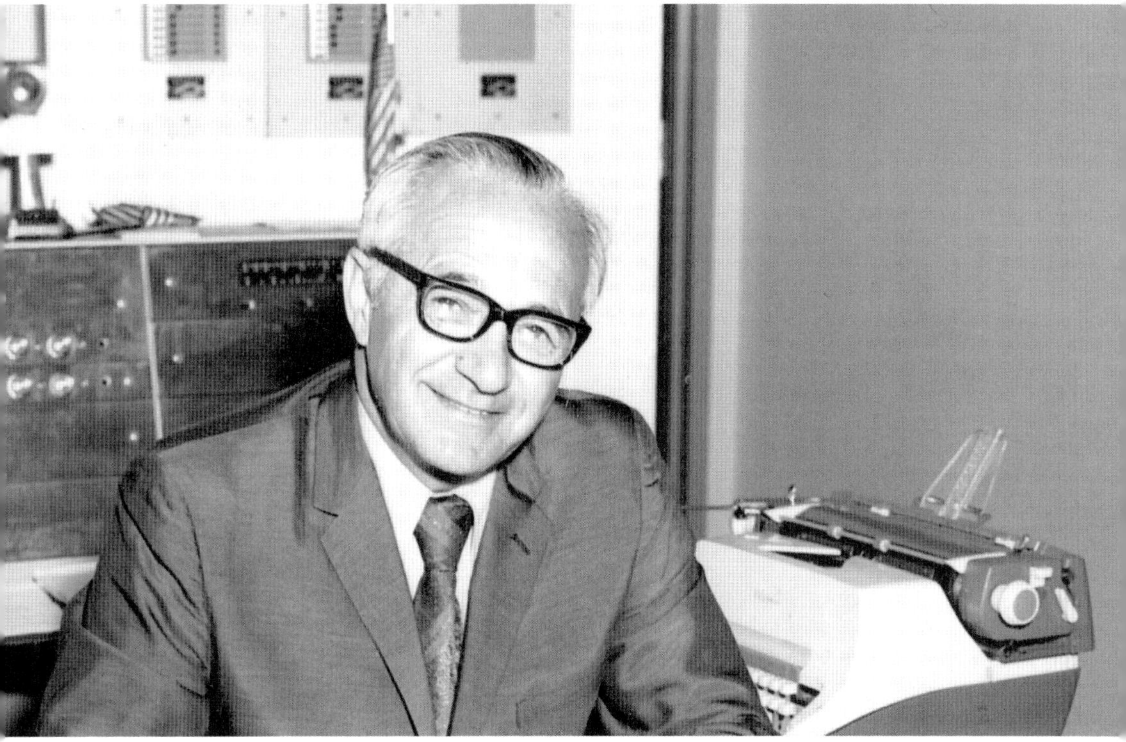

Lincoln School Principal Frank C. Monaco

Frank Monaco was born in 1909 to Italian immigrants. A graduate of Kearny High School, Monaco attended the Savage College of Health and Physical Education in Manhattan and received a master's degree from Trenton State College. After serving as Queen of Peace's first athletic director and first football coach in 1937, he became a physical education teacher at Lincoln Middle School. Monaco coached Kearny football, track, and baseball teams. He was a founder of Little League and coached American Legion baseball teams. He was principal of Emerson School before becoming principal of Lincoln School. He owned White Birch Summer Camp for Kearny boys from 1951 to 1961. He was inducted into both the Queen of Peace and Kearny High School Athletic Halls of Fame and was honored multiple times by the Marconi Fraternal Association. He died in 1993. (Courtesy of Denise Viscuso Liptak.)

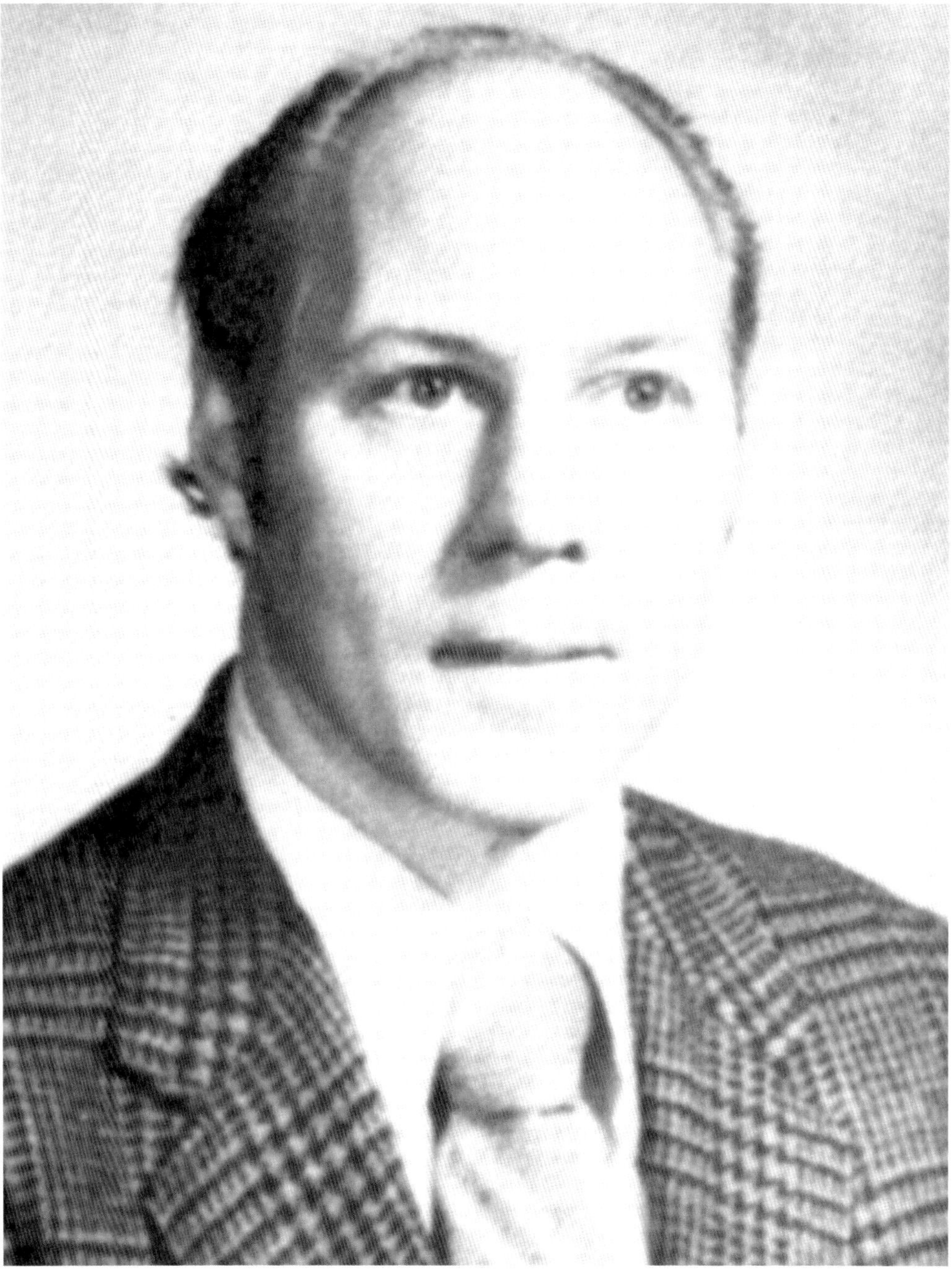

Arnold Alfred Schmidt, Artist and Teacher

Arnold Alfred Schmidt taught commercial art at Kearny High School. Born in 1930 in Plainfield, he lived most of his life in New York City and worked as an art director for an advertising agency. His own work was shown at many museums, including a painting in the permanent exhibition of the Museum of Modern Art in New York. His students recalled how he challenged them in their art, playing music on the radio for their three-period class. He emphasized the development of their portfolios, and many wish they had held on to them. He died of cancer in 1993. (Courtesy of Kearny High School.)

"Herr" Ronald Schmidt

Ron Schmidt joined the faculty of Kearny High School in the fall of 1971 to teach German. A graduate of Montclair State College, Schmidt brought fresh ideas for language instruction to his classes. He quickly became a popular teacher, and enrollment in German increased substantially. He introduced the Kearny Keglers (the German Club Bowling League), followed eventually by additional sports, including ice hockey. In 1990, Schmidt accepted a position as guidance counselor. He holds a master's degree in student personnel services from Montclair State University and spent three summers in Germany and Austria with the Georgetown University summer programs in German linguistics. He was also a Fulbright Scholar in Germany. He inspired, nurtured, and guided Kearny High students until retirement in June 2015. (Photograph by Erin Donnelly, courtesy of Ron Schmidt.)

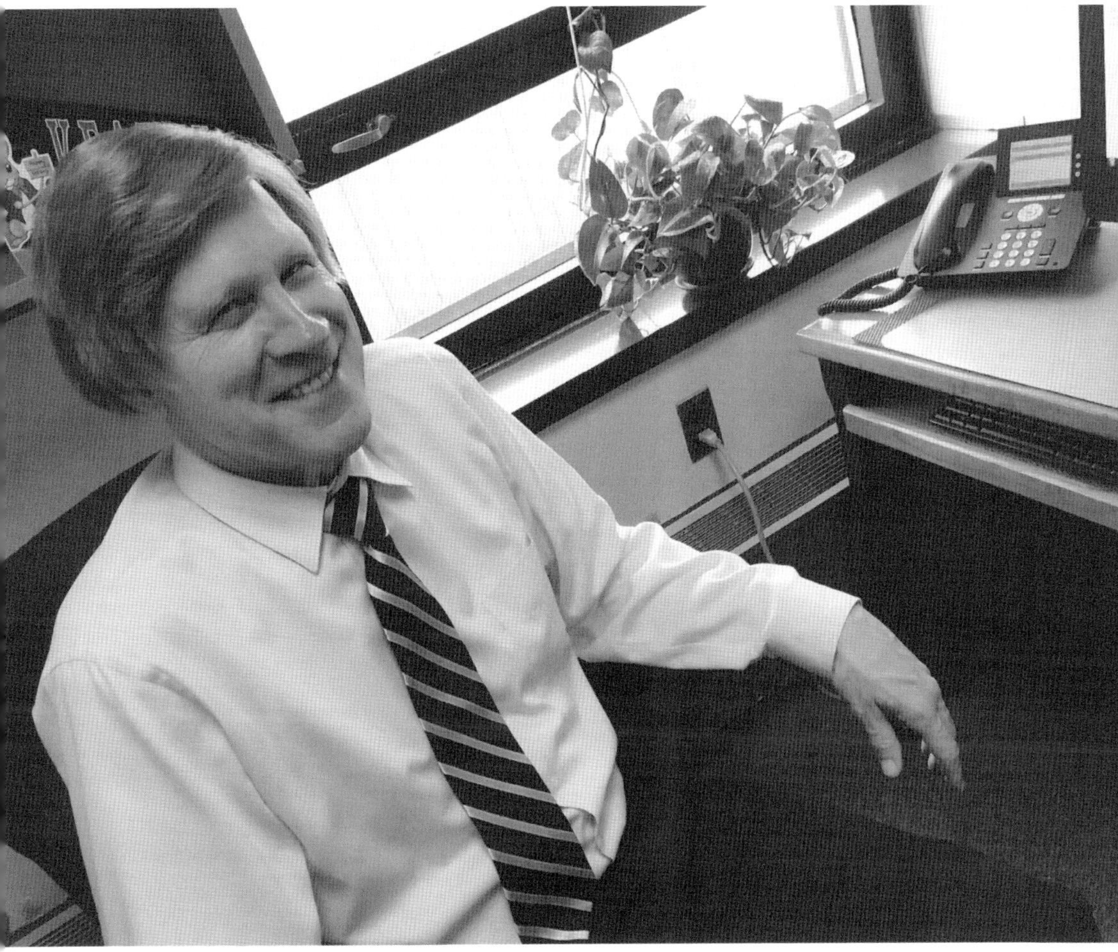

Leon Hoffman, "Yesterday" Translator

Born in 1918 in Brooklyn, Leon "Lee" Hoffman earned his bachelor's and master's degrees at New York University. Fascinated with Russian music, language, and culture, he taught Russian at Kearny High School for 30 years. He chaired the language department for several years as well. He inspired in his students a love of the Russian language and handed them his translation of the Beatles' "Yesterday" into "Ach, vchera." In 1961, he was one of 40 participating teachers in the Russian Institute Program sponsored by the National Defense Education Act. He spent five weeks in the Soviet Union to study its language and culture and returned thinking it was a miserable place to live. With more than 1,000 classical records in his collection, he could name the piece and also the orchestra and soloist. He was married to Dr. Ingeborg Schraft-Hoffman. (Courtesy of David Hoffman and Hilary Hoffman Fandel.)

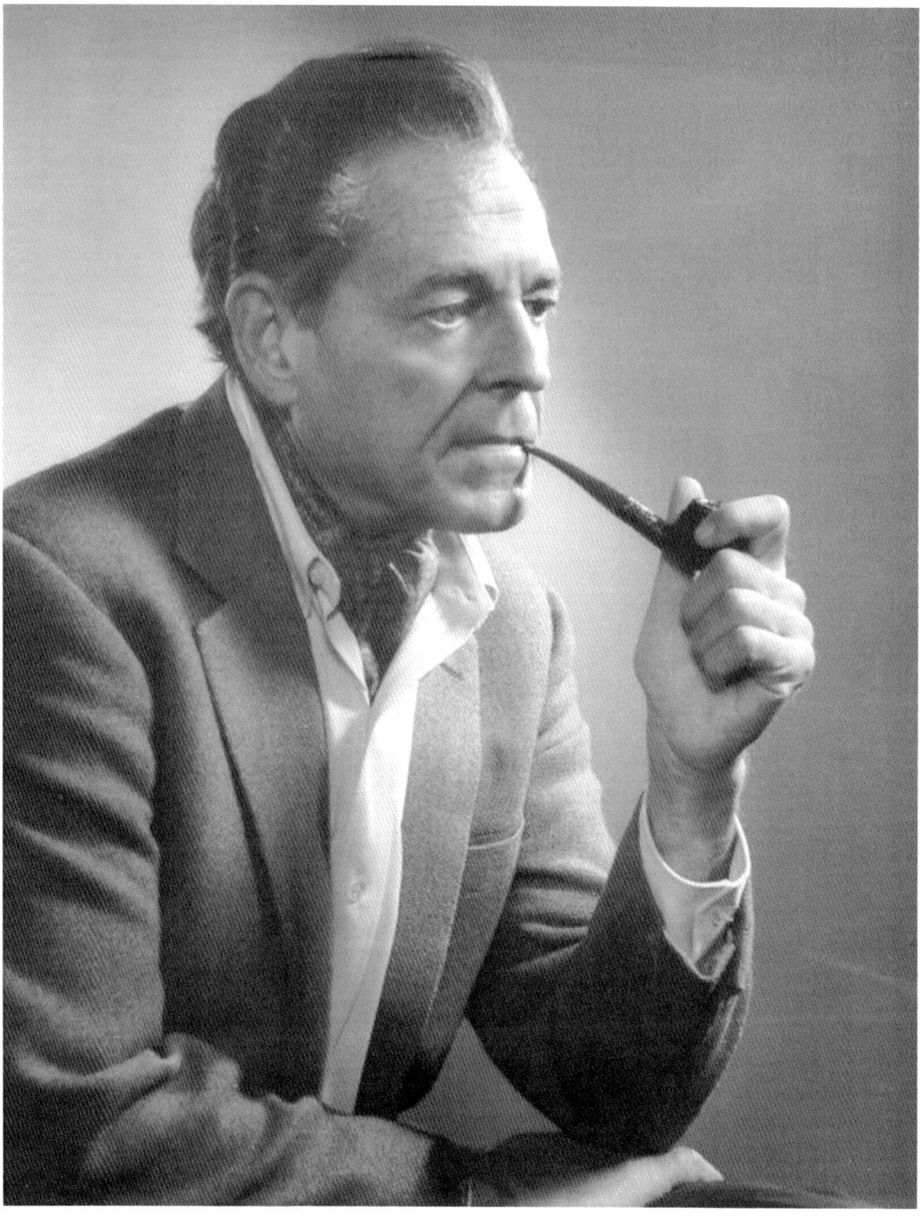

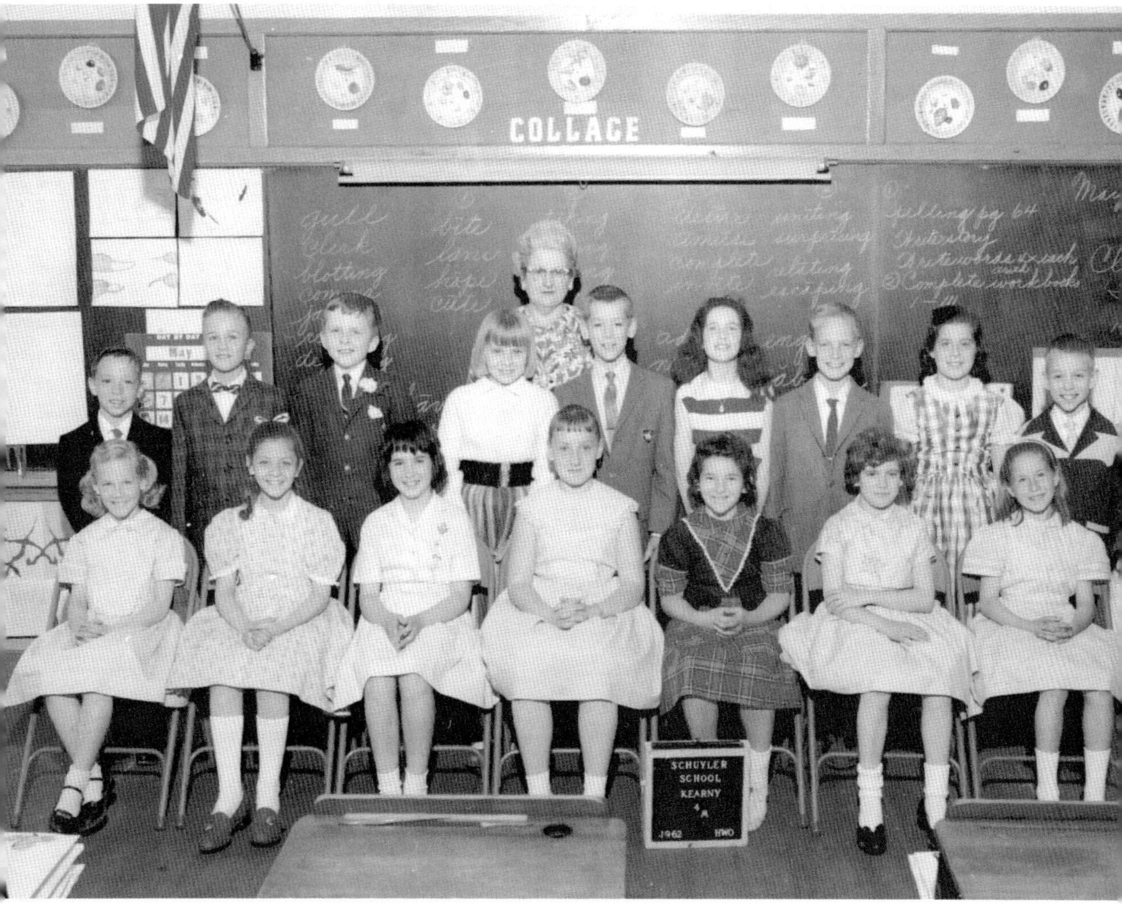

The High Standards of Mrs. Martin

If a visitor noticed a classroom of children with the best posture ever, chances were those children were students of Josephine Martin, fourth-grade teacher at Schuyler School. With her system of stars that earned books from Scholastic, she encouraged her students to become readers. She did not allow improper punctuation on compositions. By the end of the school year, children had benefited from her spirited learning community. Even today, her students lovingly and respectfully recall the ideals this educator set forth. Tough but fair, she unknowingly inspired them to become educators themselves. She is shown here with her class in 1964. (Courtesy of Evelyn Rocha Carson and Jeanne McCabe.)

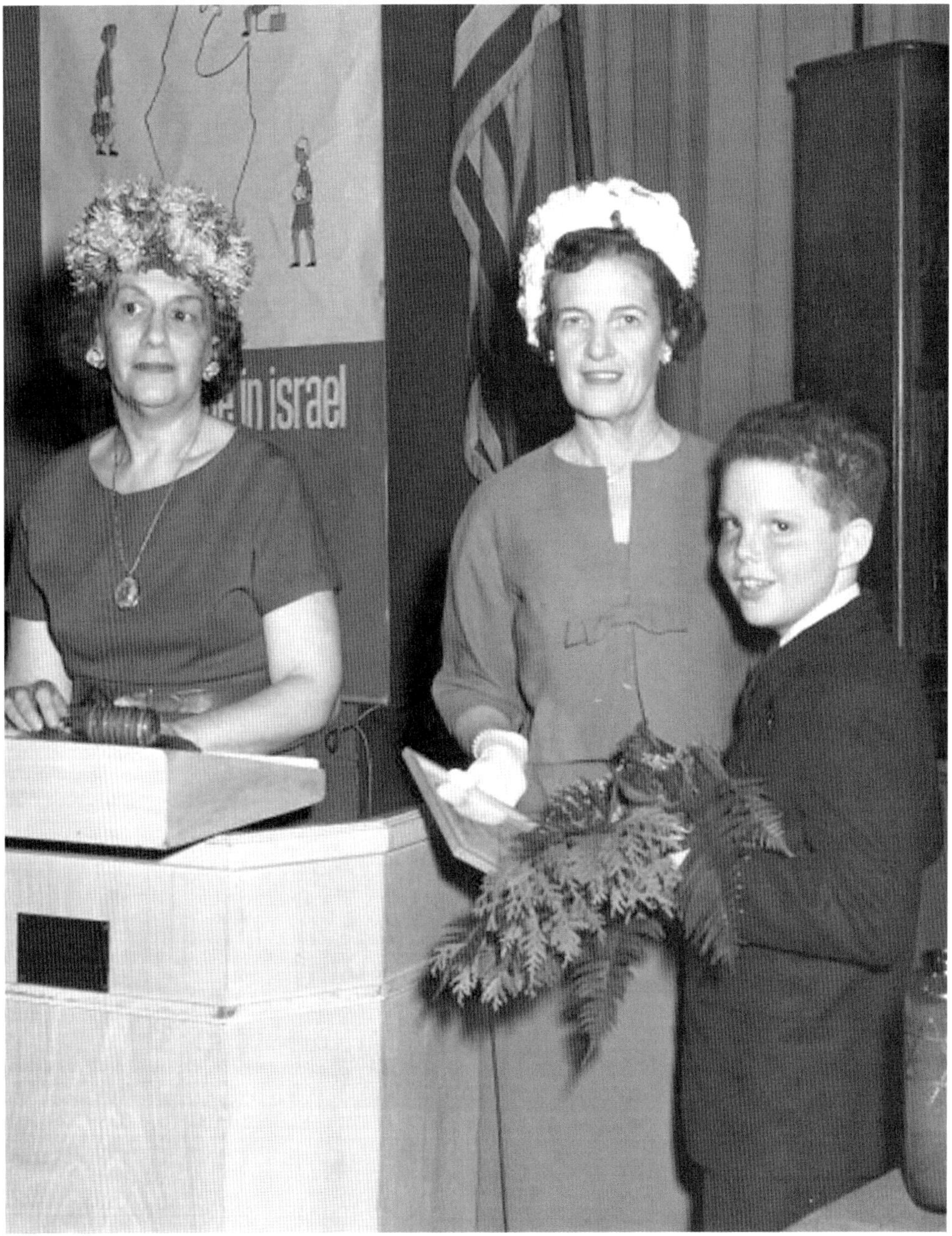

Tena Harris Nursery School We Will Always Treasure

Tena Harris operated her nursery school for at least 20 years through the 1950s, 1960s, and 1970s, in an old house on the corner of Oakwood Avenue and Beech Street. Harris gave each child a hug in the morning. Activities included nap time and trips to the triangle—where Kearny Avenue and Beech Street converge—where children played on the cannons and yearned for ice cream from the Tasty Freeze. Her husband, Herman, was a dentist with an office on Ridge Road. Active in Jewish causes, Harris is shown here accepting the 1963 Hadassah Woman of the Year award from young Tom Healey, son of the mayor. Born in 1910, she passed away in 2001. (Courtesy of Tom Healey.)

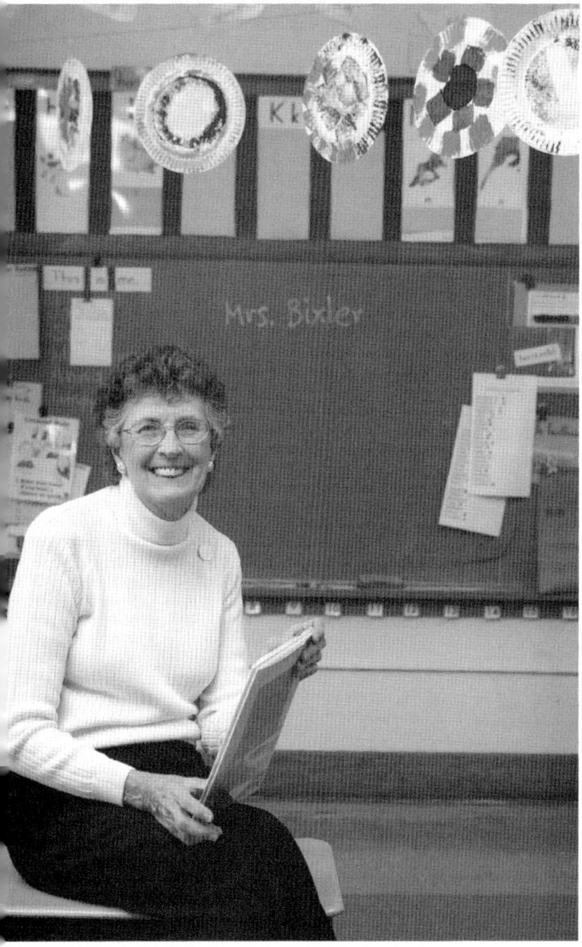

The Legendary Mrs. Bix

Margaret "Peggy" Greatorex Bixler has seen everything from men landing on the moon to the debut of the Internet. Although times have changed, to Bixler, kids will still be kids. She is the legendary teacher of Roosevelt School and a lifelong Kearny resident. She could be seen tooling around town in a big, brown Volvo with the custom plate "MRS BIX." She spent 53 years teaching first grade at Roosevelt and four years before that teaching kindergarten at Garfield School. Growing up, her family lived on Beech Street, and she attended Kearny schools herself. She always believed in the power of the town's school system and viewed teaching as an opportunity for continued learning. Her teaching style was considered to be "sheer magic." She is now retired. (Courtesy of Kearny UEZ.)

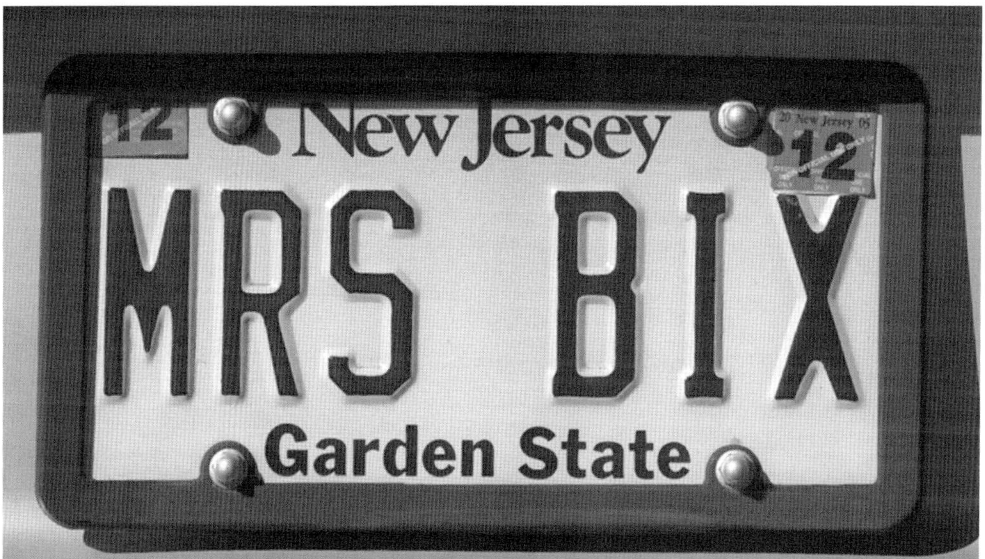

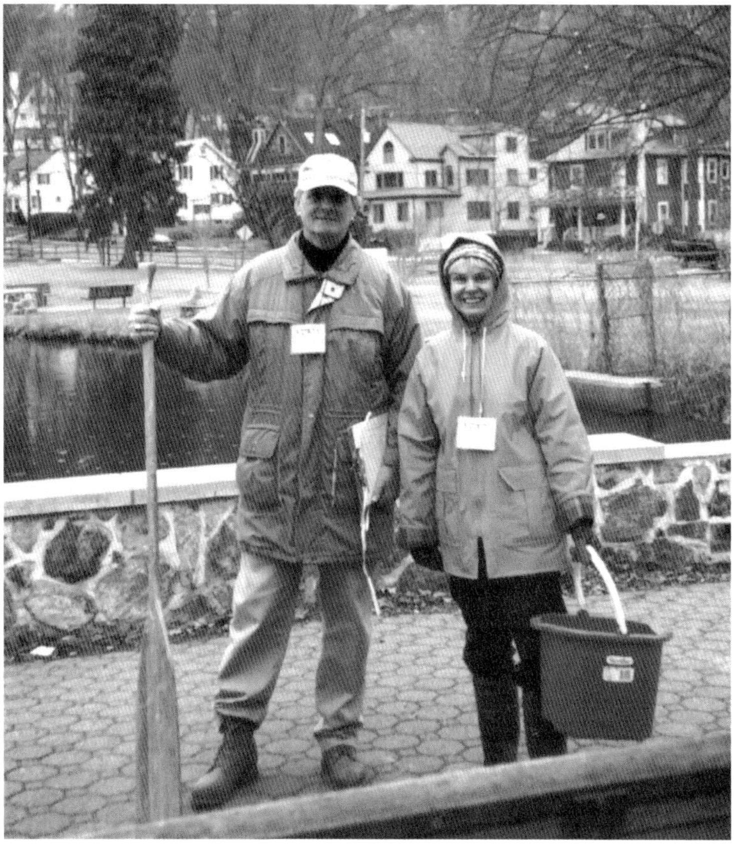

Fred and Diane Lee Gillespie, Teachers and Environmental Activists

Fred Gillespie was born in the town of Rothesay on the Isle of Bute, Scotland. At the age of five, he came with his family to America. But instead of taking to soccer like many Scots in Kearny, Gillespie took to baseball. He played on Kearny High School's varsity team. As a junior, he hit a home run in each of five consecutive games. He earned four varsity letters and was captain of the team as both a junior and senior. He also achieved four varsity letters in basketball and was named captain of the basketball team his senior year. He graduated as salutatorian and was inducted into the Kearny High School baseball hall of fame. After serving in the Army, he accepted a full scholarship to Fairleigh Dickinson University. In 1972, a banner year, Gillespie married fellow Kearny High School teacher Diane Lee and became an assistant baseball coach. He earned a master's in American history at Montclair State College. In 1976, he became head coach. He then moved into school administration as the academic vice-principal in 1992. He retired in 1999 but engaged in new activities, such as writing articles on history and hobbies for his local Sussex County newspaper.

Diane Lee began her teaching career at Kearny High School in 1968. She married Fred Gillespie in 1972. She pursued a master's degree in business education at Montclair State College and was named her program's outstanding graduate. A beloved teacher, she retired in 1999. Both she and her husband are listed in the *Who's Who of American Teachers*.

Diane and Fred Gillespie developed a passion for the environment, initiating Students Against a Vanishing Earth (SAVE). They also actively participated in the Humane Society of the United States. One of their programs resulted in the removal of sunken barges on the Kearny side of the Passaic River, receiving recognition by the New Jersey General Assembly and the governor. Diane's knowledge of gardening has transformed the Gillespie property into a wildlife habitat, recognized as a sanctuary by the National Wildlife Federation. (Courtesy of Fred Gillespie.)

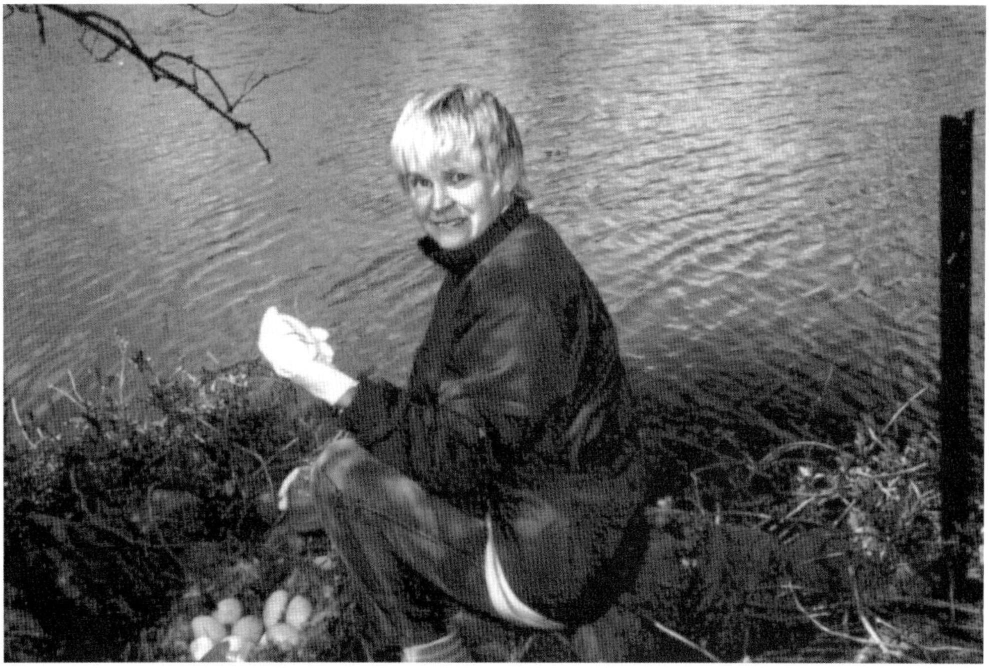

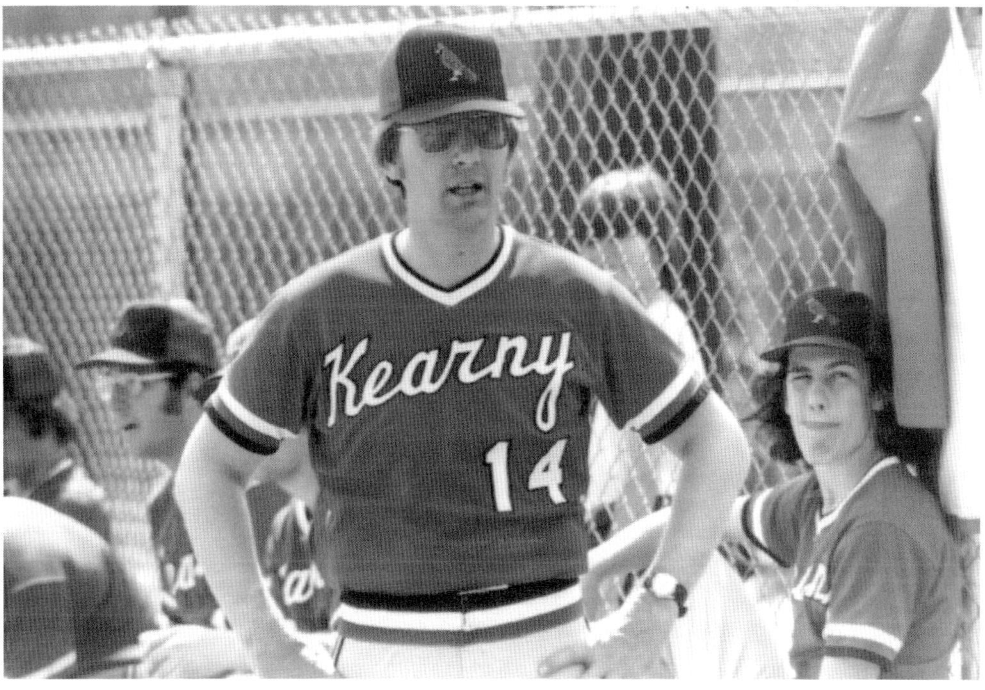
Kearny
14

Dr. Edmund L. Tink

Dr. Tink served as the Kearny School District superintendent for many years. Born in Wisconsin in 1901, he earned distinction on the Lawrence College (Wisconsin) debate team. He and his wife, Hester, lived in the Fairlawn Manor section of Kearny. He became superintendent of schools in Kearny on July 1, 1932, and remained in this post for 37 years until he retired on December 31, 1969. He played a major role in Kearny's centennial celebration. He also was fond of birdhouses, and when he summered in Maine, he brought birdhouses made by students in shop. He passed away in 1977. He is shown here on the right with Mayor Healey. (Courtesy of Kearny Museum.)

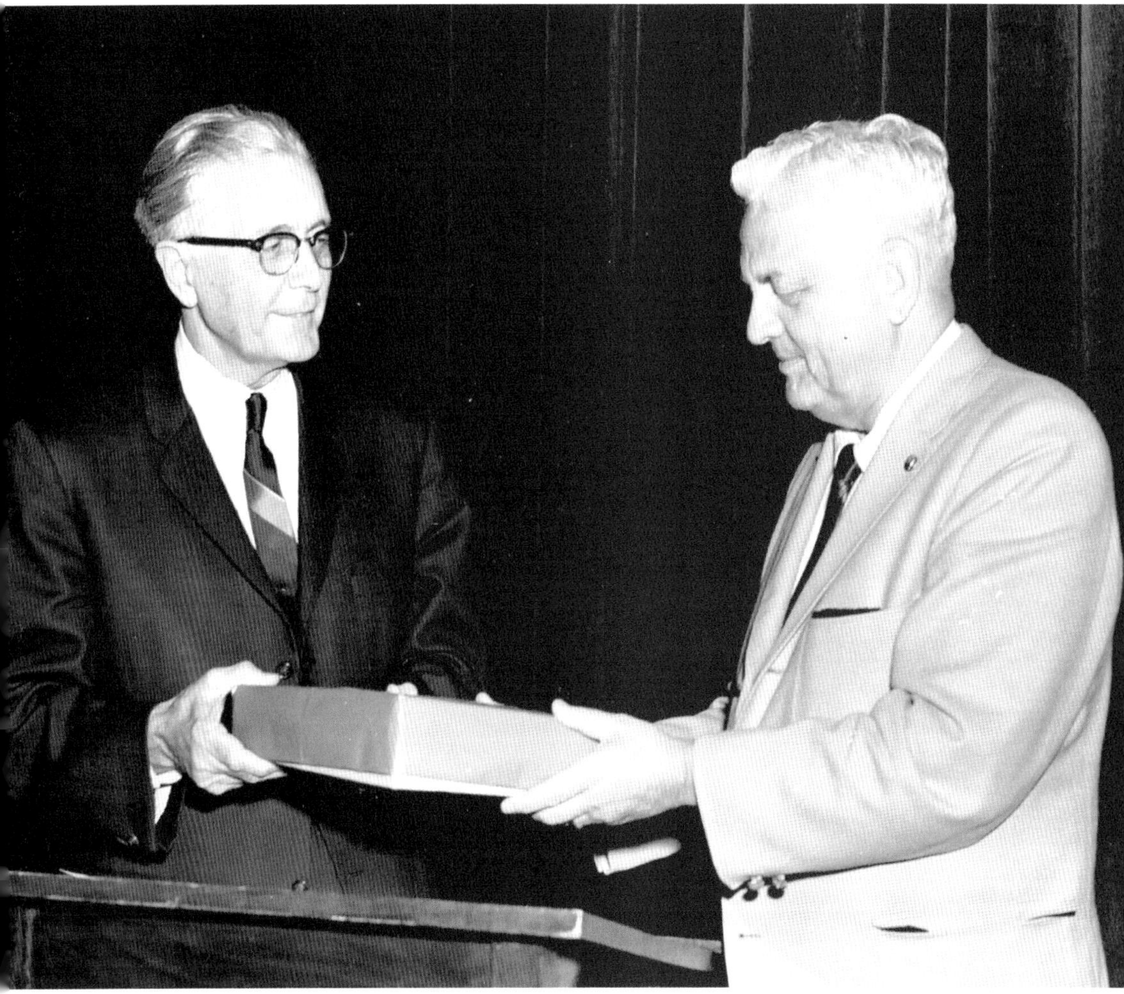

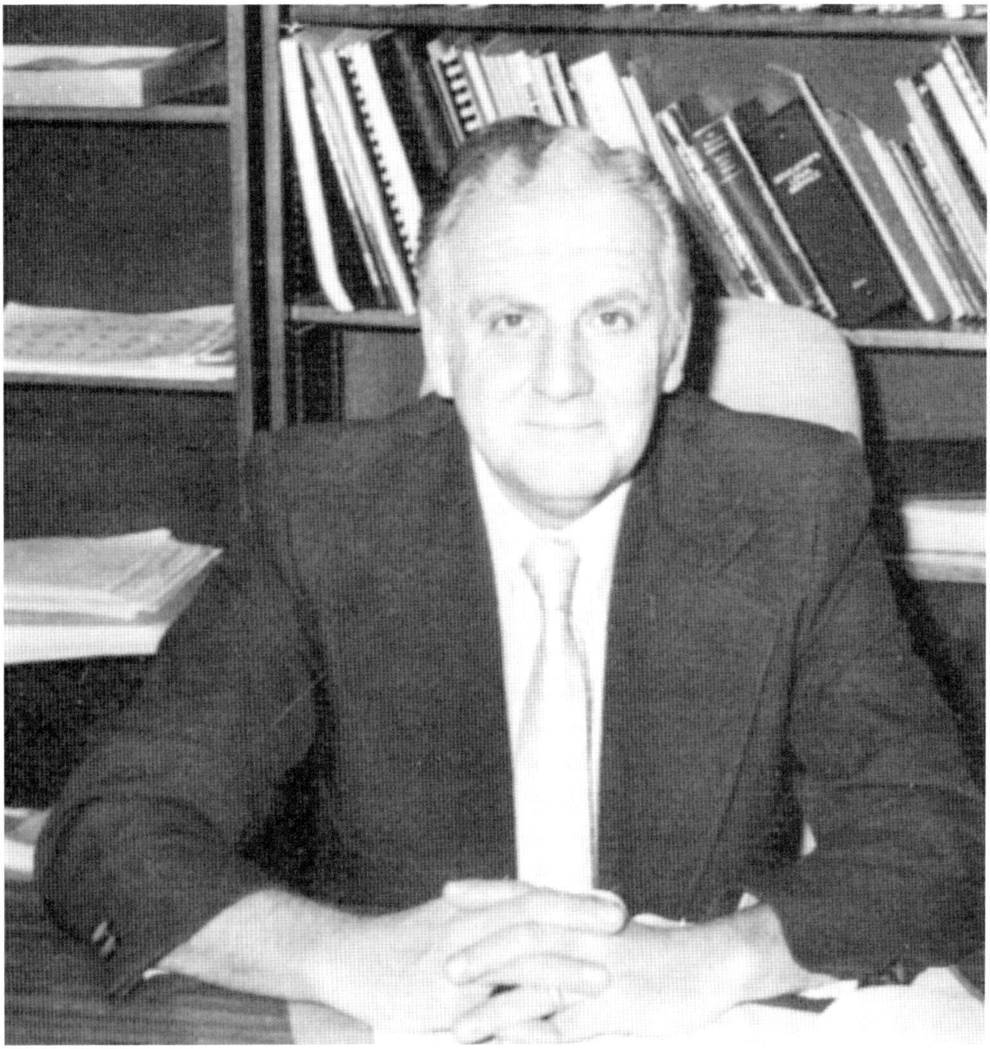

Dr. John Onnembo Ran the Distance

John Dominick Onnembo was born in Kearny in 1927. At Kearny High School, he was one of New Jersey's top half-milers. After a stint in the US Army in Germany, he received his bachelor's degree from Fordham University and ran track. He earned two master's degrees from Seton Hall University and a doctorate from Fordham University.

Onnembo served Kearny students for 40 years from 1953 until 1993, first at Washington School as a social studies teacher, then principal, and later at Franklin School. In 1970, he became assistant superintendent of schools and then superintendent for 13 years. He was beloved by students and colleagues for his patience, leadership, and dedication to Kearny. The high school gymnasium and a crew team skull are named after him. His estate donates a $1000 scholarship each year to worthy Kearny High School graduates. (Courtesy of Kearny High School.)

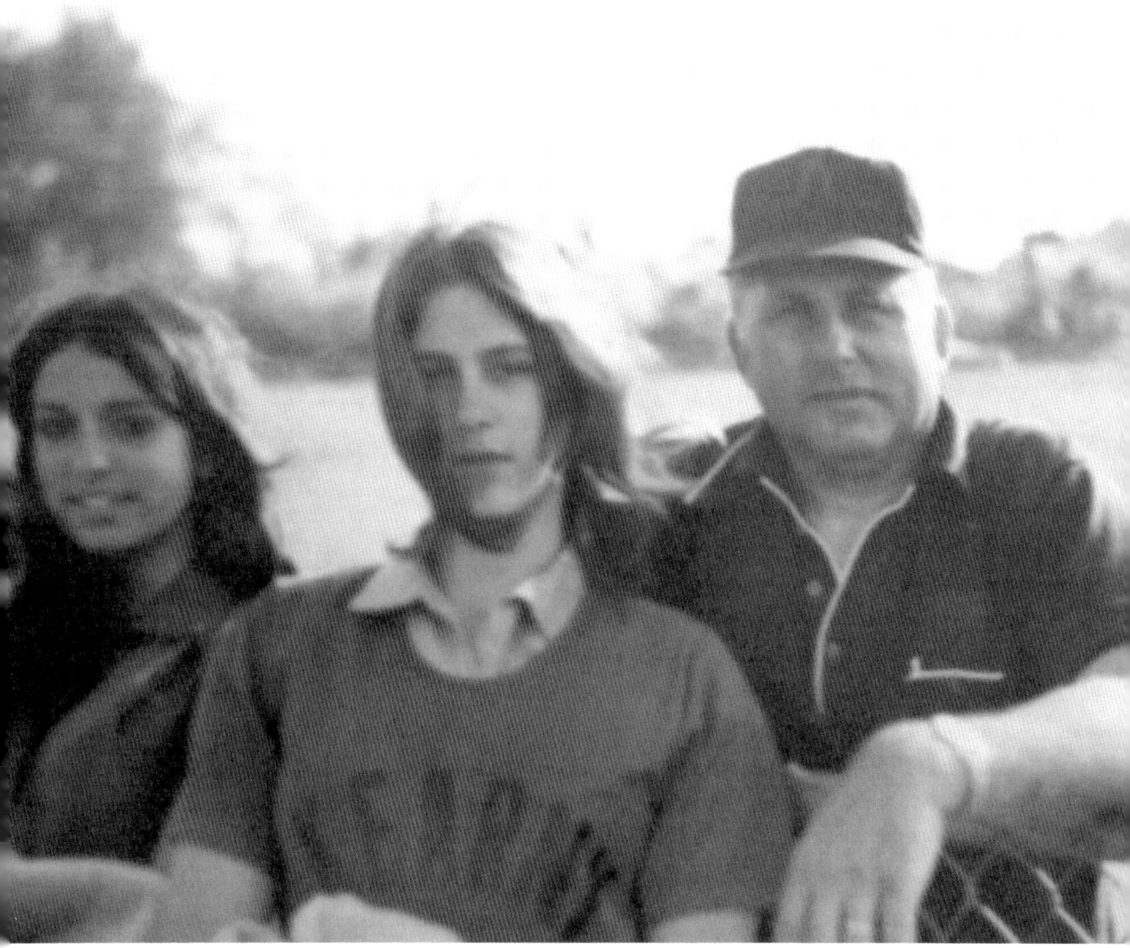

The Short Season of Thomas Krulik

Tom Krulik died at the age of 45. He was born in 1929 in Kearny to Ukrainian immigrant parents. He taught math and coached track at Kearny High School. When he died in 1974, the *Lamp Post* yearbook for the class of 1975 dedicated a page to his memory. He knew what it took to win, and he brought many championships to the school's distinction. As Geoff Burt says in the yearbook, "If life goes on, let us stop for maybe just one minute and look at the life that was divided into three seasons: fall, winter, and spring. Because as it was for Brian Piccolo, Mr. Krulik also had a short season." He is shown here with Geriann Silvestri Rotando and Renee Dudley. (Courtesy of Lisa Krulik.)

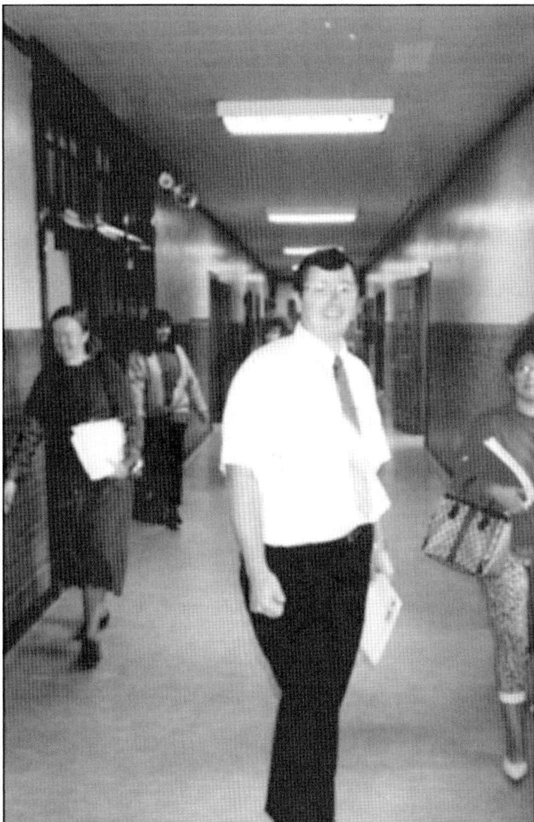

The Gentle Spirit of Ed Morrell

Born and raised in Kearny, Ed Morrell was the class of 1966 Kearny Kardinal mascot at Kearny High School. He went on to attend Fairleigh Dickinson University and Montclair State University and receive his teaching certification, inspired by his Kearny High School teachers. He joined the faculty in 1970 and taught in the business department. At first, he taught typing and various business subjects. Eventually, he taught computer technology, which he enjoyed the most, until he retired in 2005. He passed away in 2005 at age 57 from cancer. Eleven $1,000 scholarships have been awarded in his name to Kearny High School graduates who plan careers in either education or technology. A tribute in the 2006 Kearny High School yearbook said, "He was large in life, a beacon of caring, he was a kind, gentle soul." (Courtesy of Diane Morrell and Kearny High School.)

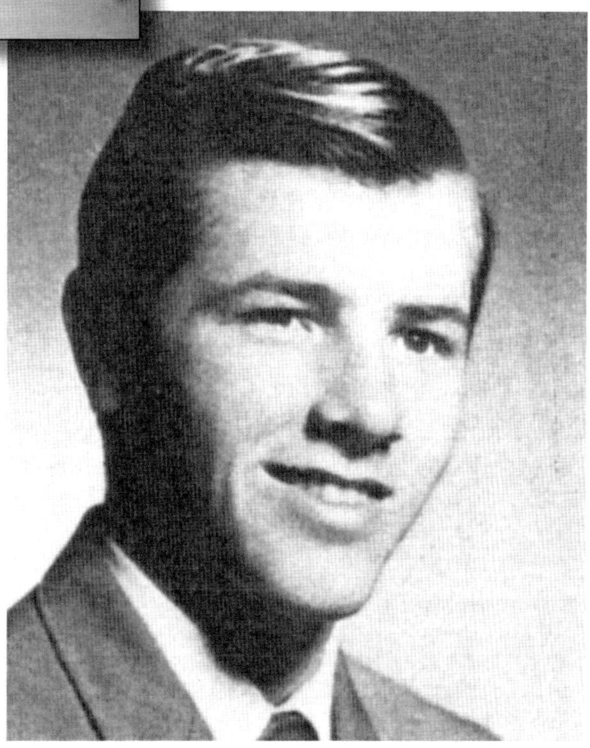

Robert Sprague, Teacher, Administrator, Coach

Bob Sprague, now retired, was with the Kearny School District for 40 years. He was born and raised in Kearny, graduating from Kearny High School in 1964. After nine years as a physical education instructor, he went on to serve six years as vice-principal and 24 years as principal at Franklin School. In 2010, he became assistant superintendent to interim superintendent Frank Digesere. Sprague was president of the PSA Union for many years. In addition to teaching and school administration, Sprague coached football, girls basketball, and golf. He was head baseball coach at Monmouth College for 12 years. He also spent five years at Fairleigh Dickinson University as head coach before starting his tenure as vice-principal. In 2014, the Franklin School PTA dedicated the school gymnasium as the Robert C. Sprague Gymnasium. (Courtesy of Kearny School District.)

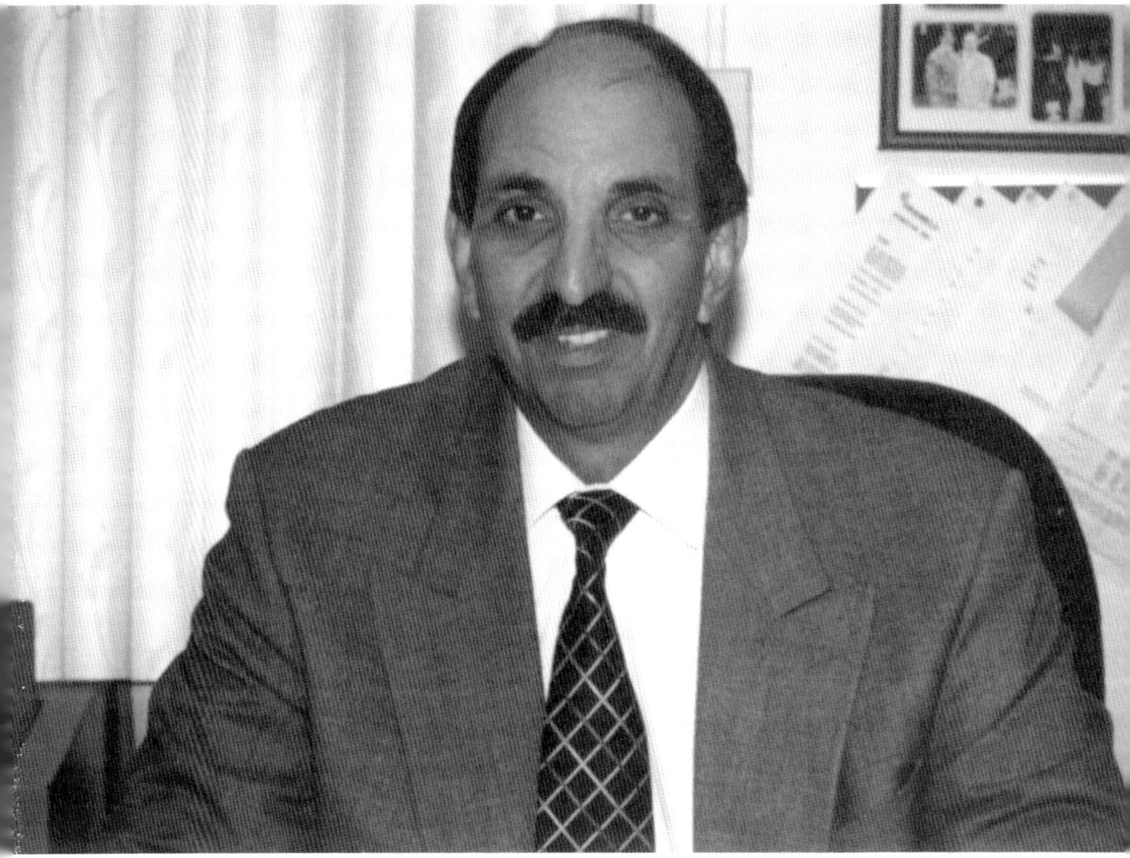

CHAPTER FOUR

Sports Heroes

Say "Soccer Town, USA" and Kearny, New Jersey, comes to mind. The town's love of soccer began with the influx of workers from Scotland and Ireland to work in the mills and factories. The Clark Thread Company sponsored Kearny's first great soccer team: ONT (Our New Thread, one of the company's products). The American Football Association formed in 1884 at Clark Thread. The ONT team became the association's first champion. Kearny, then, became the first national champion of soccer. More teams formed, including the Kearny Rangers and the Kearny Scots. By 1907, eight of the national team's 11 members came from the Clark and Kearny Rangers teams. The US World Cup team in 1990 and 1994 had three players from Kearny: John Harkes, Tony Meola, and Tab Ramos. The National Soccer Hall of Fame has a large number of players (not already mentioned) connected with Kearny. These include Fred Shields, Wally Peters, Edward McIlveney, Shamus O'Brien, Thomas Dugan, and Amos Dick.

Soccer players seemed to have one characteristic in common: they follow in the tradition of their fathers, who also played in their home countries. That is as much true today as it was more than 100 years ago.

Kearny loves soccer but also gives serious credence to other sports. Football great Alex Webster and his brother "Jiggsy" got their start in Kearny. Baseball shaped the careers of Ed Halicki, Bob Stanley, Howie Muderski, Ownie Carroll, and Sam Dente. Basketball brought out the best in Bill Raftery. Kearnians have made Olympic teams, such as crew members Jeff Klepacki and Jen Dore Terhaar.

From the playgrounds to recreational leagues to Kearny High School teams, dedicated coaches have been instrumental in spotting and nurturing talent. John DeVincenzo and Sandy Juliano have both been honored with Gunnell Oval clubhouse names.

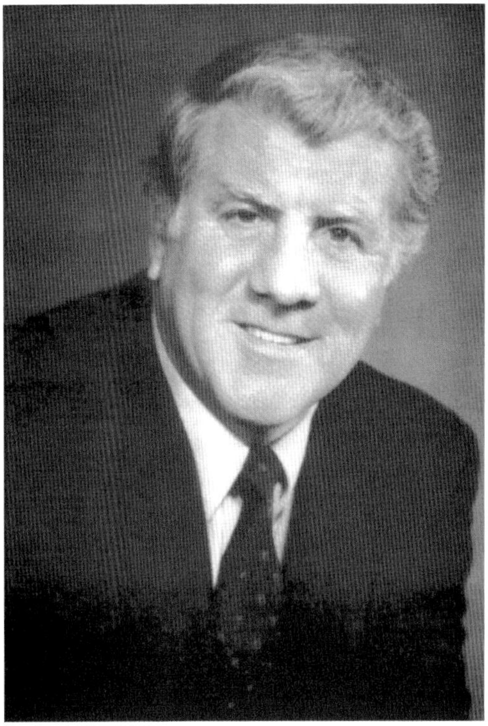

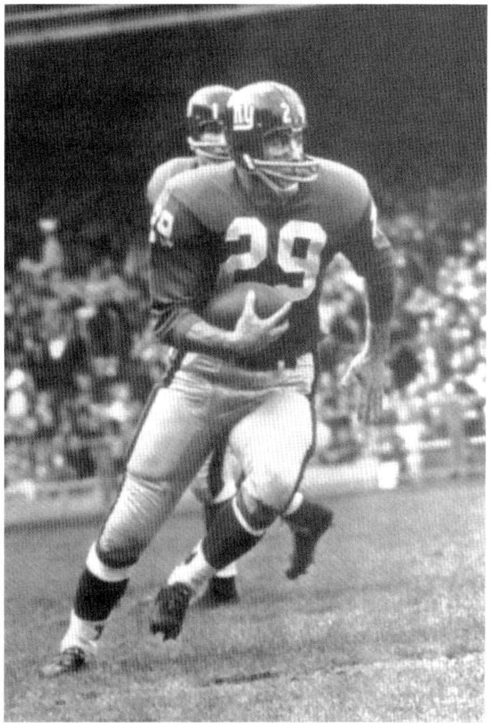

The Webster Brothers, Football Legends

Born in Kearny in 1931, Alex Webster, star of the Kardinals football team, helped his Kearny High School team win the New Jersey High School State Championship. After graduating in 1949, he played at North Carolina State University on a full scholarship. The Washington Redskins picked him during the 12th round of the draft in 1953 but cut him before the season began. He became a star in Canada and returned to the NFL in 1955 as a free agent with the New York Giants. He became assistant coach in 1967–1968 and was named head coach in 1969. He was voted Coach of the Year in 1970. He resigned in 1973 and passed away in 2012 in Port St. Lucie, Florida.

Alex's brother "Jiggsy" (James) played No. 22 on the football team at Kearny High School and graduated in 1953. Then, he joined the US Army and played football for Fort Bliss in El Paso. He received a scholarship to play at Milwaukee's Marquette University and earned team MVP in 1959. The New York Giants drafted him in 1960, but he did not make the team. Soon, a UFL team picked up his contract, and he moved to Michigan, where he played for five years and won two league championships. A respected teacher, coach, and school administrator, he succumbed to Alzheimer's—attributed to football-related head injuries—in 2013.

Photographs above show Alex and Alex in action. On the next page are Jiggsy in play, and the two brothers together at The Thistle in 2003. (Above left, courtesy of Alex Webster; all others, courtesy of Mark Webster.)

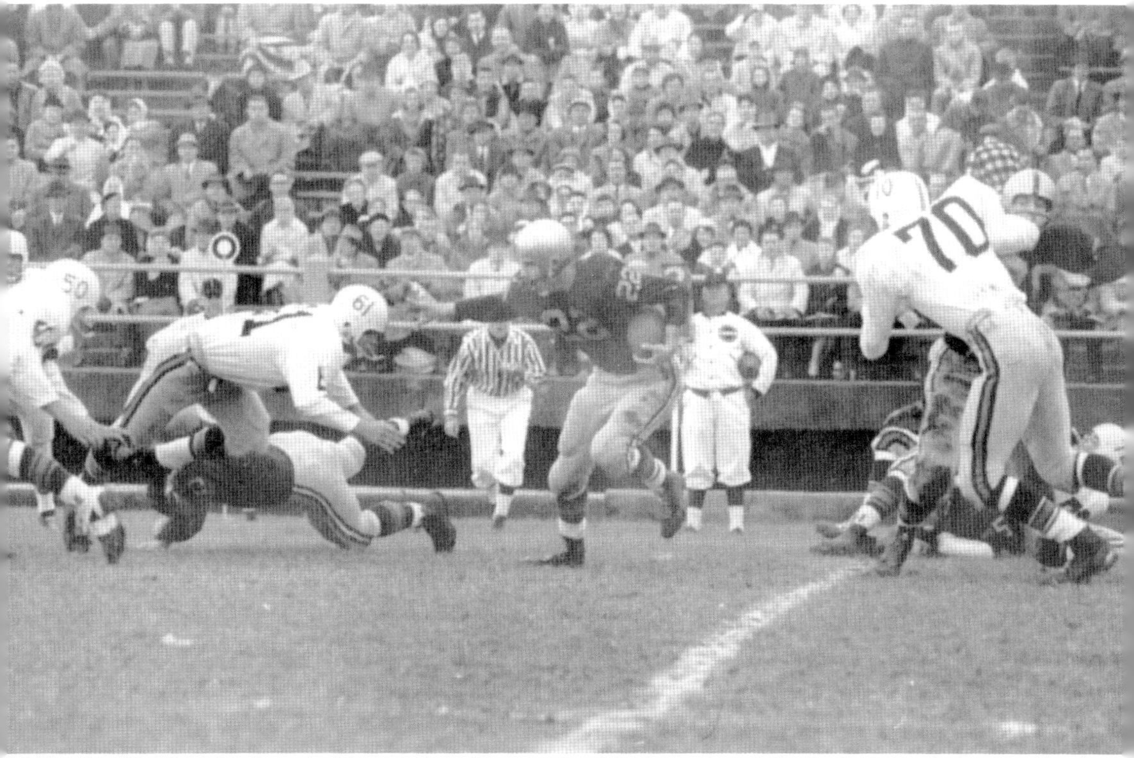

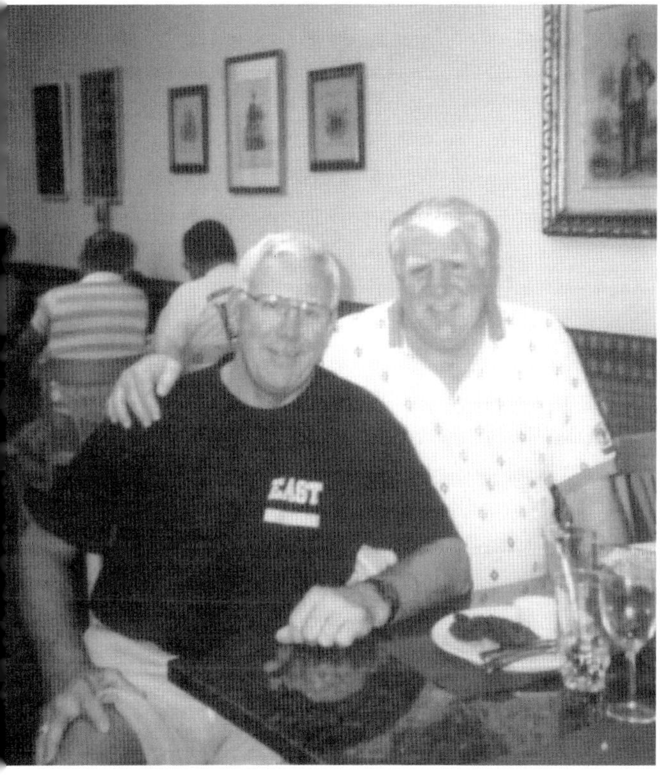
EAST

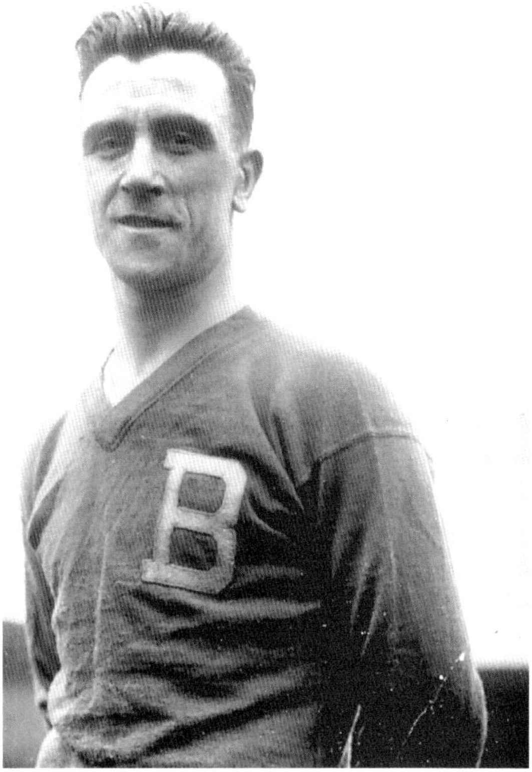

Archie Stark, Soccer Hall of Fame
Archibald MacPherson Stark arrived in America from Glasgow, Scotland, around 1912 at the age of 14. He played for Kearny's Scots American and Irish American soccer teams as well as the United States team in 1925. He later played for the Bethlehem Steel team, its "B" insignia on his uniform. Called the "number one goal scorer," he was inducted into the National Soccer Hall of Fame in 1950. He died in Kearny in 1985. (Courtesy of Kearny Museum.)

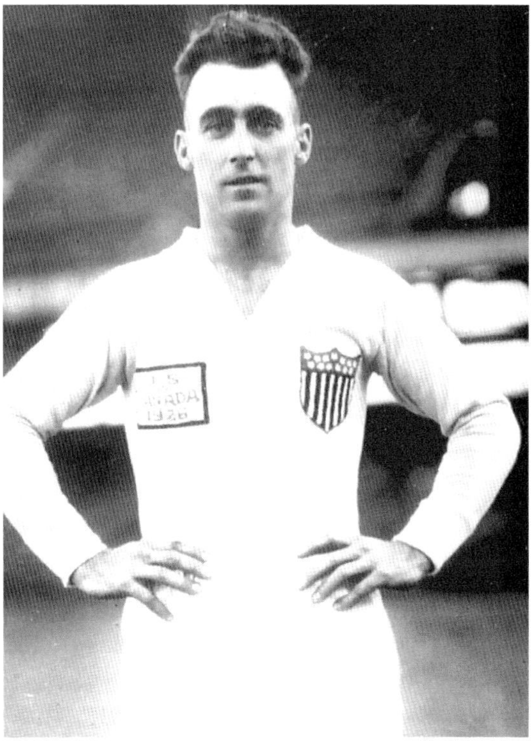

Davey Brown, Soccer Hall of Fame
David Brown was born to Scottish immigrants and lived on Dukes Street. He played soccer in international games in 1925 and 1926. He is shown here in his uniform in a game against Canada in 1926. Called the "number two goal scorer," he was inducted into the National Soccer Hall of Fame in 1951 and died in Kearny in 1970. (Courtesy of Kearny Museum.)

Billy Gonsalves, the Babe Ruth of American Soccer

Born in Rhode Island in 1907 to Portuguese immigrant parents from the island of Madeira, Adelino "Billy" Gonsalves represented the United States in the World Cup in 1930 and 1934. He also played in 11 US Open Cup finals in 15 years. Although he grew up in New England, he lived in Kearny in his later years. He lived on Columbia Avenue and played with Kearny's Scots American team in 1941–1942. He was one of the first inductees into the National Soccer Hall of Fame in 1950. Gonsalves was considered to be one of the best soccer players in the first half of the 20th century. He died in Kearny in 1977. (Courtesy of Kearny Museum.)

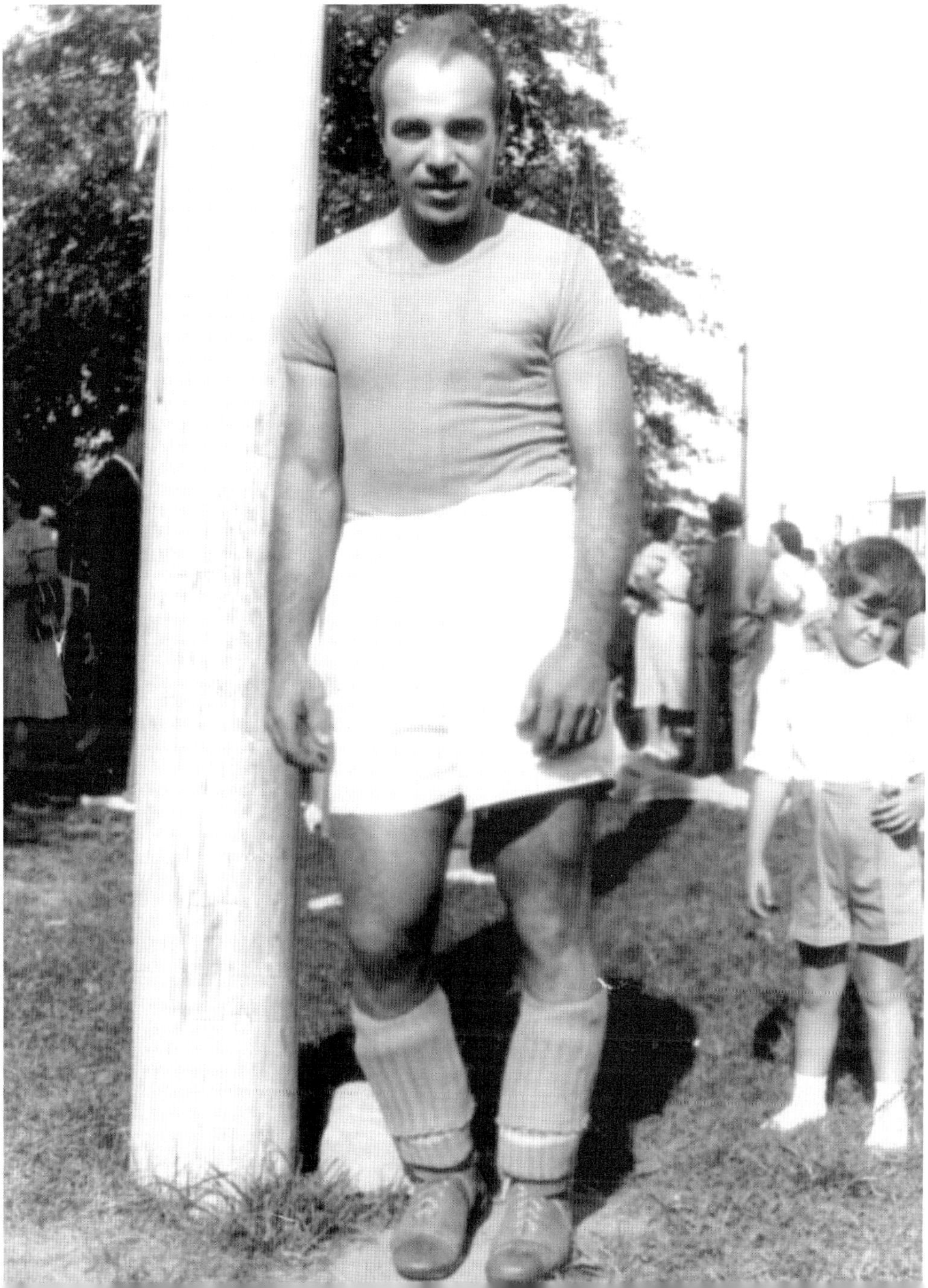

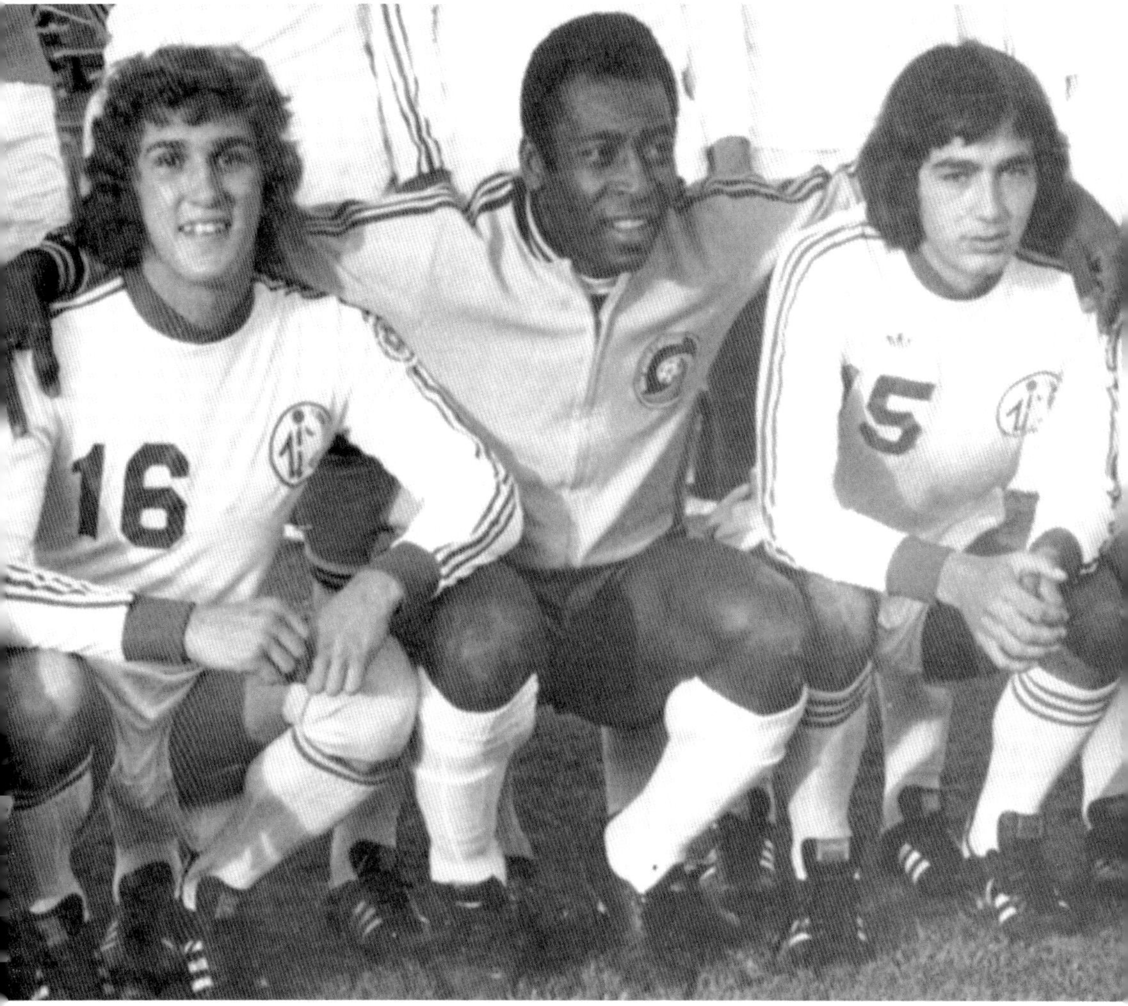

Santiago Formoso, "One of the Most Talented Players in America"
Born in Vigo, Spain, in 1953, Santiago Formoso graduated from Kearny High School in 1973. He went on to attend the University of Pennsylvania but was tapped in 1976 to play soccer with the Hartford Bicentennials in the North American Soccer League. He later played with the New York Cosmos and other teams. Along with Hugh O'Neill, he was on the 1976 US Olympic Soccer Team. From 1988 to 2001, he worked in the Metrostars marketing department and is now creative director at *USA Today*. He is shown here (far right) with Pele and Bicentennial team member Hugh O'Neill in 1977. (Courtesy of Hugh O'Neill.)

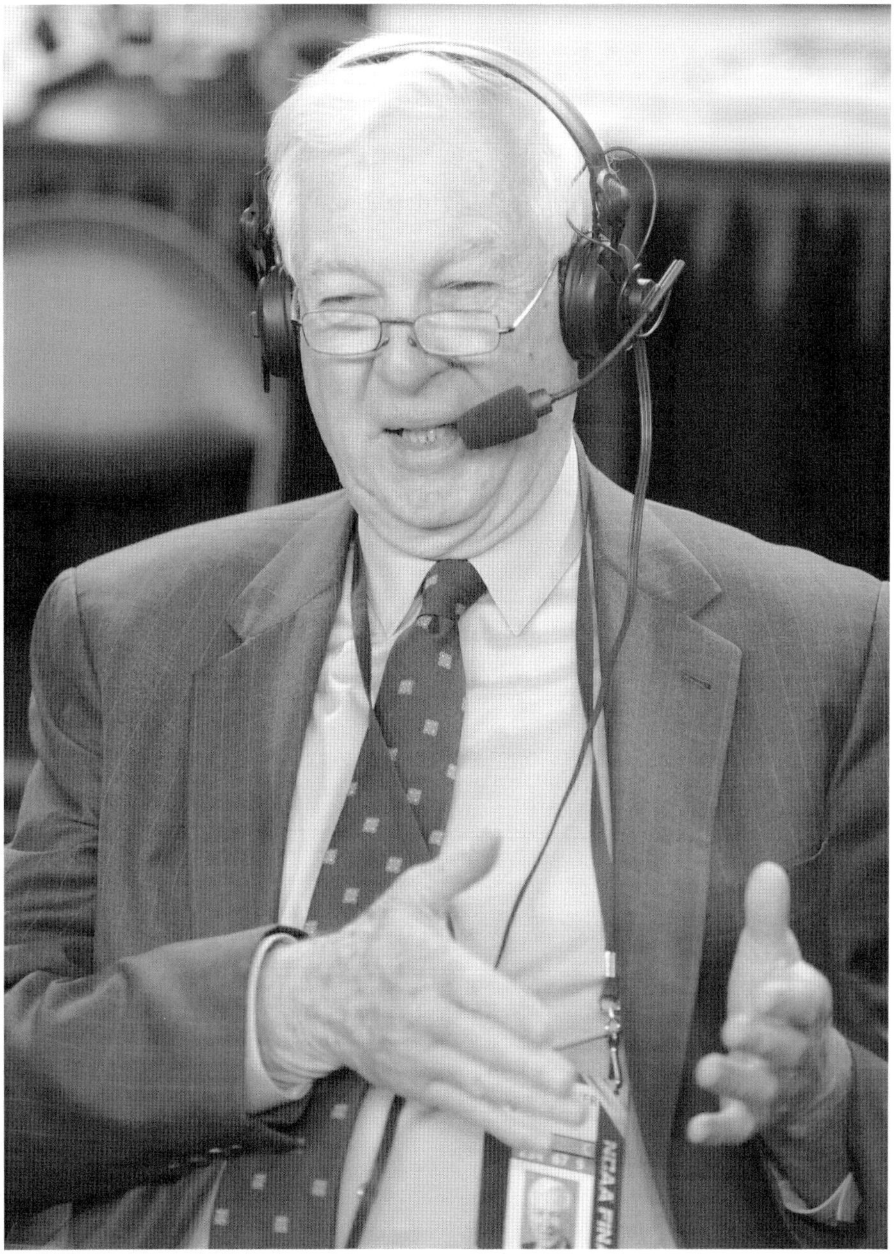

Bill Raftery, Sports Announcer

Along with recreation director Sam Hagen and Hugh O'Neill, basketball All-American Bill Raftery started the Kearny Recreation Soccer League for the town's youth. It was part of a deal he struck with Mayor Joseph Healey while working to launch his professional basketball career. A three-sport athlete—soccer, basketball, and baseball—at St. Cecilia High School, he graduated from La Salle University. He was drafted by the New York Knicks but never played in the NBA. He did, however, serve as head basketball coach at Fairleigh Dickinson University and Seton Hall University. For more than 30 years, he has been a basketball analyst and announcer on television, including CBS and Fox. (Courtesy of Sean Dougherty, *USA Today Sports*.)

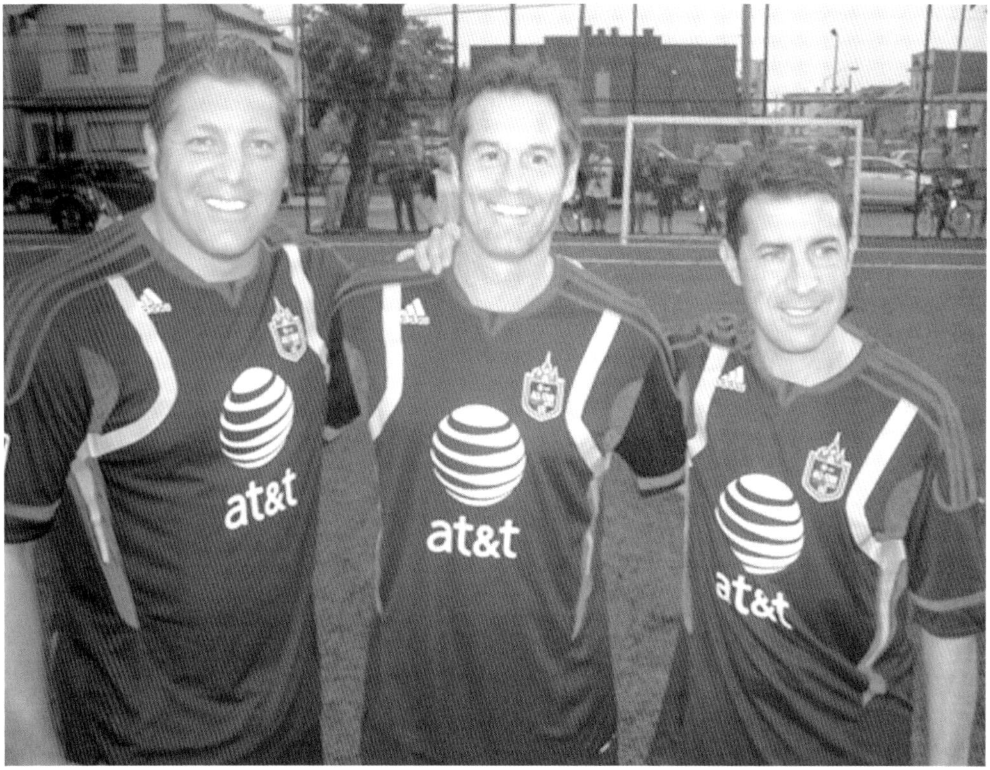
at&t
at&t
at&t

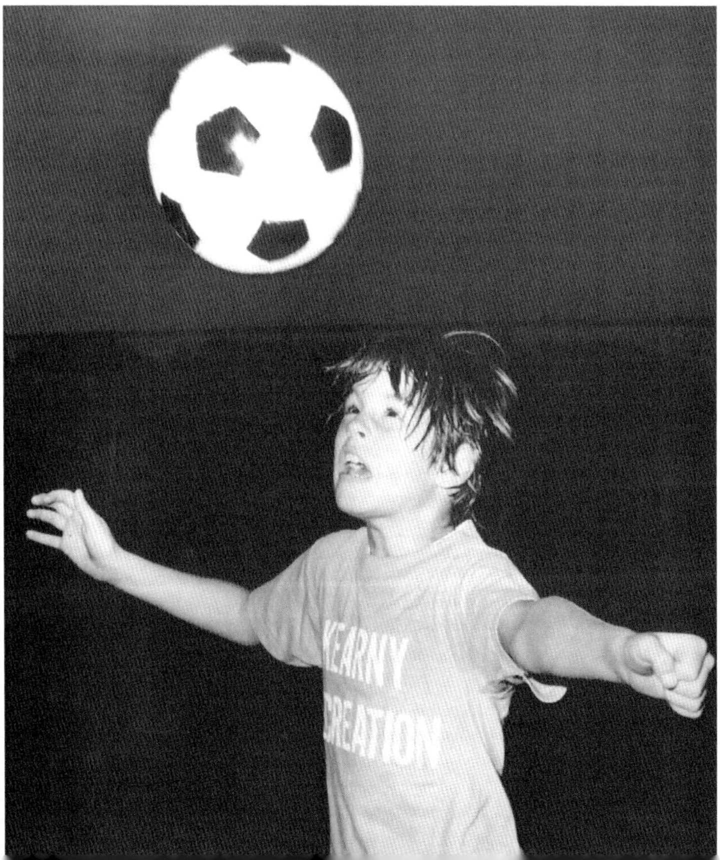
KEARNY

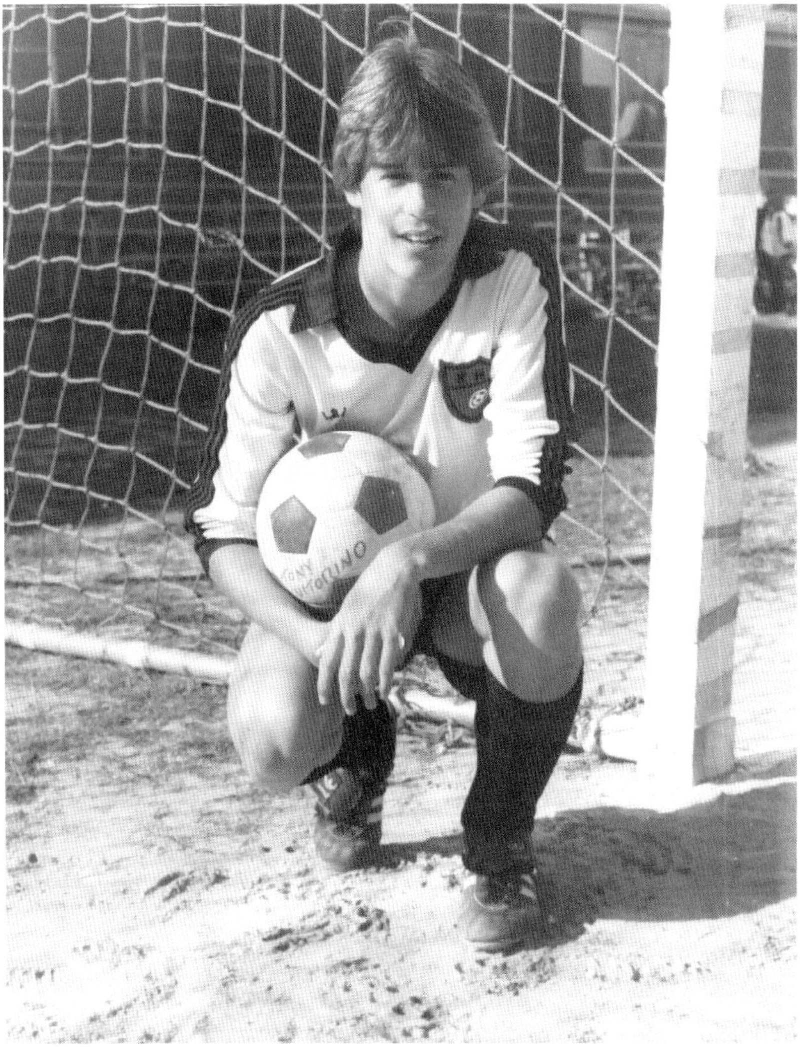

The Triple Threat of John Harkes, Tony Meola, and Tab Ramos

John Harkes is one of several "Soccer Town USA" inductees into the US Soccer Hall of Fame. When Harkes was four years old, he pulled on big brother Jimmy's Thistle jersey and followed him and his father to the soccer field. His father, Jim, played for the Scots American Club team for 16 years. Harkes attended Kearny High School and played on the US World Cup team in 1990 and 1994. He was inducted into the National Soccer Hall of Fame in 2005. He is shown here as a youngster, already with a passion for the sport.

Continuing in the tradition of his father, who had played professional soccer in Italy, Belleville-born Tony Meola played soccer for Kearny High School (with teammate John Harkes) and went on to play in the 1990 and 1994 World Cup games as goalkeeper. After playing for the Metrostars for many years, he retired in 2002. He was inducted into the National Soccer Hall of Fame in 2012.

Born in Montevideo, Uruguay, Tab Ramos followed in his father's footsteps to play professional soccer. He arrived in America in 1978 at the age of 11 and became a US citizen in 1982. The Kearny resident played on the US team in the World Cup games in 1990, 1994, and 1998. He was inducted into the National Soccer Hall of Fame in 2005. Since 2014, he has served as the assistant coach to the US men's soccer team. (Courtesy of Jim Hague and Kearny UEZ.)

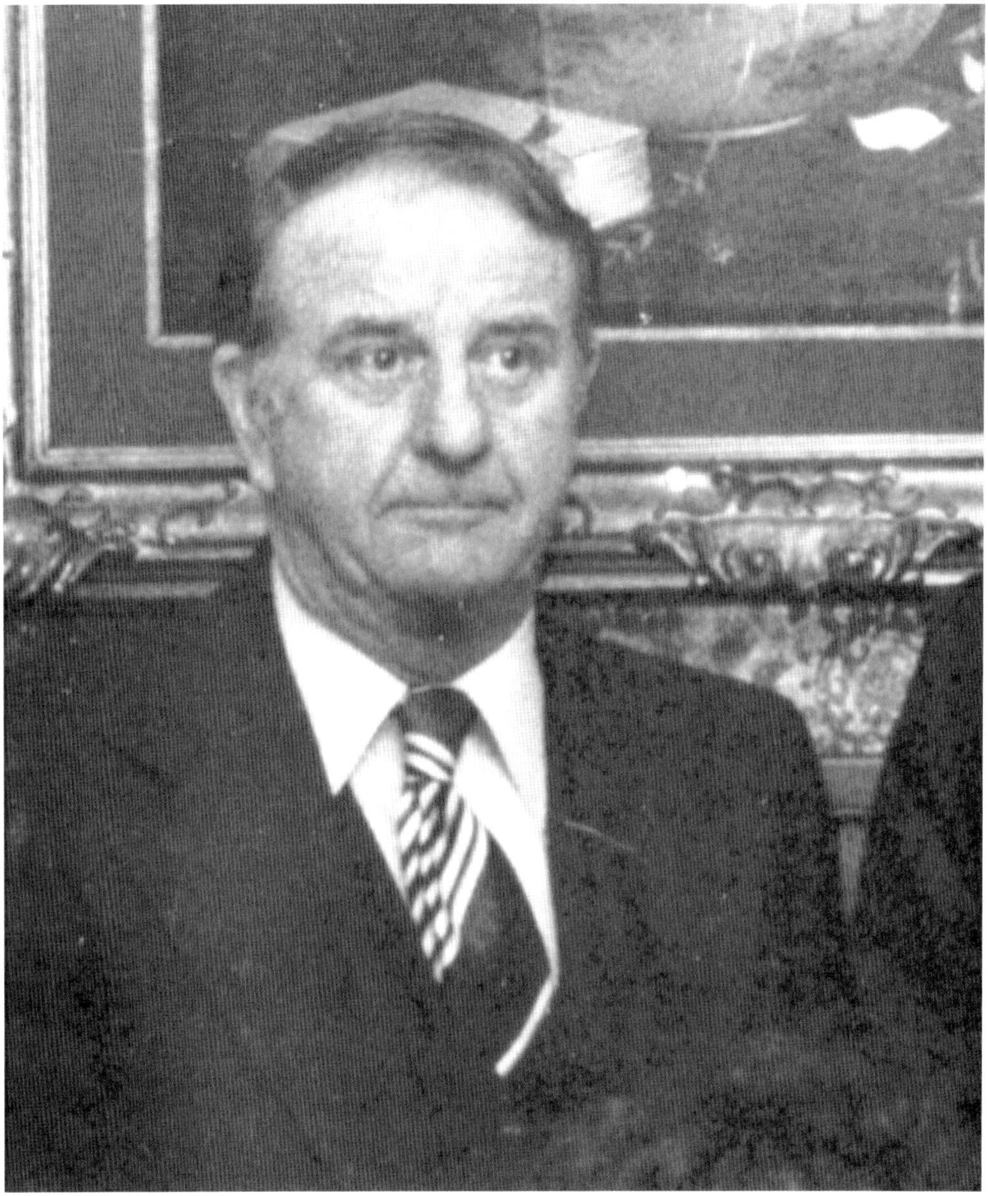

Hugh O'Neill Jr., Founder of Kearny Recreation Soccer

Hugh O'Neill Jr. came to Kearny from Paisley, Scotland, like thousands of others. Born in 1920, he served in the British 8th Army, Royal Corps of Signals in World War II. In Scotland, he was a bricklayer and mason until his 1948 emigration. He continued that work in Kearny. While he served leadership positions in many civic organizations, such as president of the Irish American Club, vice president of the Scots American Club, and councilman, he is perhaps best remembered for his contribution to Kearny youth sports. In 1961, he noticed many Kearny youths were playing soccer without the benefit of supervision or guidance. He founded Kearny Recreation Soccer. A plaque on the exterior of the recreation soccer field house at Gunnell Oval honors him. He died in Kearny in 1982. (Courtesy of Hugh O'Neill.)

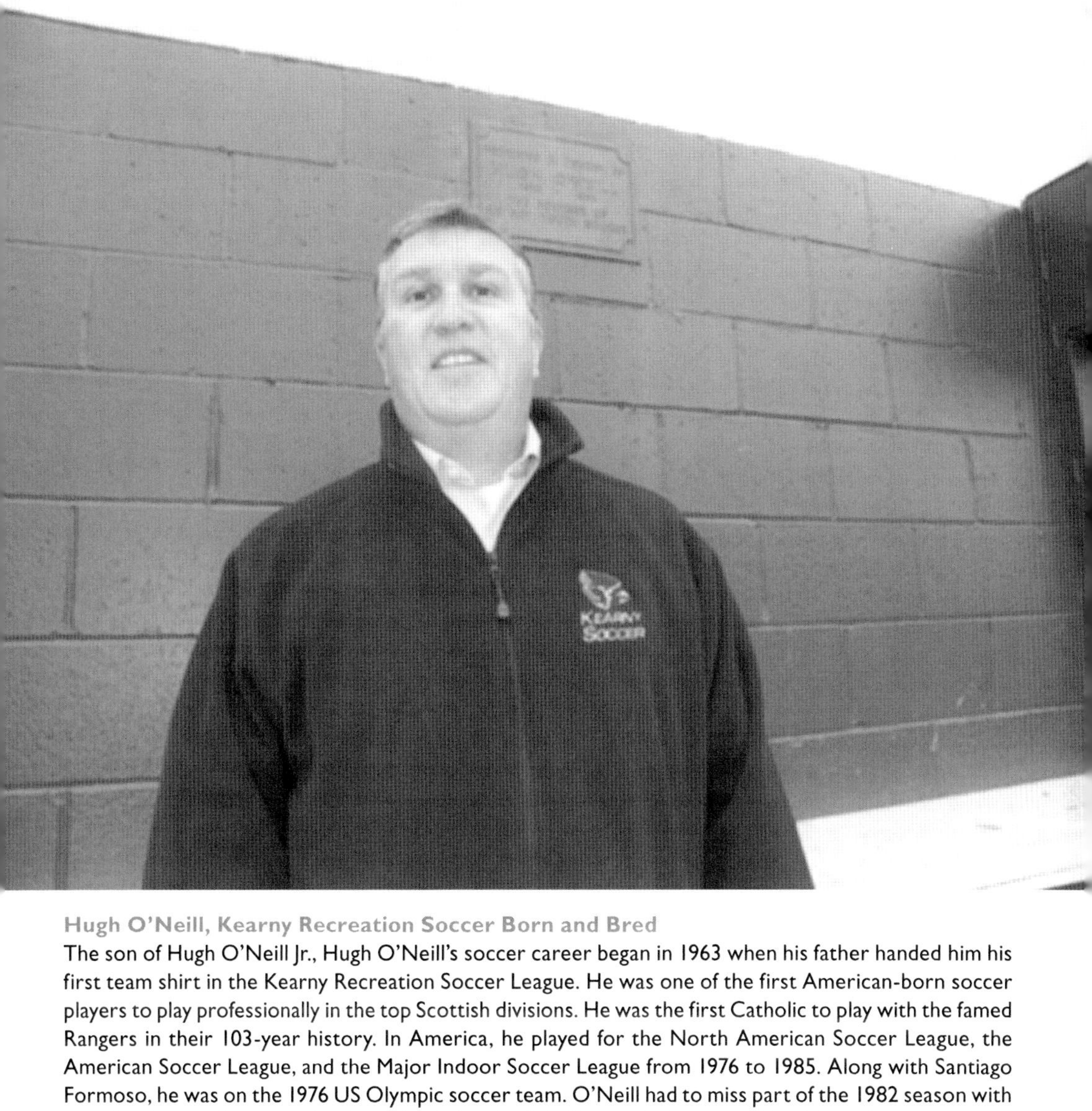

Hugh O'Neill, Kearny Recreation Soccer Born and Bred
The son of Hugh O'Neill Jr., Hugh O'Neill's soccer career began in 1963 when his father handed him his first team shirt in the Kearny Recreation Soccer League. He was one of the first American-born soccer players to play professionally in the top Scottish divisions. He was the first Catholic to play with the famed Rangers in their 103-year history. In America, he played for the North American Soccer League, the American Soccer League, and the Major Indoor Soccer League from 1976 to 1985. Along with Santiago Formoso, he was on the 1976 US Olympic soccer team. O'Neill had to miss part of the 1982 season with Carolina Lightnin' to attend to his dying father back in Kearny. (Courtesy of Jim Hague.)

Jennifer Dore Terhaar, Two-Time Rowing Olympian

At 15, Jen Dore Terhaar started rowing on the Passaic River while attending Kearny High School. She graduated from Kearny High School in 1989 and was a part of the class of 1993 at Rutgers University. Terhaar became a 10-time National Team member and two-time Olympian in the 1996 and 2000 games, winning silver medals in the Eight at the 1993 and 1994 World Rowing Championships and the US gold medal in 1995. In 2003, she returned to elite rowing and represented the United States at the World Championships in the Women's Eight. She is considered the most decorated female rower from Rutgers. She was inducted into the National Rowing Hall of Fame in 2012. (Courtesy of Kearny High School.)

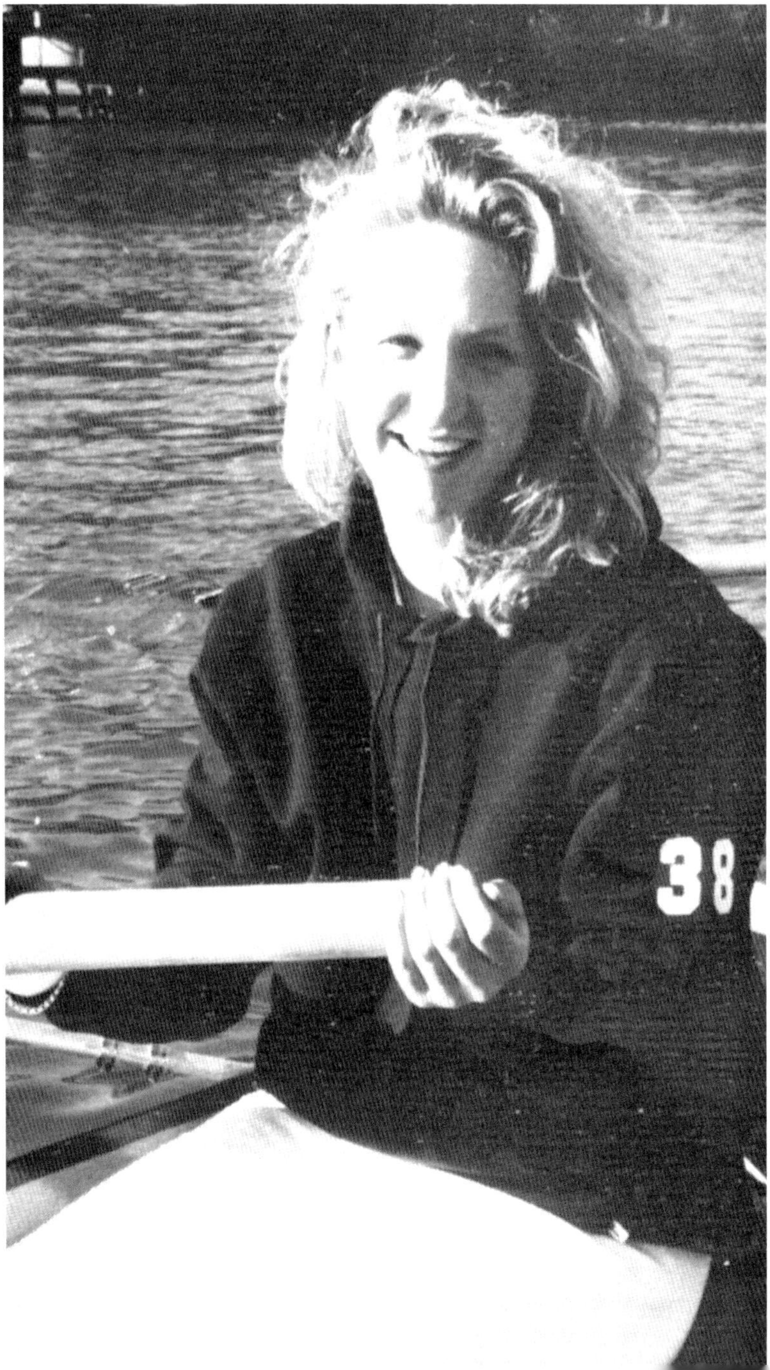

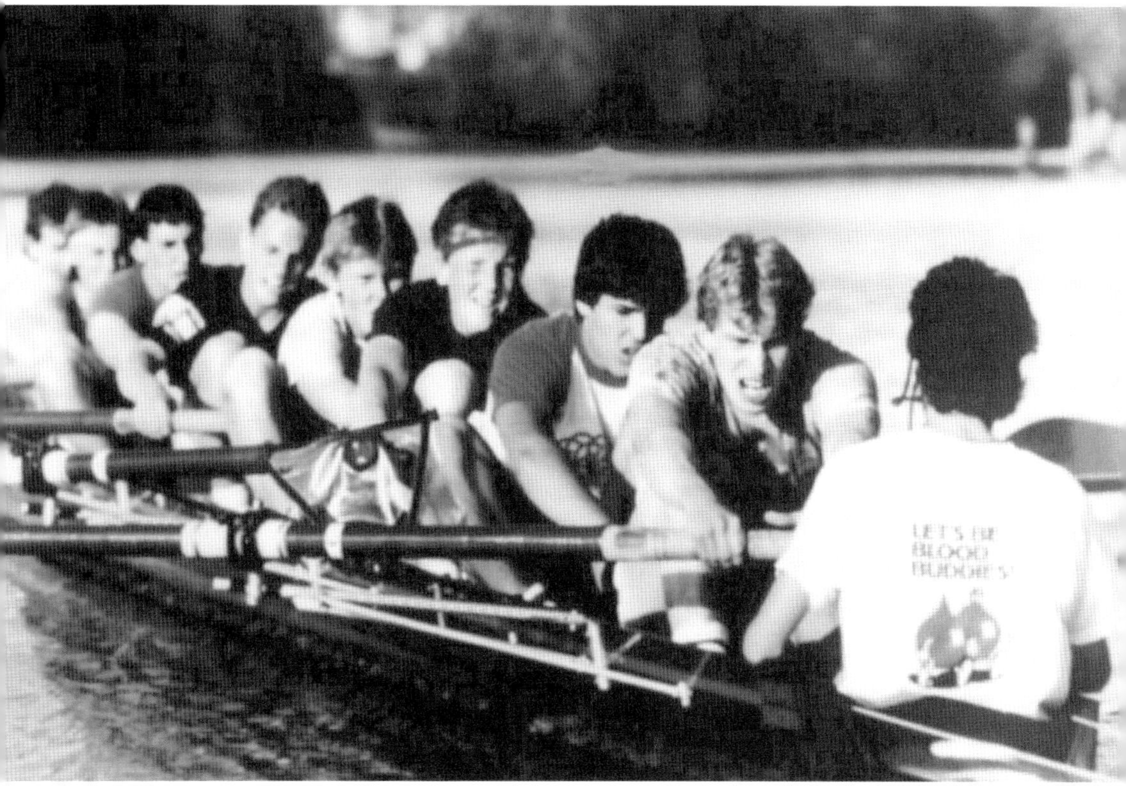

Jeff Klepacki, Three-Time Olympian in Crew

Jeff Klepacki credits Kearny High School for being one of the few New Jersey high schools with a crew program. Born in 1968, Klepacki took up crew on the Passaic River at Kearny High School in his senior year. He was a member of the Rutgers University crew team and graduated from Livingston College with a bachelor of arts degree in economics in 1990. He led his team in the World Rowing Championships in the US Men's Heavyweight 8+ to gold medal victory in 1994, 1998, and 1999. He also participated in the Olympic Games in 1992, 1996, and 2000. He was inducted into the National Rowing Hall of Fame in 2012. He is shown here on the Kearny High School crew team during the spring of 1986 as the fourth rower, wearing a headband. (Courtesy of Jeff Klepacki.)

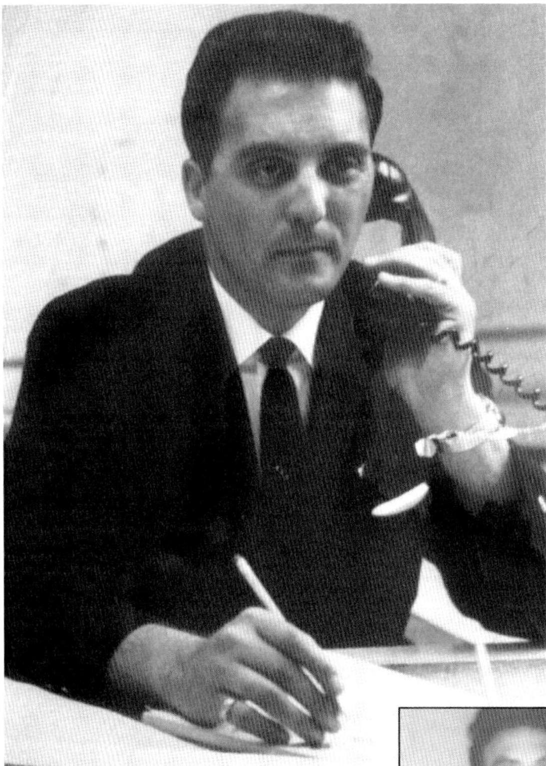

John F. DeVincenzo, Little League Coach, Big League Dedication

Born in Newark in 1927 to Italian immigrant parents, John DeVincenzo graduated from Barringer High School in 1945 and enlisted in the US Navy, where he served for two years in the Coast Guard. He had a flourishing career in the paper industry, but perhaps DeVincenzo is best known in Kearny for Little League. "Mr. Dee" started as a minor league coach for his sons in 1958. His commitment lasted 51 years. He coached the Kearny Federal Savings Little League team to many championships before he became the president of Kearny's Little League organization. In 2010, he received the Hudson County Sports Hall of Fame Community Service Award. The eastern field of Gunnell Oval has been named in his honor. (Courtesy of John R. DeVincenzo.)

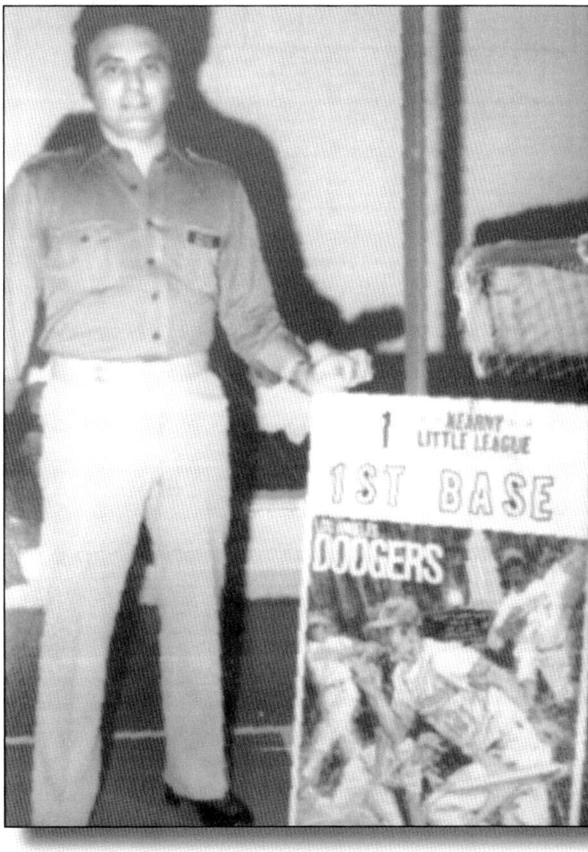

CHAPTER FIVE

Healers

Kearny's Board of Health debuted in June 1892. An outbreak of typhoid in 1894—caused by a drought that polluted the Passaic River—became the board of health's first real challenge.

In 1913, Kearny laid claim to its own hospital, Stumpf Memorial, at the corner of Bergen Avenue and Elm Street on land donated by German immigrant Jacob Stumpf in honor of his late wife, Mary Hahn. In attendance were surgeons August Strasser and Widmer Doremus, assisted by James Bramley and Howard Dukes. Other attending physicians included Henry Allers, Marcus Squire, Alfred Mutter, and Stanley Goudy. The hospital eventually took on the name of West Hudson Hospital, now a rehabilitation center that is part of the Clara Maas hospital system.

Of course, not all of Kearny's healers treated patients in the hospital. Physicians like E. Holden Goldberg had private practices. Notable among such physicians were also Maclyn Cagan, Franklyn Saracino, Victor Rudomanski, John Long, Irving Friend, Daniel Garfinkel (and the itty-bitty rubber animals he gave out to children), and S. Lewis Kook. Several doctors tended to the needs of the schools and Kearny High School's sports teams as E. Holden Goldberg had done decades before. Pediatrician John Elkas attended to the Newark school system and operated his private pediatric practice on Kearny Avenue.

Many former students may recall their school nurses, such as Rosalind Bellini, who long serviced Roosevelt School. Other Kearnians also fondly remember the staff at doctor offices, like Ann Rudomanski, a registered nurse in her husband's pediatric practice, and Grace Hartigan, who worked for Irving Friend and Daniel Garfinkel.

Then, there were the dentists, like Milton Lerner, with offices on Kearny Avenue, and Peter Young on Kearny Avenue but farther south across from town hall.

Although the days of doctors making house calls and, thankfully, the days of dental work without the benefit of modern technology are long gone, Kearny takes pride in its healers and their service to the overall community.

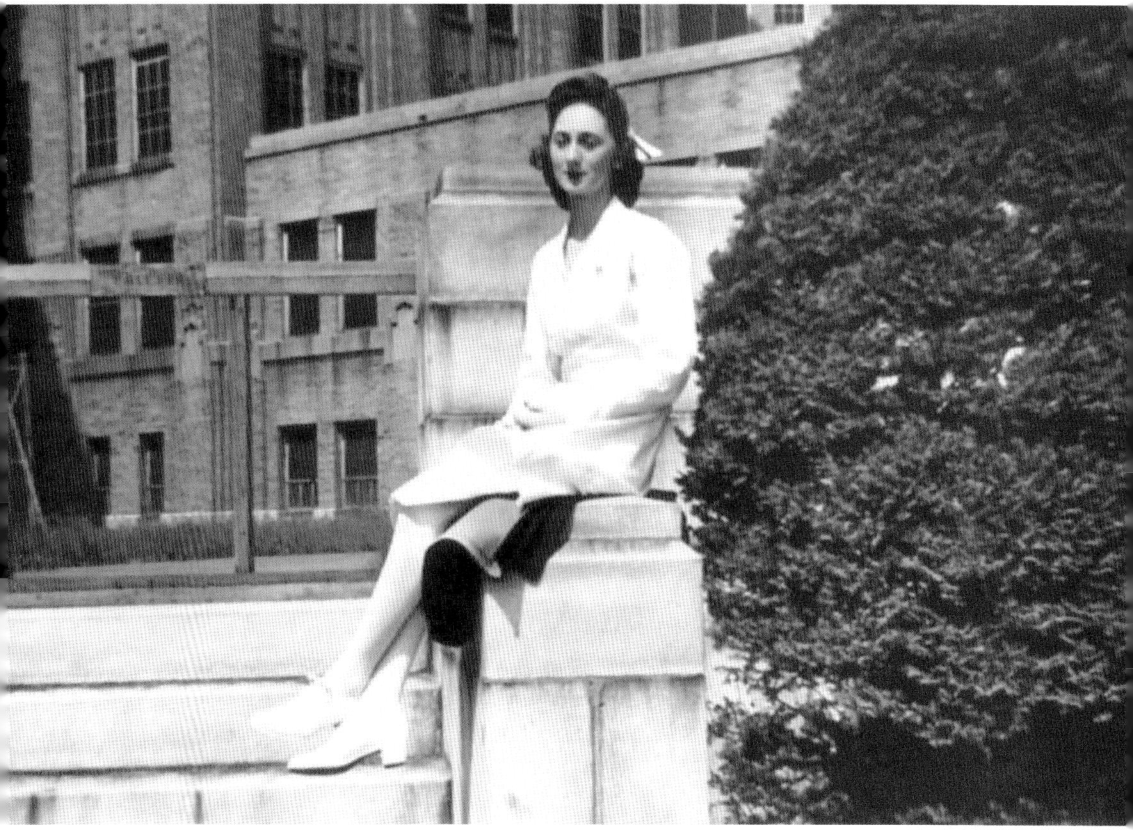

Nurse Rosalind Bellini

Rosalind Weiss Bellini, born in Perth Amboy in 1920, earned her nursing degree at Beth Israel Hospital in Newark. She first demonstrated her dedication in both the operating room and emergency room at West Hudson Hospital in Kearny. Then, she returned to school to earn her bachelor of science in nursing degree and spent the next 25 years, from 1963 to 1978, as the school nurse at Roosevelt School and Schuyler School. She and her husband, Joseph (known as Vic), lived on Seeley Avenue. Vic joined the Kearny police force after World War II and retired in 1978 as deputy chief. The Bellinis moved to Pompano Beach, Florida. They died within 18 days of each other in 2010 after 67 years of marriage. (Courtesy of Barbara Hagan.)

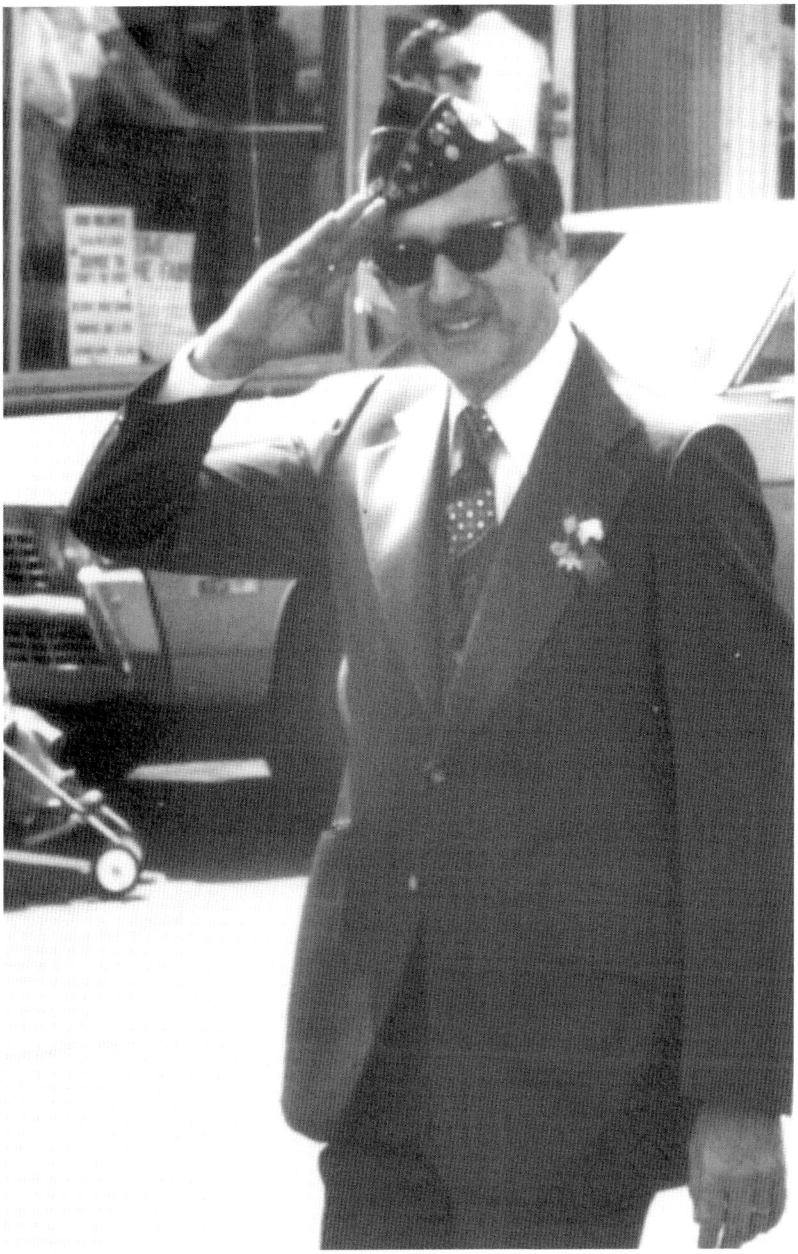

Milton J. Lerner, Dentist

Milton Lerner was born in 1922 to Abe and Dora Lerner, who moved to Kearny from Bridgeport, Connecticut, when an opportunity opened up to own a candy store on Elm Street and Midland Avenue. Lerner attended Carnegie Mellon University to become an engineer. When war was declared in 1941, he joined the US Army Air Corps as a radio operator, flying the China-Burma-India hump. He met his wife, Beverly Perlstein, on a blind date set up by their mutual friend, Norman Bass. Lerner attended dental school in Philadelphia and opened a dental practice on Kearny Avenue near Midland, where he practiced for 40 years. He was a dedicated member of the Jewish War Veterans and Congregation B'nai Israel. He passed away in 2006. (Courtesy of Vicki Lerner Megna.)

Irving W. Friend

Born in 1928 in Passaic to Russian-Jewish parents, Irving Friend attended Passaic High School and graduated from New York University in three years. While still in medical school, he married and had two of his four sons. He practiced primarily in Kearny, taking over the practice of Phil Grundfest with Daniel Garfinkel in 1958. The family lived on Livingston Avenue. On any given day, Friend cared for minor injuries and colds, major illnesses, surgery, and orthopedics. But perhaps the most exciting medical service he performed was delivering babies. He was a great fan of Kearny High School sports, especially football. He died in 1974 at the age of 45. (Courtesy of Friend family.)

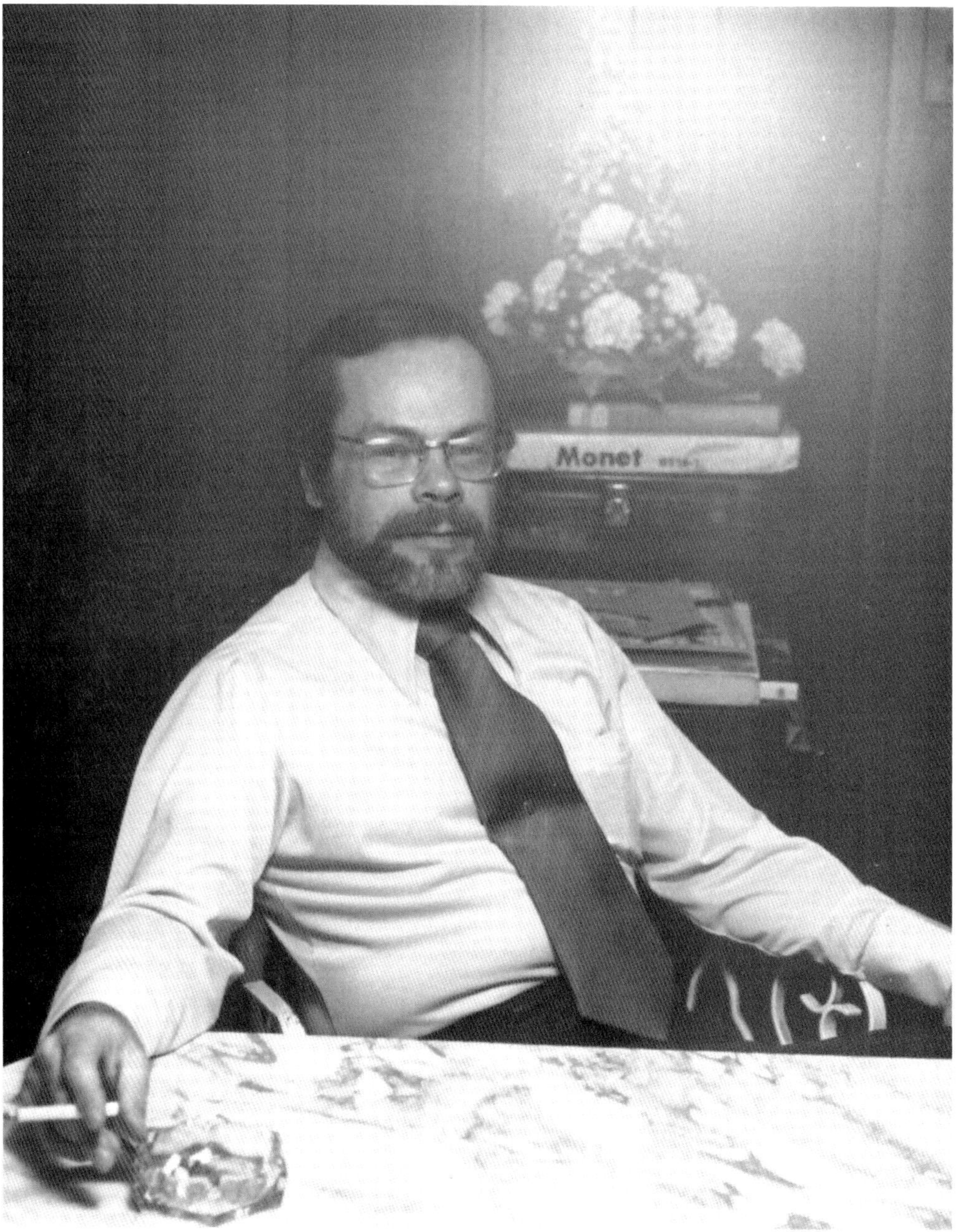

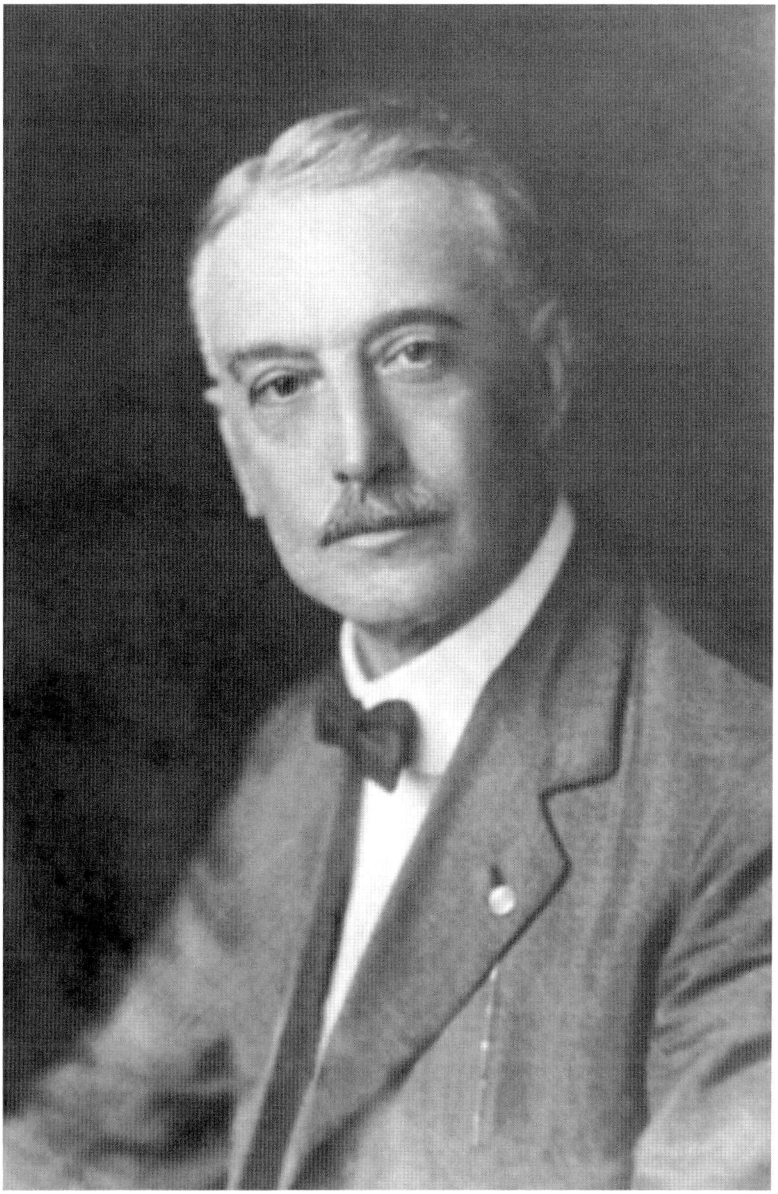

Eugene Holden Goldberg, Doctor and Kearny's First Mayor
Eugene Holden Goldberg wore many hats in Kearny. Born in 1868 in Newark, Goldberg attended Afton, Morris County, and the schools of Harrison and Kearny. He earned his doctor of medicine at Columbia University College of Physicians and Surgeons in New York in 1889. After a residency at Newark City Hospital, he opened his private practice in October 1891 at 18 Kearny Avenue. His reputation, aided by his large and successful practice, helped him achieve many positions of leadership, including town treasurer in 1896 and 1897. He was elected alderman by a landslide and then elected mayor in 1903. He served four years.

Goldberg, a Methodist, lived at the southeast corner of Kearny and Bergen Avenues. By 1910, however, his family took up residence at the New Jersey Home for Disabled Soldiers, presumably to better tend to their medical needs. (Courtesy of Kearny Museum.)

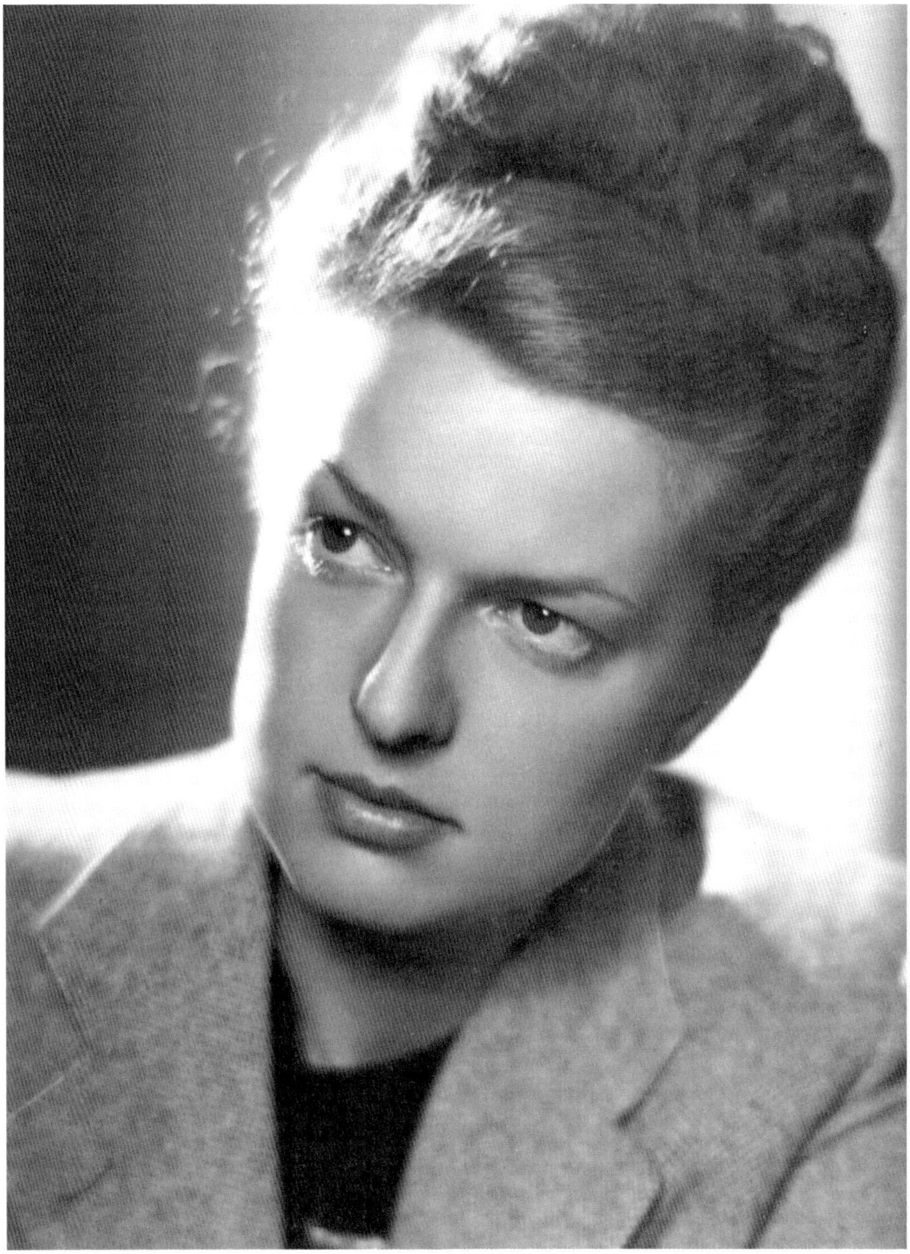

Ingeborg Schraft-Hoffman, All-Weather Doctor
Ingeborg Schraft-Hoffman was known to ski to her patients if necessary. Born in Stuttgart, Germany, Schraft-Hoffman also loved to fly. She earned a glider pilot's license in Germany and needed to study science to satisfy the demands placed on females in the Third Reich. She chose medicine. Kicked out of university for listening to BBC, she was able to continue her studies in Vienna. After World War II, she married US Army officer Leon Hoffman, moved to New York, and passed her medical boards. She joined the practice of William Nemzek in Kearny in 1954. She eventually opened her own pediatric practice. She was fond of botanical gardens, ballet, and the opera. Schraft-Hoffman passed away at the age of 91 in 2014 while listening to the song "Come Fly with Me." (Courtesy of Hilary Hoffman Fandel.)

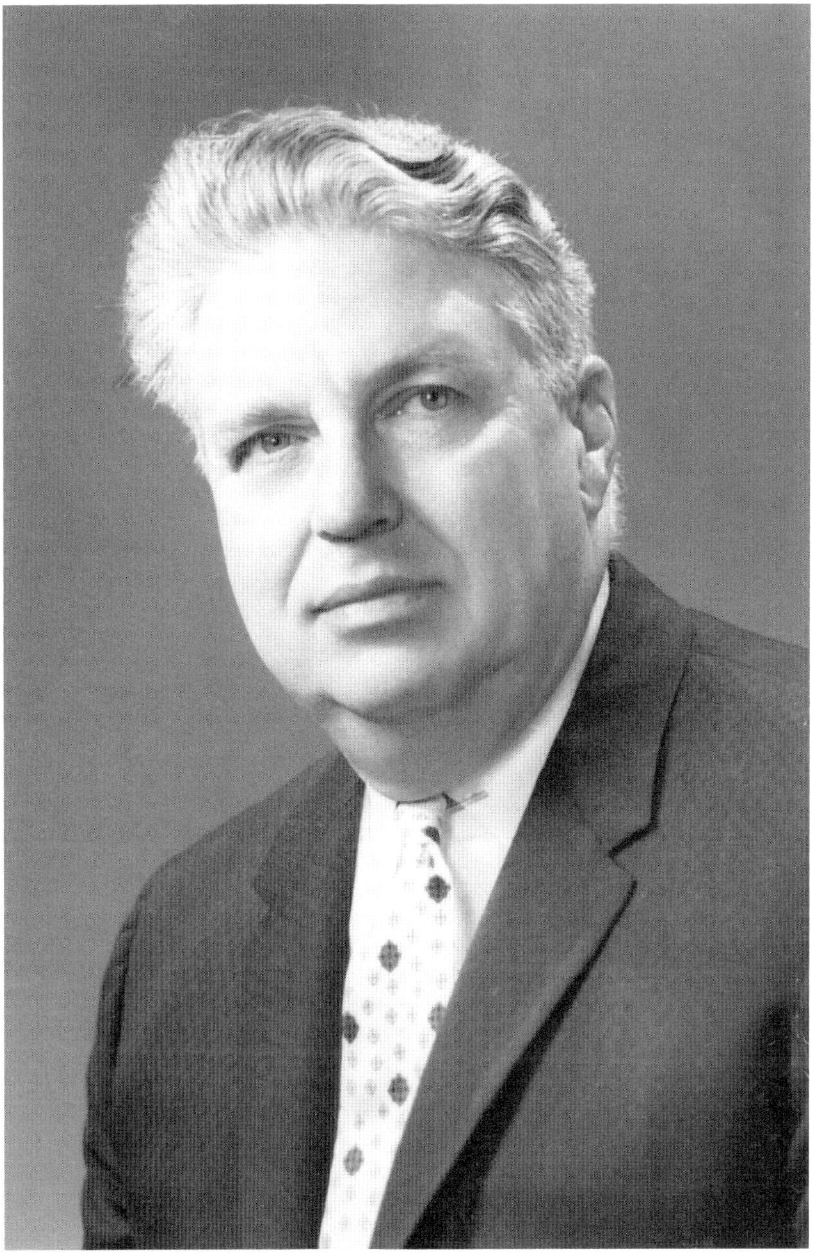

J. Lawrence Gillespie, "Dr. G"

Born in 1910 and raised in Kearny, J. Lawrence Gillespie was a family physician, surgeon, and philanthropist. He earned his medical degree from the University of Maryland in 1937 and maintained his practice for more than 50 years. He founded the first local drug abuse clinic. He was medical director of the Kearny school system for more than 40 years. But he was a man of service in other ways, too. He founded the West Hudson/South Bergen Boys Club and had a long association with the Boy Scouts of America. Gillespie was the first Boy Scout in the West Hudson area to receive the coveted Eagle Scout Award. He was a charter member of the Kearny Optimist Club and held several leadership positions during his 50-year affiliation. He passed away in 1987. (Courtesy of Cilla Gillespie Nagy.)

Morton Kessler

Morton Kessler, born in New York in 1919, graduated from New York Medical College and interned in pathology and was a resident surgeon at Cleveland City Hospital. Settling in North Arlington, Kessler opened his practice on Ridge Road. He then had a house built on Livingston Avenue in Kearny, and the family moved. Many people remember him fondly because he paid house calls until his early death in 1975. He received the Community Leadership Award from the Essex-West Hudson CIO Community Service Committee. He was also a president of the Men's Club of Congregation B'nai Israel, a trustee of the synagogue, and a division chairman of the United Jewish Appeal of Essex County. (Courtesy of Wendy Kessler.)

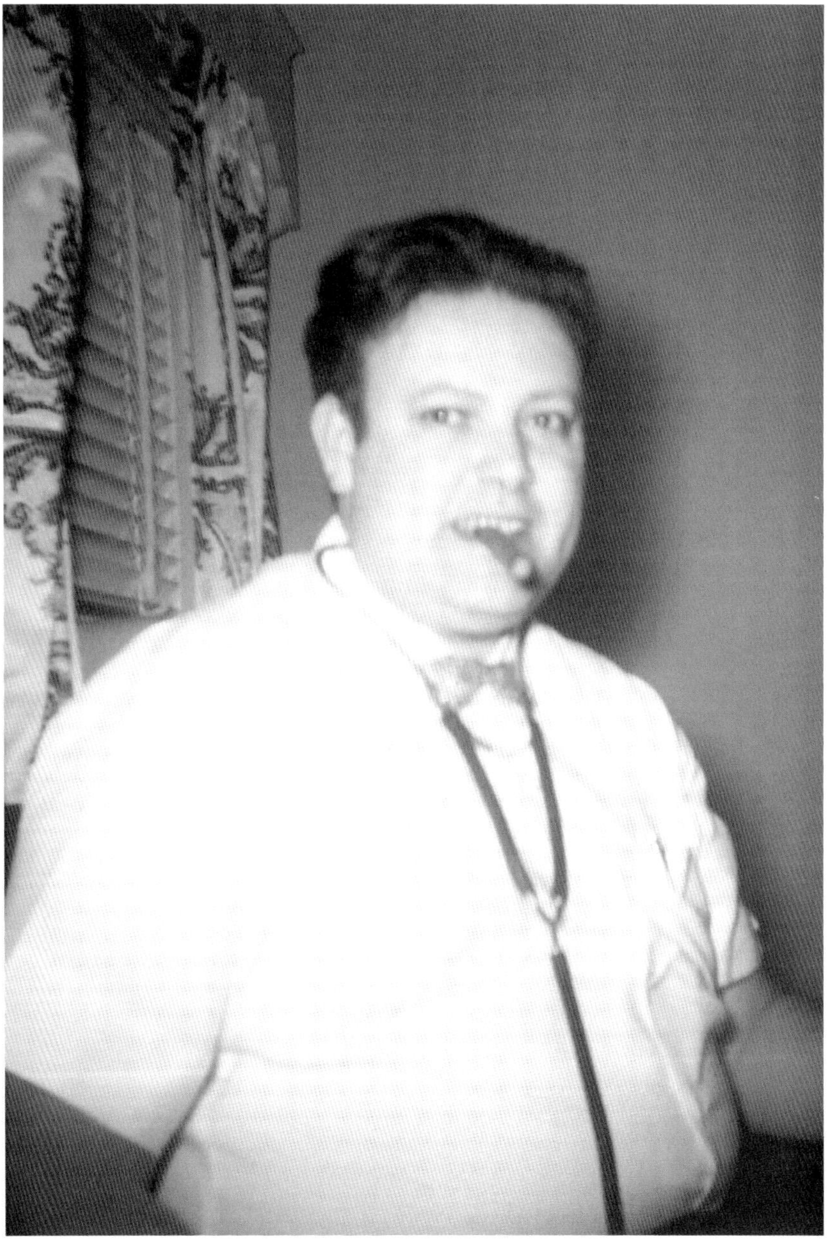

CHAPTER SIX

Musicians, Artists, and Writers

To create art, some say, requires focus, space, and talent. But proximity to New York City certainly helps as well. Creative talents in music, visual arts, performing arts, and literature have long taken advantage of Kearny's location. However, the town has been known to give birth to talent, too.

One day in 1933, three Kearny High School classmates got together to form a jazz band. Jazz became the career of guitarist Tony Mottola, saxophonist George Paxton, and saxophonist Herbie Haymer.

Kearny also provided the breeding ground for other arts and artists, including eccentric Louis Eilshemius, who had homes in both Kearny and Manhattan. Graphic artist Al Hartley, son of the congressman, benefited from his father's encouragement and pursued drawing. Anyone who read Archie comic books probably came across Hartley's artwork. Award-winning children's author Jim Murphy credits his St. Stephen's teacher with inspiring his craft. Songwriter and novelist Lynn Gillespie Chater attributes the start of her singing career to the Kearny High School group, The Lamplighters.

School could not suppress Dave Morrell's unquenchable desire for all things Beatles. He parlayed his passion into a music career from coast to coast, putting him in touch not just with John Lennon and Paul McCartney but also with other musical legends.

Kearny has also shaped literature. Scarlett O'Hara of Margaret Mitchell's *Gone with the Wind* has Kearny resident Harold Latham to thank for changing her name from the bland Pansy. Latham was heavily involved in the Kearny Free Public Library, and the library itself has been an exhibitor of the arts. Summer programs at the library and around town encourage the creation of art, especially among youngsters. The town offers classes in art, dance, theater, and acting. Kids still attend dance class, but now they might be learning hip-hop, Broadway, and Zumba instead of the Highland fling.

Jazz Guitarist Tony Mottola

Tony Mottola was born at home on Elm Street in 1918 to Neapolitan parents. According to his son, Tony Mottola Jr., he cared about two things: music and family. He formed a band in 1933 with fellow Kearny High School students George Paxton and Herbie Haymer. In 1936, Paxton arranged for him to audition for the George Hall band at the Taft Hotel in New York City. Mottola got the job, and he left to go on the road the following week, earning about $275 a week, more than his father made as a tool and die worker. He remained in Kearny, because his work took place mainly in Manhattan. He recorded with Frank Sinatra and worked with the Doc Severinsen orchestra on *The Tonight Show*. He died in 2004. (Courtesy of Tony Mottola Jr.)

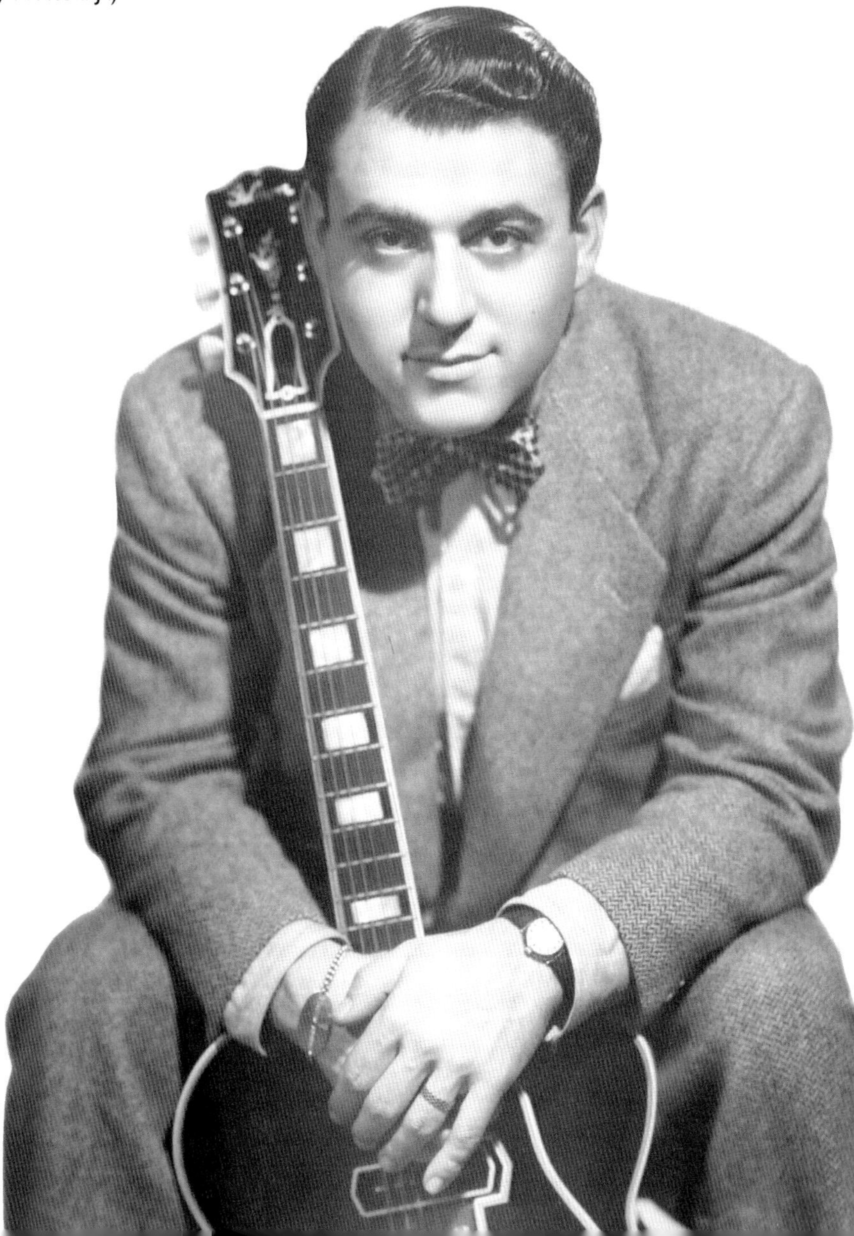

Jazz Saxophonist George Paxton

Born in Jacksonville, Florida, George Paxton moved to Kearny and formed a band with Kearny High schoolmates Tony Mottola and Herbie Haymer. He learned to play the saxophone at a young age and later attended Juilliard. In New York City, he was hired to arrange music for the owner of the Meadowbrook Inn, a New Jersey hotspot for top musical talent. He formed his own swing orchestra in 1944. That experience came in handy when, together with Marvin Cane, he formed a record label, Coed Records, in 1958 with offices in the famous Brill Building in Manhattan. Among his recording artists were the Crests and the Duprees. He died in Palm Beach, Florida, in 1989. (Author's collection.)

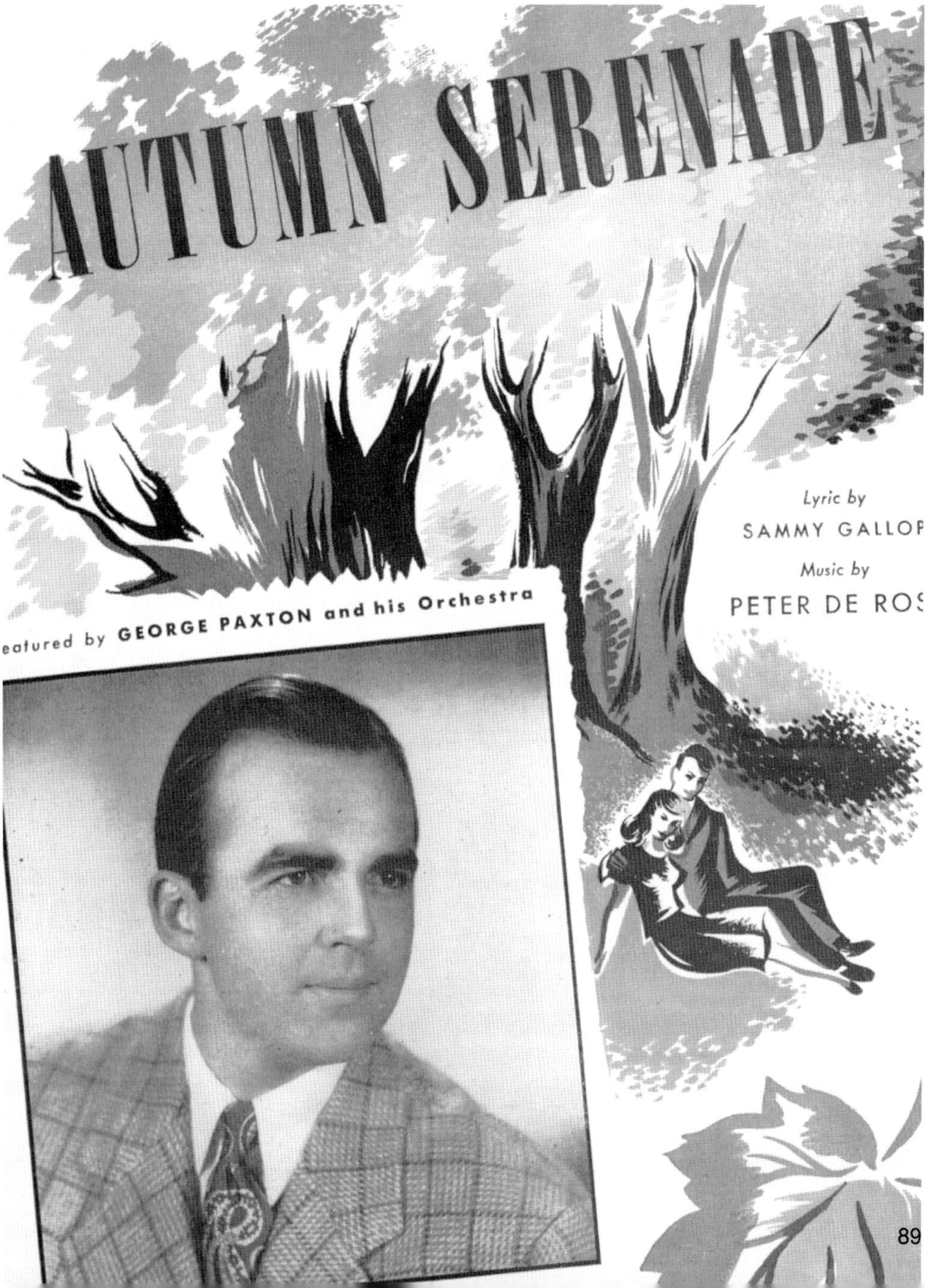

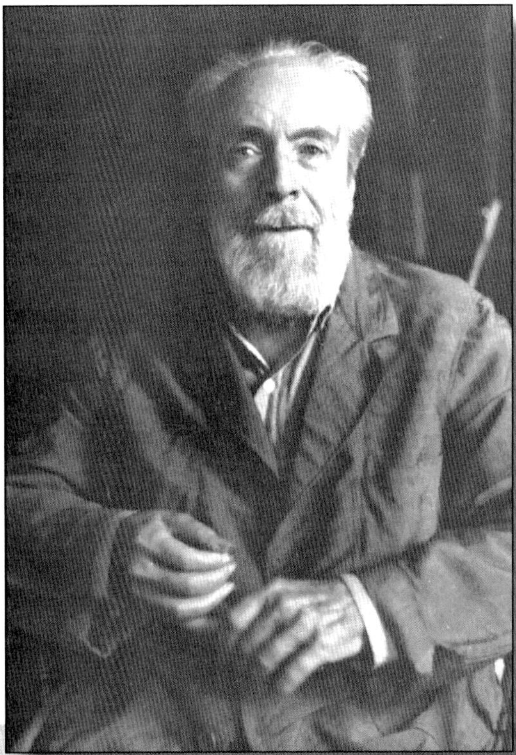

Louis Michel Eilshemius, the Self-Professed "Spirit Painter Supreme"

Louis Michel Eilshemius was born in 1864 at Laurel Hill, an Arlington estate owned by his father, wealthy Dutch importer Henry Gottfried Eilshemius, who owned tracts of land on both sides of Kearny Avenue. The youngest son of eight children, Louis studied in Germany and, by 17, had become a skilled illustrator and painter. He tried to follow his father's ambitions for him and enrolled at Cornell University to study agriculture. However, his own ambitions clamored for art. His father eventually allowed Louis to study art in Paris. Fame, however, eluded him. Many critics believed him to be a bit mad. Following an auto accident, he became a recluse in his family-owned Fifty-Seventh Street brownstone, where he lived with a deaf older brother and a housekeeper. He died in December 1941 at age 77 in Bellevue's psychopathic ward. (Left, author's collection; below, photograph by the author.)

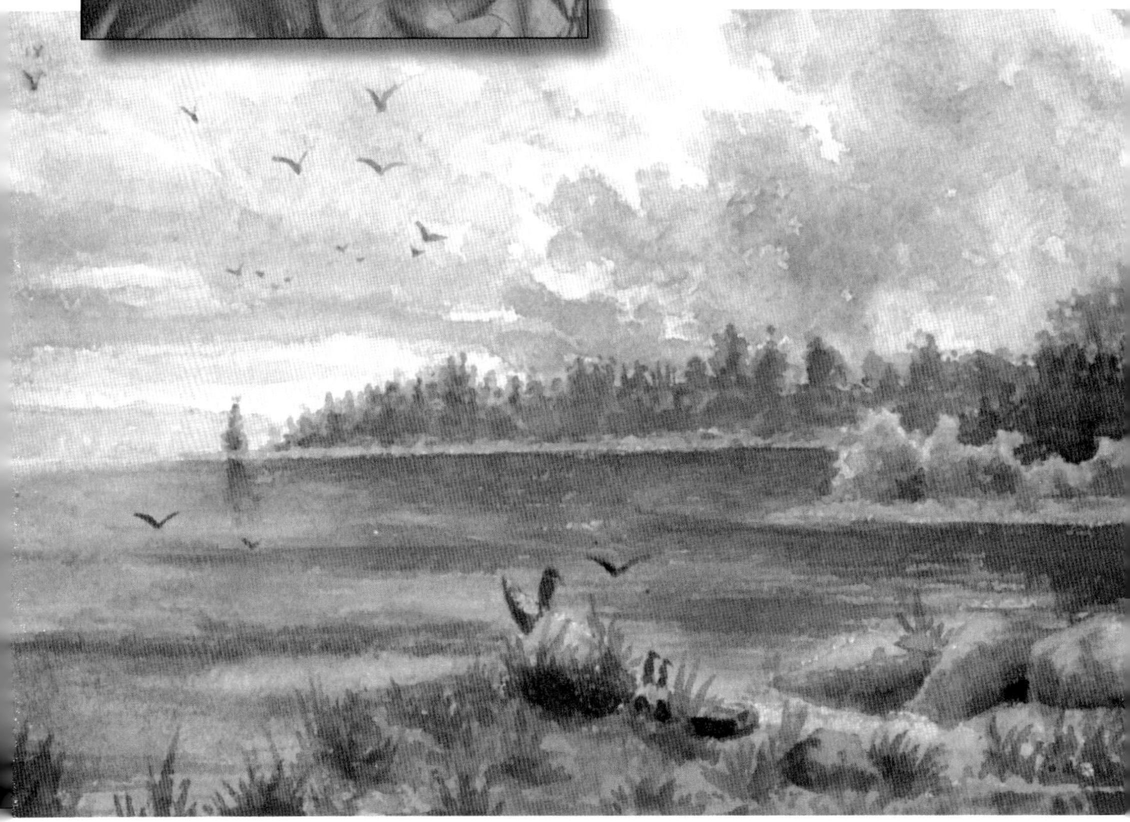

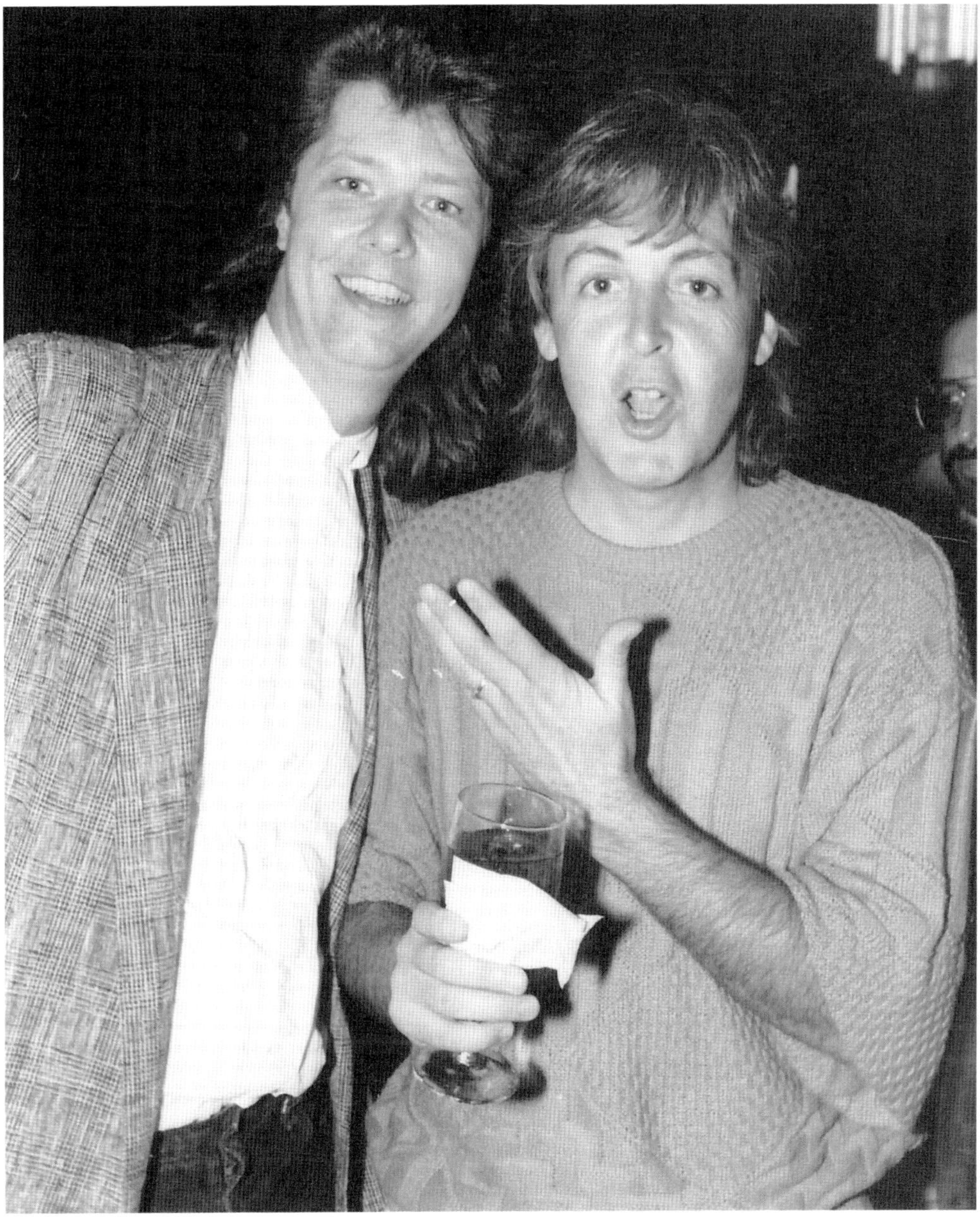

Beatlemania and Dave Morrell
"I woke up one cold day in Kearny . . . I felt different . . . this music was like candy . . . it was more powerful than my parents or my school teachers . . . 'Beatlemania' . . . The doctor said, 'Mrs. Morell, there is no cure.' " Dave Morrell grew up on Rutland Avenue and later Bennett Avenue. He officially entered the music business in June 1972, a year after he graduated from Kearny High School. He worked for Capitol Records from 1980 to 1990. Lured out to Los Angeles by Concord Music Group in 2005, he has since been an independent promoter for 429 Records and Lakeshore Entertainment. He wrote about his early experiences of meeting his heroes in *Horse-Doggin': The Morrell Archives Volume 1*. He is shown here (left) with Paul McCartney in 1986 in the Radio City Music Hall foyer in New York City. (Courtesy of Dave Morrell.)

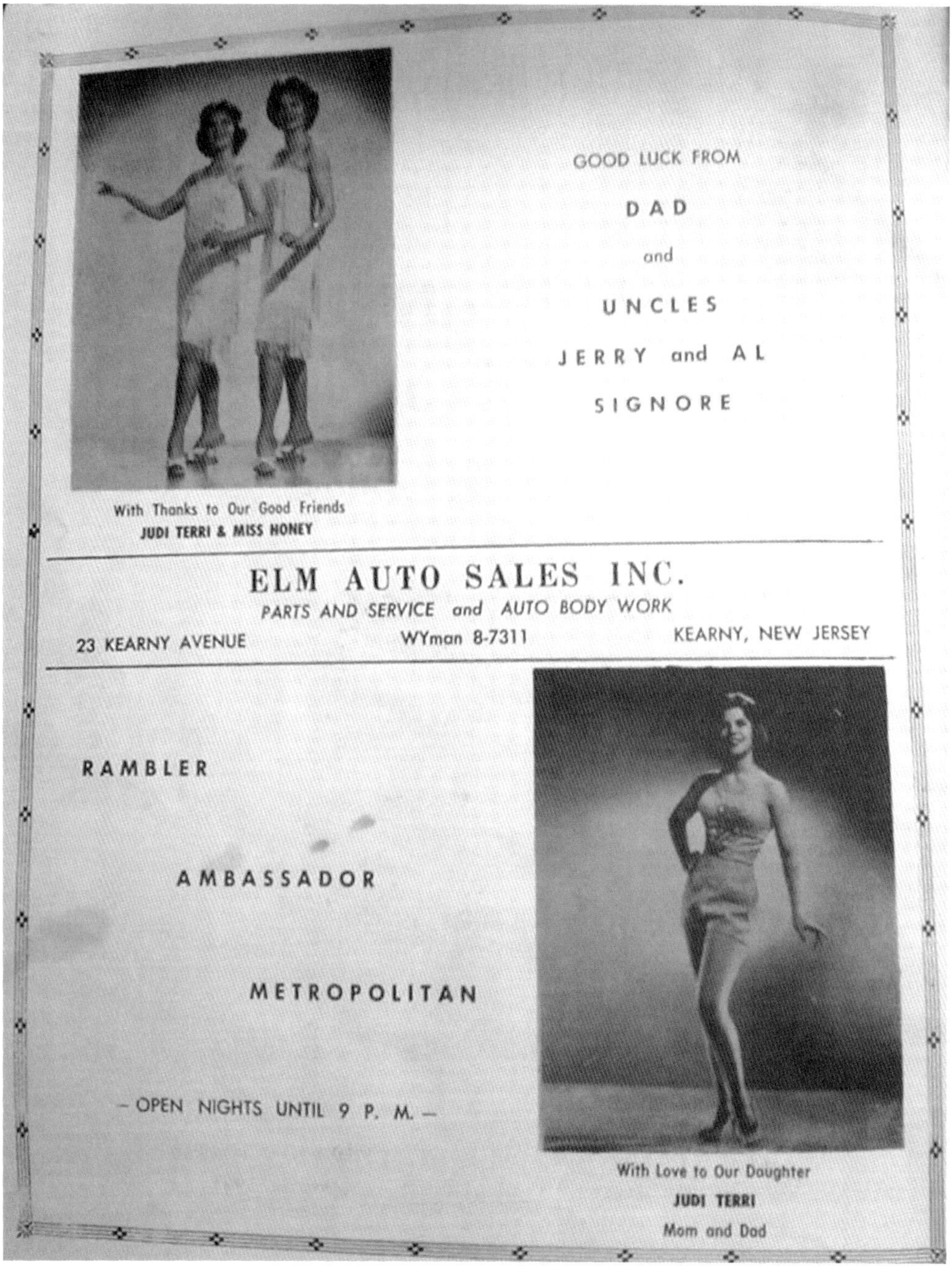

Miss Honey, Nurturing Dance Teacher

Honey Novelli ran the Judi-Terri School of Dance above the Lincoln Theater on Kearny Avenue starting in 1954. Novelli was born in 1924 in Pennsylvania and died in 2009. Her students remember her fondly for her instruction in ballet, tap, and jazz—and for her kindness, patience, and understanding. They also recall that her pinky nails were very long, that she could not drive (her husband, Alex, drove her), and that she could play anything on the piano. One student recalls her appearance on the *Ted Mack Amateur Hour* around 1955. Recitals were held on the Lincoln Theater stage. (Courtesy of Susan Harsley.)

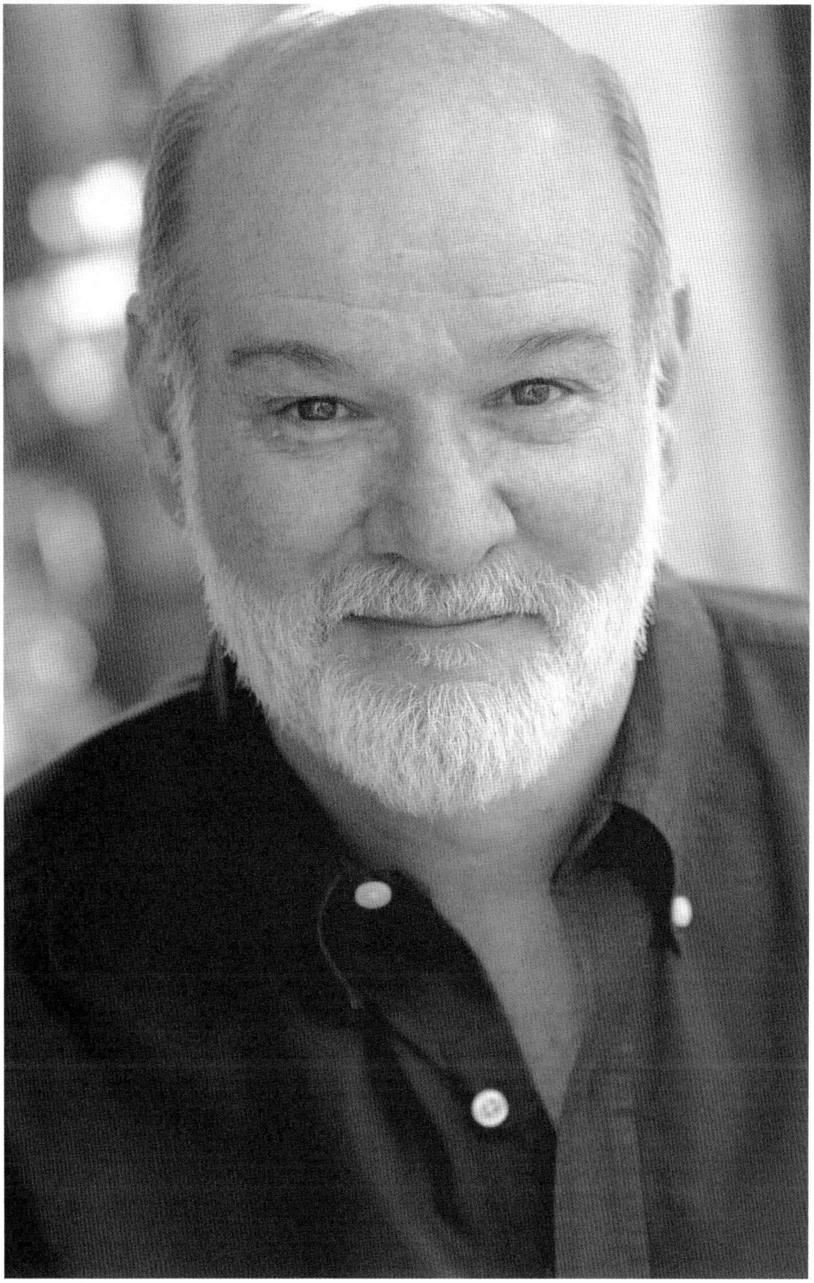

Children's Author Jim Murphy

In an acceptance speech for the Boston Globe–Horn Book Awards, Jim Murphy mentioned growing up in Kearny. He and his friends explored the Meadowlands and invented adventures. He had not been much of a reader until a teacher at St. Stephen's named a forbidden book. Murphy read the book and kept reading, which later translated to writing. His more than 30 books for children and young adults have earned him a variety of awards, including the Sibert Award for nonfiction and two Newbery Honors. He graduated from Rutgers University and became a managing editor in children's publishing. (Photograph by Arthur Cohen, courtesy of Jim Murphy.)

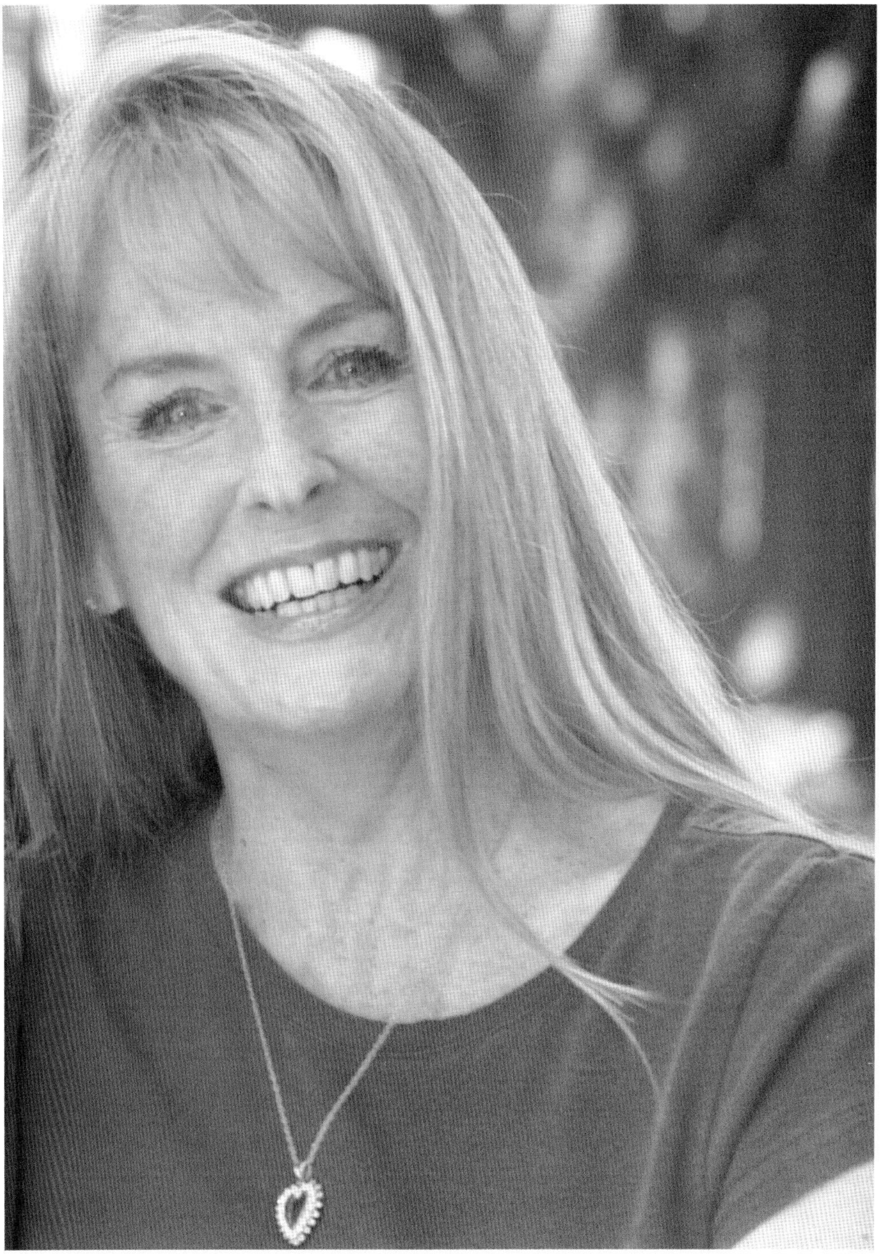

Lynn Gillespie Chater, Kearny Girl Makes Good in Nashville

Kearny High School 1967 graduate Lynn Gillespie persisted to make a go of it in the Nashville music scene. Masquerading as a male songwriter to increase her odds of success, Gillespie got her—or his (as alter ego Jesse Read)—first three cuts in Nashville and a mention in *People* magazine. The masquerade didn't last long, but one producer decided to take a chance on her. Two years later, Gillespie had a cut on Mindy McCready's *Ten Thousand Angels* CD, which went triple platinum. Together with her husband, Kerry Chater, formerly of the popular Gary Puckett and the Union Gap musical group, she has written two Christian musicals (performed in Nashville) and many songs. The couple now writes thriller novels, and they look forward to one adapted for a made-for-television movie. (Courtesy of Lynn Gillespie Chater.)

Harold Latham, Cultivator of Literature and History

Literary editor Harold Strong Latham lived on Pleasant Place. Born in 1887, he worked at Macmillan Publishing Company in New York City. In 1935, he visited Margaret Mitchell at her Atlanta home. He took her *Gone with the Wind* manuscript home with him. It became a runaway bestseller the following year and won the Pulitzer Prize. Some say it was Latham who convinced Mitchell to change her heroine's name from Pansy to Scarlett. He retired in 1952 after serving as editor in chief and vice president.

Latham was an active participant in Kearny activities. He organized the Presbyterian Boys Club in 1909 and served as president of the West Hudson Hospital Association. He was a trustee of the Kearny Museum and Historical Association. He was heavily involved in Kearny's centennial celebration. He died in 1969. (Courtesy of Kearny Museum.)

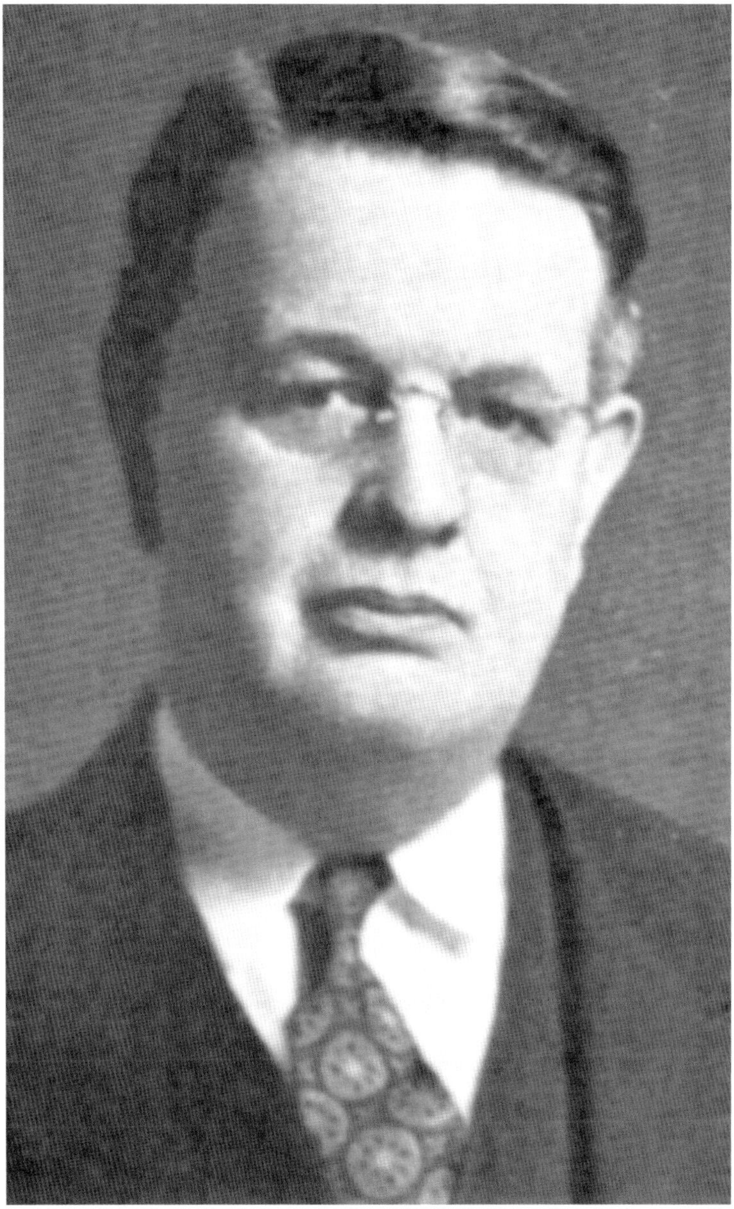

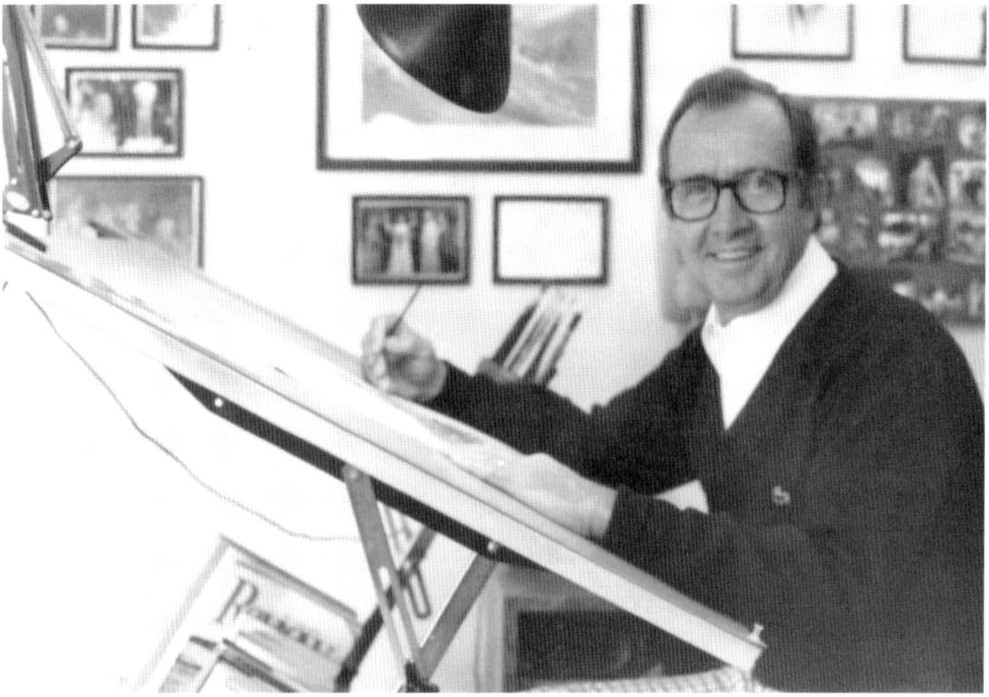

Al Hartley and the Comics

Al Hartley, the son of Congressman Frederick Allan Hartley Jr., was born in 1921 and raised in Kearny. With encouragement from his father, he pursued drawing and attended the Arts Student League of New York. World War II interrupted his studies. He served as a bomber pilot in the US Army Air Corps. When he returned, he became a commercial artist and freelanced for Stan Lee and Marvel Comics. There and at Atlas Comics, he drew some of the best-known comic book characters and their stories, including Thor, Iron Man, Patsy Walker, and Archie. He died in Florida in 2003. (Courtesy of Fred Hartley.)

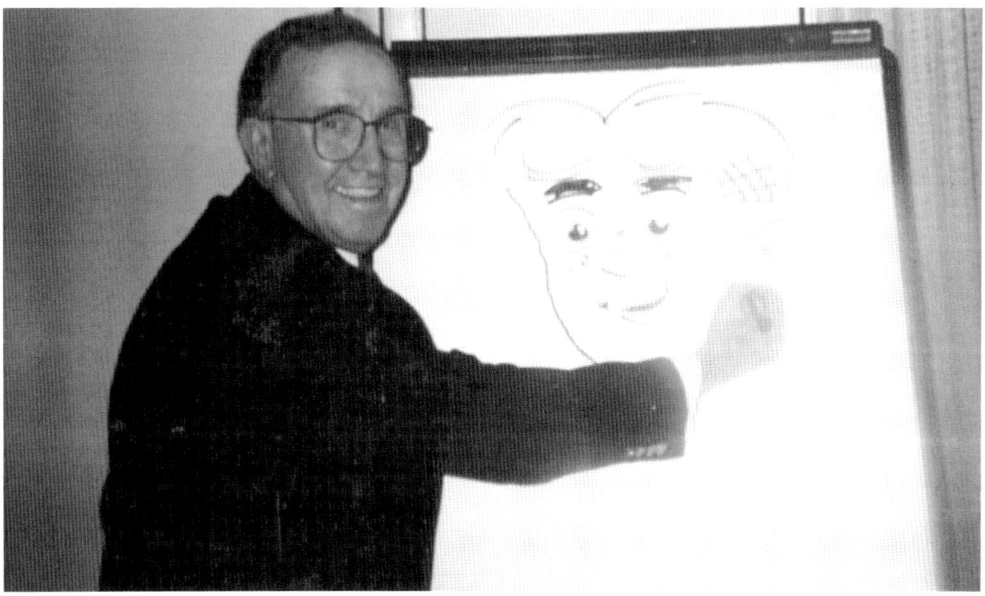

CHAPTER SEVEN

Neighbors

Elected and appointed civil servants have not been the only people dedicated to Kearny. Young and old ordinary residents volunteer their time and skills to help others. Gabriela Salvador has helped the Kearny Museum restore historical costumes while a university student, whereas many senior citizens engage with church, school, and other organizations. Retirees Ed and Peg Bixler have been integral to the success of the community garden along Passaic Avenue. Eleanor Flavell opened her home to foster children again and again. Mary Lynn Pettigrew opened a consignment shop at the First Presbyterian Church to ease others of financial burdens.

But the town has its share of characters, too. John McCloud owned an entire block of property and became the man about town after his wife died. Albert Gonzalez gained notoriety as a major-league computer hacker. At the same time, other individuals have shaped Kearny's character and history. George Rogers, his son Paul, Sebastian "Zibbie" Viscuso, and Chalie Dolan have demonstrated the meaning of lovingly giving back to the community. William Styple's passion for history gave Kearny incredible insights into Maj. Gen. Philip Kearny.

Still others have moved away from town but act on the values they learned while growing up in Kearny. Michelle Kraus, for example, created a consulting career that brings her into the circle of Pres. Barack Obama, 2016 presidential hopeful Hillary Clinton, and high-technology VIPs. Her fellow Douglass College graduate, Donna Caputo Shandle, became one of the earliest women engineers in the US Navy civil service. Heidi Yamaguchi devoted her time to training FEMA rescue dogs before her untimely death.

Many religious leaders could easily be termed legendary locals, including Msgr. Joseph Carroll of St. Cecilia Church, Rev. Robert L. Blackwell of the First Presbyterian Church, Fr. Robert Egan of New Jersey Boystown on Belgrove Drive, and Rabbi Sidney Bogner of Congregation B'nai Israel. They gave tirelessly to their constituencies.

It is these neighbors, families, and leaders who make our time in Kearny memorable.

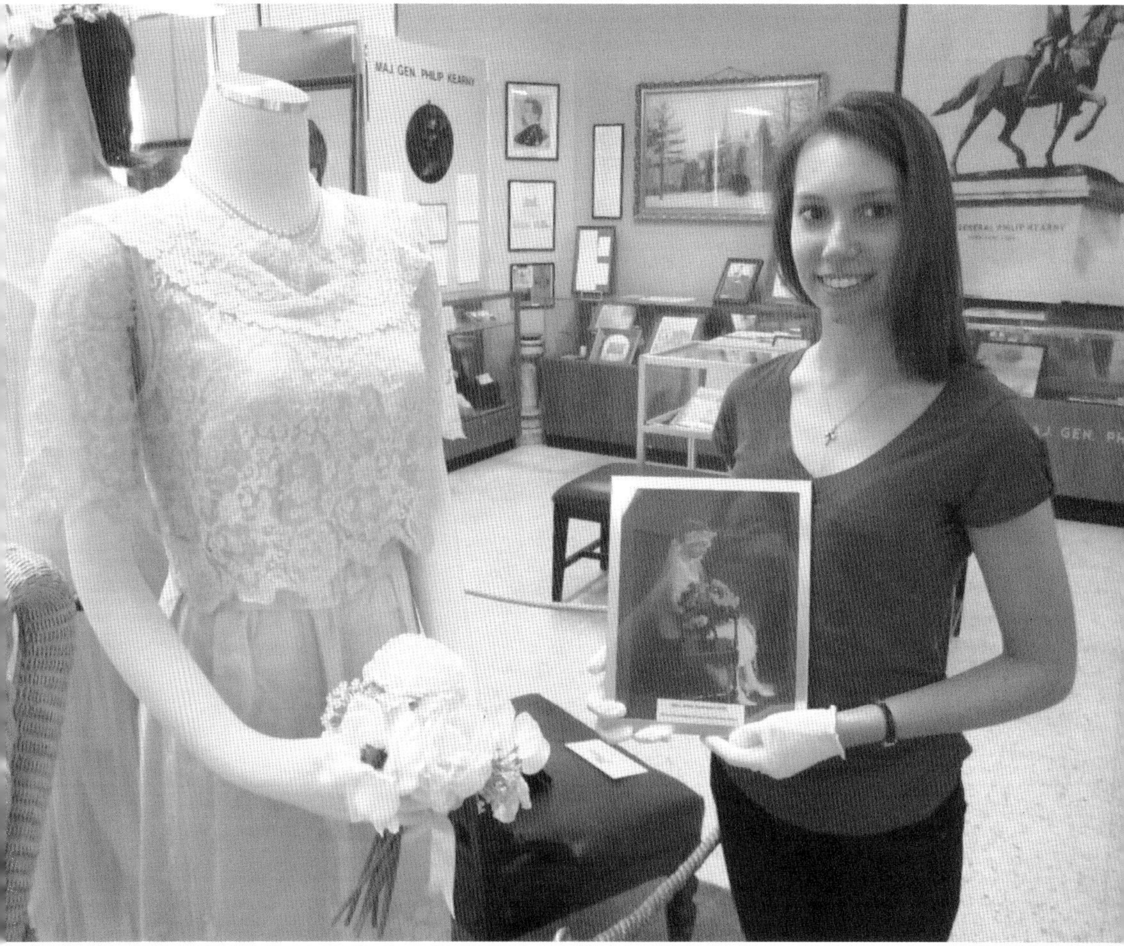

Historical Costumes by Gabriela Salvador

Born in 1993 to parents of Portuguese descent, Gabriela Salvador attended Schuyler School and Kearny High School. While at Kearny High School, she became fascinated with different periods of history and the associated clothing. She conducted her own independent study and taught herself to sew. One day at the Kearny Museum, she noticed how the costumes were improperly displayed. She contacted library director Josh Humphrey and came in to meet with the Museum Committee. Armed with the committee's approval and a budget, Salvador set about to professionally restore the museum's costumes. The first outfit she worked on was a World War II WAVE uniform. Currently a double major at William Paterson University studying journalism/public relations and writing, Salvador is also an honors-track history student. She continues to restore the past through historical clothing. (Photograph by the author.)

Building the Community Garden with Ed and Peg Bixler

Margaret (Peg) Bixler and her husband, Ed, are core members of a team establishing Kearny's Community Garden along the Passaic River just south of South Midland Avenue. The Cub Scouts and 50 families have dedicated plots among 250 bales of straw to grow their own vegetables and gardens. In March 2014, the project received a $2,000 Sustainable Jersey Capacity-Building grant from the Public Service Electric and Gas Foundation. In its first year, 2013, this urban beautification and education project's members learned to cultivate the organic straw bale garden. Kearny Public Works designed the water system that irrigates the bales laid out in 11 parallel rows. Woodchips between the rows came from Superstorm Sandy. (Photograph by the author.)

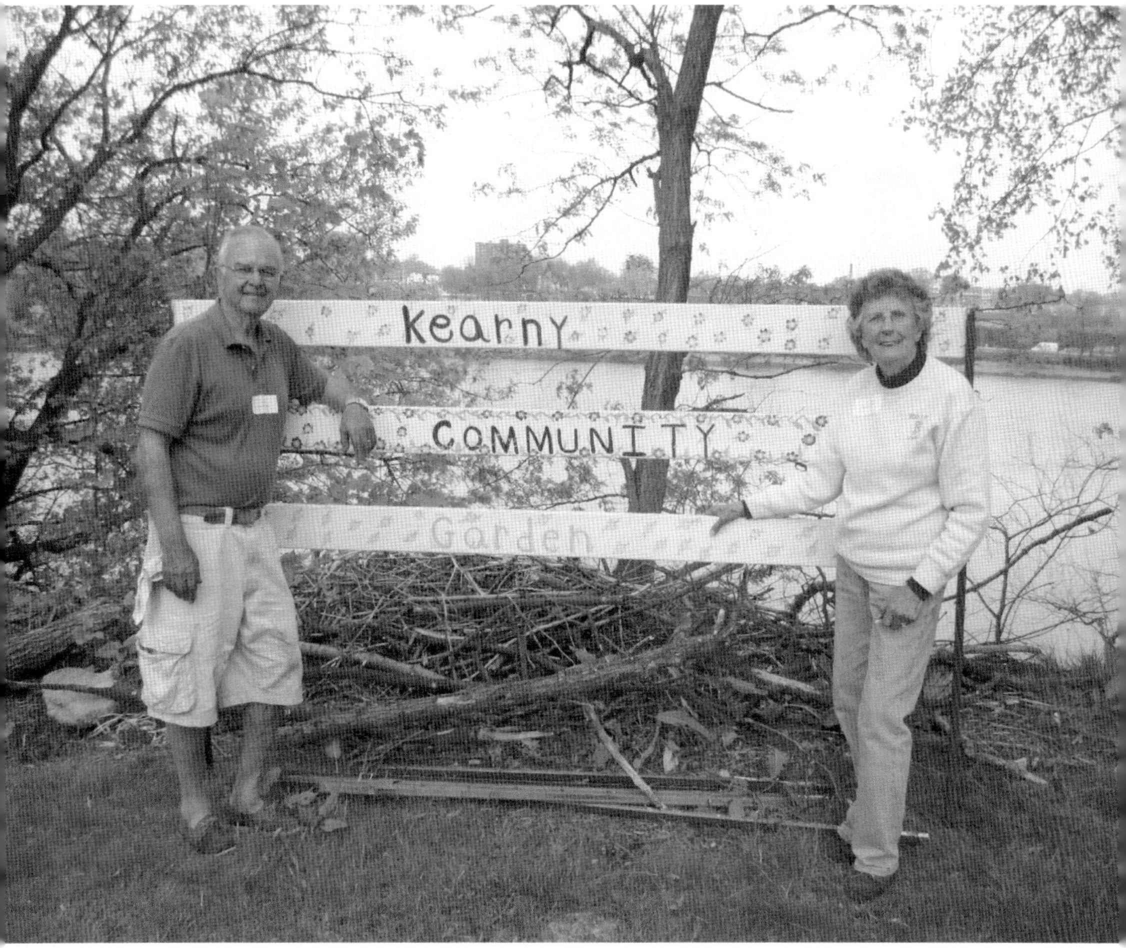

John McCloud and the McCloud Block

John Leonard McCloud was born in Sussex County, New Jersey, about 1847. He operated a blacksmith business at 475 Elm Street and owned many buildings on one block of Elm Street, earning it the name of McCloud Block. His gelding was named Major, and it was said the horse knew the route home and stopped at every corner tavern. McCloud was also a justice of the peace. Legend has it he jilted a woman at the altar and, after his wife's untimely death, was quite the man about town. McCloud built a house at 568 Devon Street, which remained the family home for decades to come. (Courtesy of Karen McCloud.)

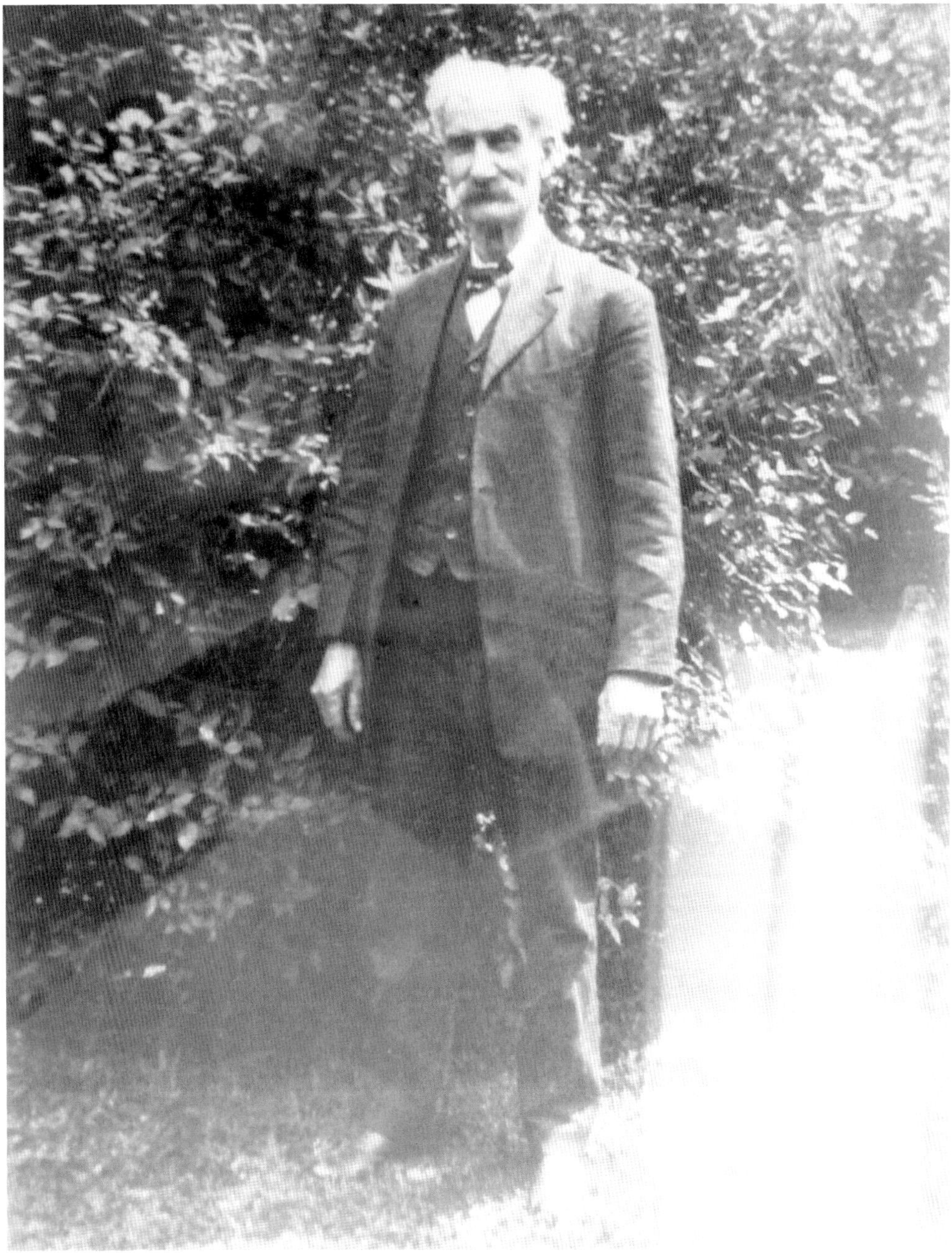

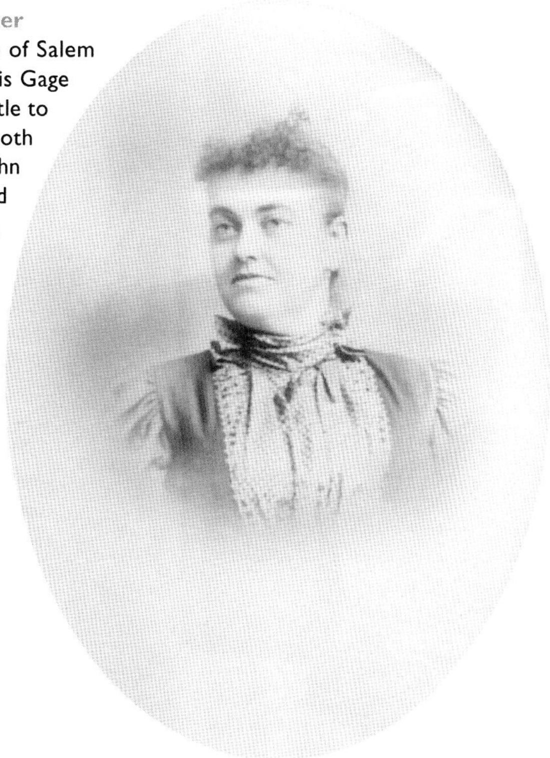

Mary Francis Gage McCloud, Child Baker

After her father's 1863 death in the Battle of Salem Heights, Virginia, three-year-old Mary Francis Gage came with her mother to Arlington. With little to live on from the Civil War widow's pension, both worked in an Elm Street bakery across from John McCloud's blacksmith shop. Gage and McCloud married in 1880 and had five children. At 46, she died suddenly from a massive stroke. (Courtesy of Karen McCloud.)

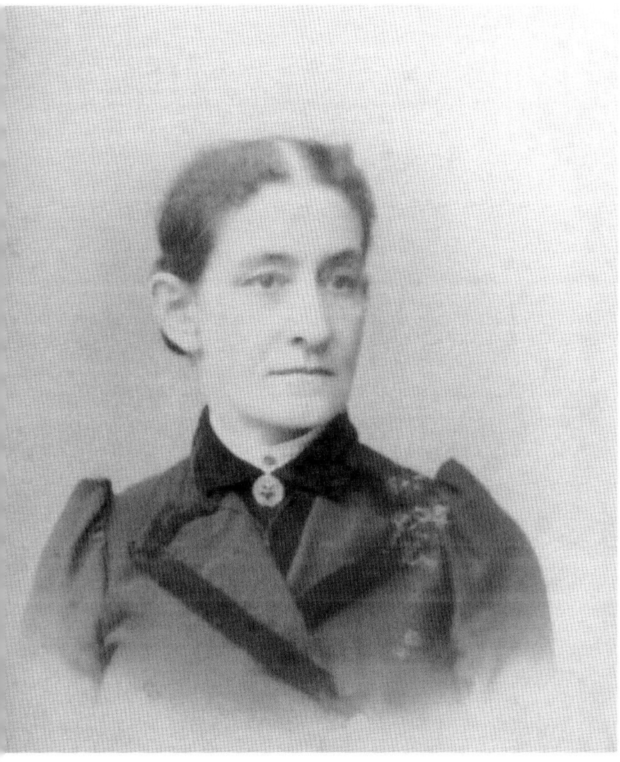

Theresa Estler Gage, the Civil War Widow

Theresa Gage moved with her young daughter, Mary Francis, to Kearny after her husband died in the Civil War. She worked at a bakery on Elm Street and lived with her daughter and her husband on Devon Street. She continued to dress in mourning clothes. She was predeceased by her daughter. She died in 1917 and is buried with her husband in Boonton. (Courtesy of Karen McCloud.)

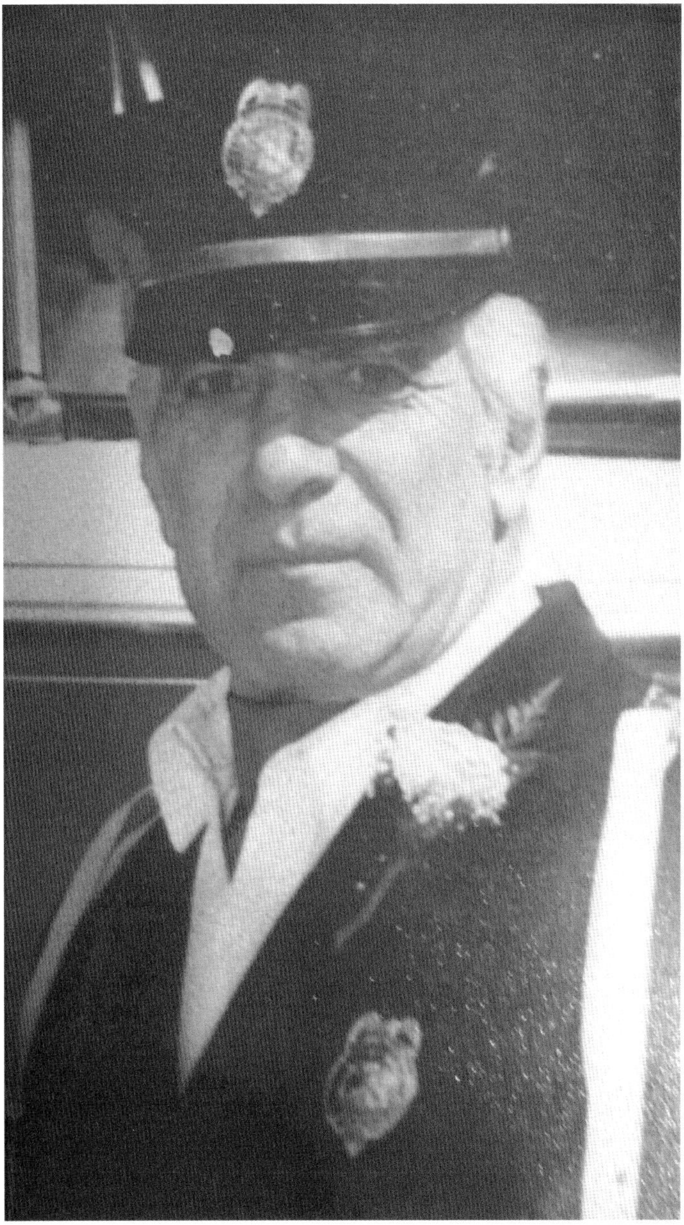

Sebastian "Zibbie" Viscuso

Born in 1937, Sebastian "Zibbie" Viscuso played football and baseball, served on student council, and was engaged in many other activities at Kearny High School as a member of the class of 1954. He married Mildred Monaco, daughter of principal Frank Monaco. His commitment to Kearny is clear through his public service and dedication to local organizations. He served as a Kearny firefighter from 1966 to 1996 and was vice president of the Fireman's Mutual Benevolent Association (FMBA) for 20 years. He was a member of the Kearny Board of Education from 1987 to 1994 and is on the board once more, beginning his term in 2010. He was inducted into the Kearny High School Hall of Fame for football and for his contributions to the Hall of Fame for 30 years of service. He still regularly attends school and sporting events. (Courtesy of Denise Viscuso Liptak.)

Strategic and Political Adviser Michelle Kraus

Dr. Michelle Kraus grew up on Livingston Avenue in Kearny. She attended Roosevelt School, Lincoln School, and Kearny High School, graduating in 1971. She then attended Douglass College and continued her education by obtaining a master's degree at the University of Michigan and her PhD at Carnegie Mellon University. She currently serves on Pres. Barack Obama's National Finance Committee. A technology executive, she has helped digital technology companies survive and thrive. Kraus also serves as a board member of She Heroes, a nonprofit dedicated to engaging young girls with diverse, professional role models. Furthermore, she is a member of the National Advisory Council on STEM Education. (Courtesy of Michelle Kraus.)

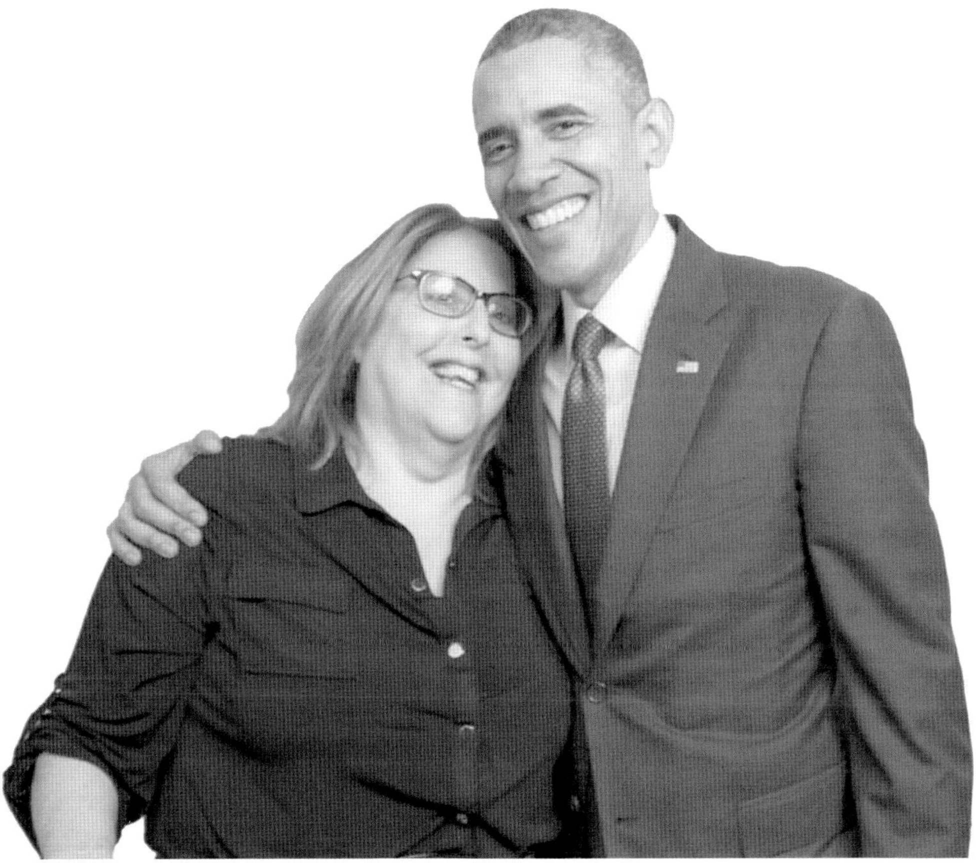

The Steadfast Mary Margaret "Mae" Swetell

Hard work with heart and soul was at the core of Mary Margaret Swetell (1902–2003), affectionately known in the community as "Mae." She owned the Town Hall Tavern in Kearny along with her husband, Michael ("Micky"), from 1950 until the tavern's closing in 2003 when she was 98. Both Mary's and Micky's families emigrated from Lithuania at the turn of the 20th century. Mary played an instrumental role in running the business while raising four children and managing her quarter-acre property in Belleville. In the 1970s, Mary attended the Broadway show, *No, No, Nanette*, starring Zsa Zsa Gabor. Gabor asked her what her beauty secret was, and Mae responded, "Ivory soap!" (Courtesy of Laura Williams.)

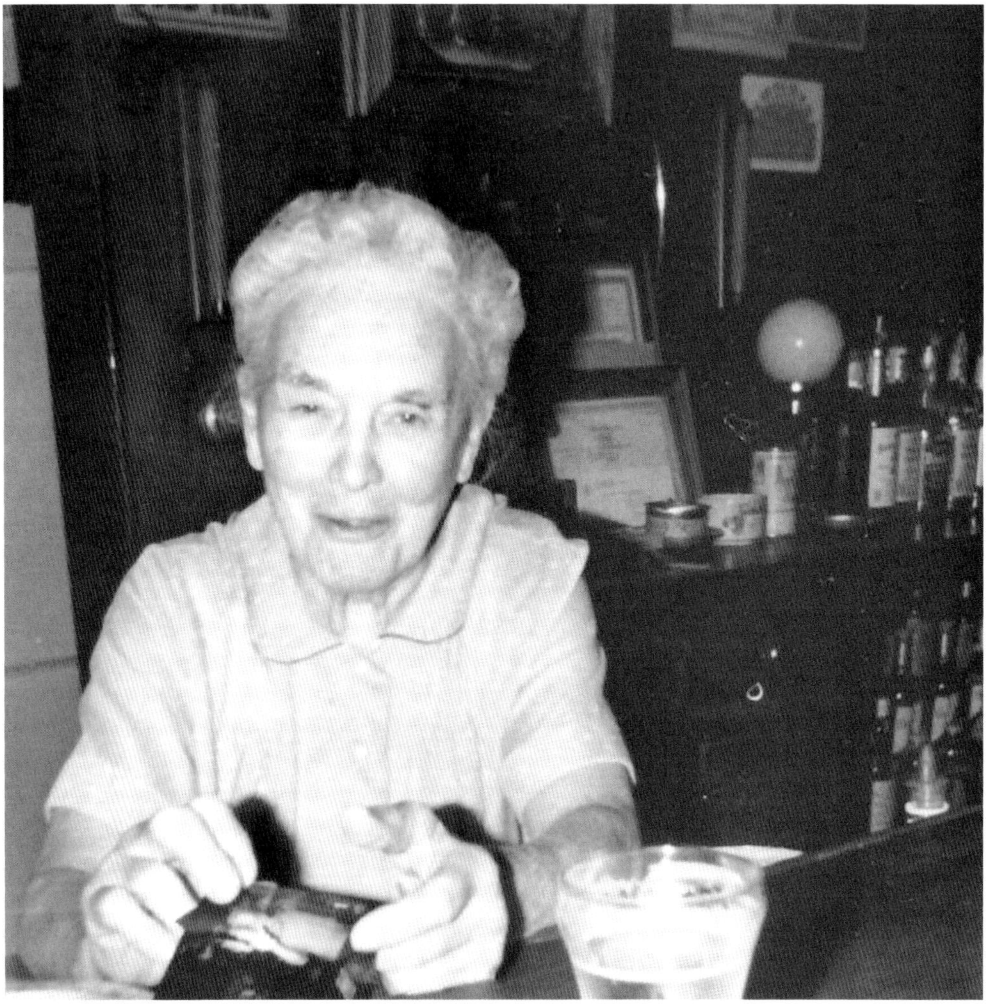

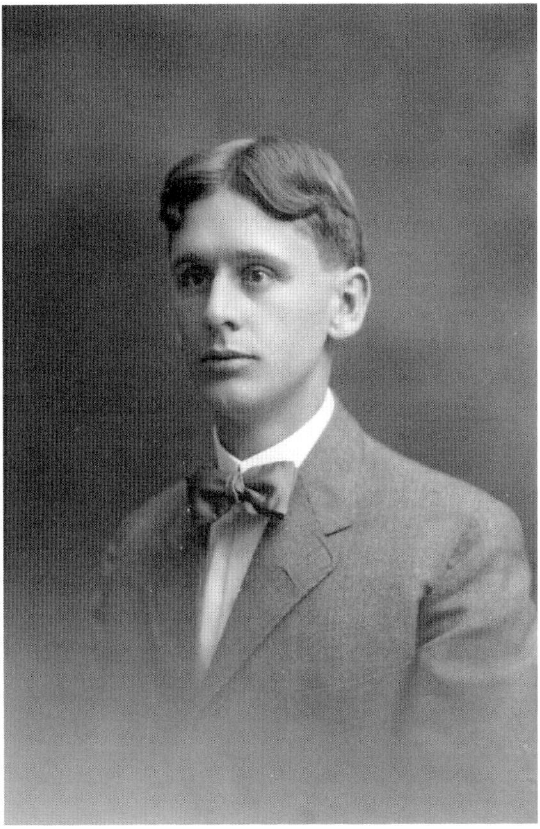

Waldemar Lindblom and a Revolutionary Find

Son of real estate developer Louis Lindblom, Waldemar and his son, Norwood, unearthed a 12.5-pound cannonball from their backyard at 162 Midland Avenue in 1936. The cannonball dated back to 1777 and the Revolutionary War, a remnant of the Battle of Second River when the British Army's Captain Drummond crossed the cedar swamp of the Kearny meadows and took his position at Fairlawn Manor, the Schuyler mansion in Arlington. (Courtesy of Rich Wall.)

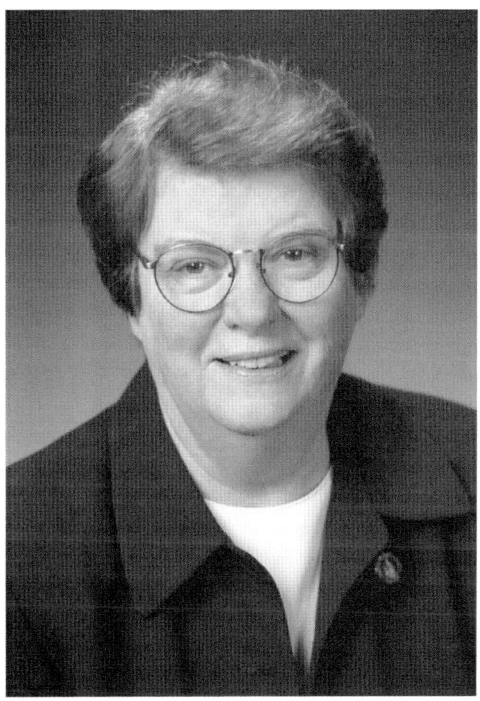

Francis Raftery, College President

Sr. Francis Raftery stepped down as president of the College of St. Elizabeth in Convent Station in 2013 after 38 years of service. She grew up in Kearny as a child of Irish immigrants, alongside younger brother and All-American, Bill Raftery. A leader in education, she entered the Sisters of Charity after earning her bachelor's degree in early childhood education from New Jersey City University. (Courtesy of College of St. Elizabeth.)

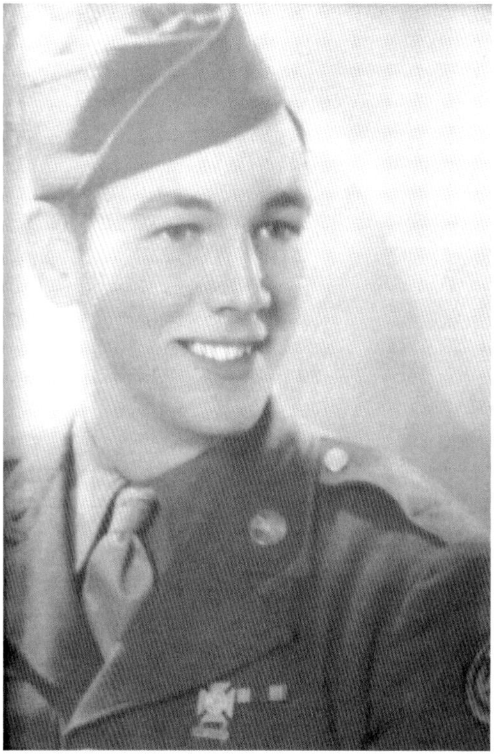

The Helping Hand of William Leahy

Bill Leahy was the son of West Hudson Park caretaker Michael Francis Leahy and Hannah Carroll Leahy. Bill, A World War II veteran, lost his hand in an industrial accident at his workplace of T. Shriver & Company in Harrison. Yet, the loss did not stop him. When it snowed, he would spread ashes from his coal furnace along Maple Street where he lived so no one would slip. (Courtesy of Carole Leahy Miller.)

Mary Lynn Pettigrew Helping Those in Need

Mary Lynn Pettigrew, a Kearny High School class of 1975 graduate, serves as a deacon and thrift store operator at the First Presbyterian Church of Arlington on Kearny Avenue. The consignment shop sells clothing, appliances, knickknacks, and many other items. Located on the second floor of the church, the store has proved to be a successful contribution to the community. (Photograph by the author.)

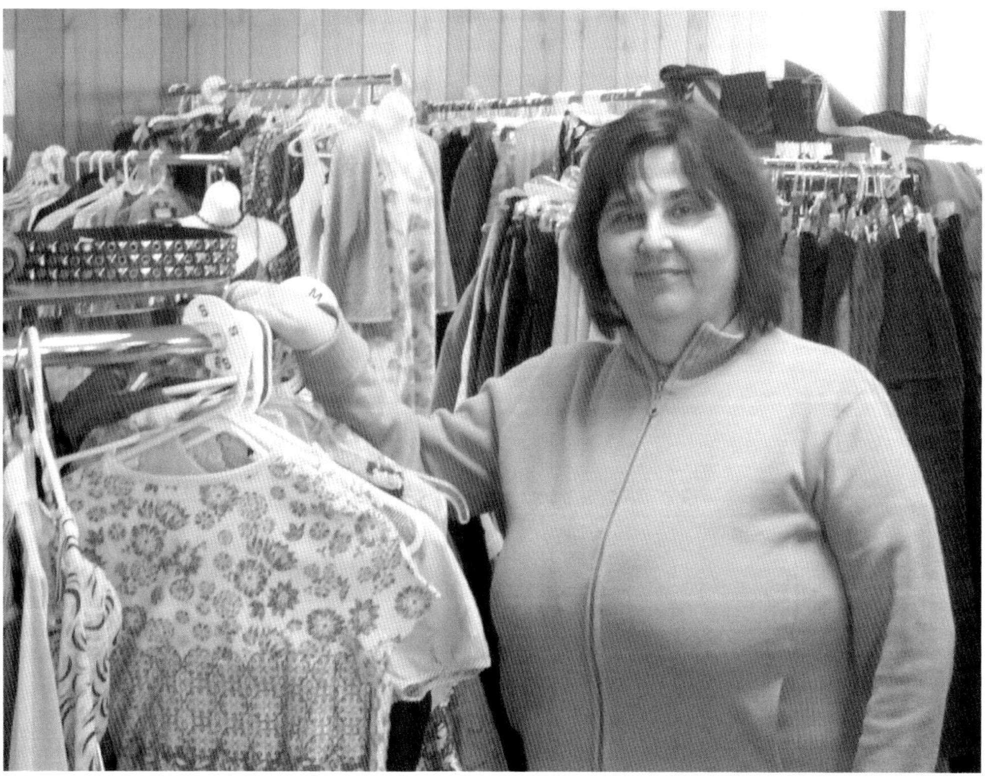

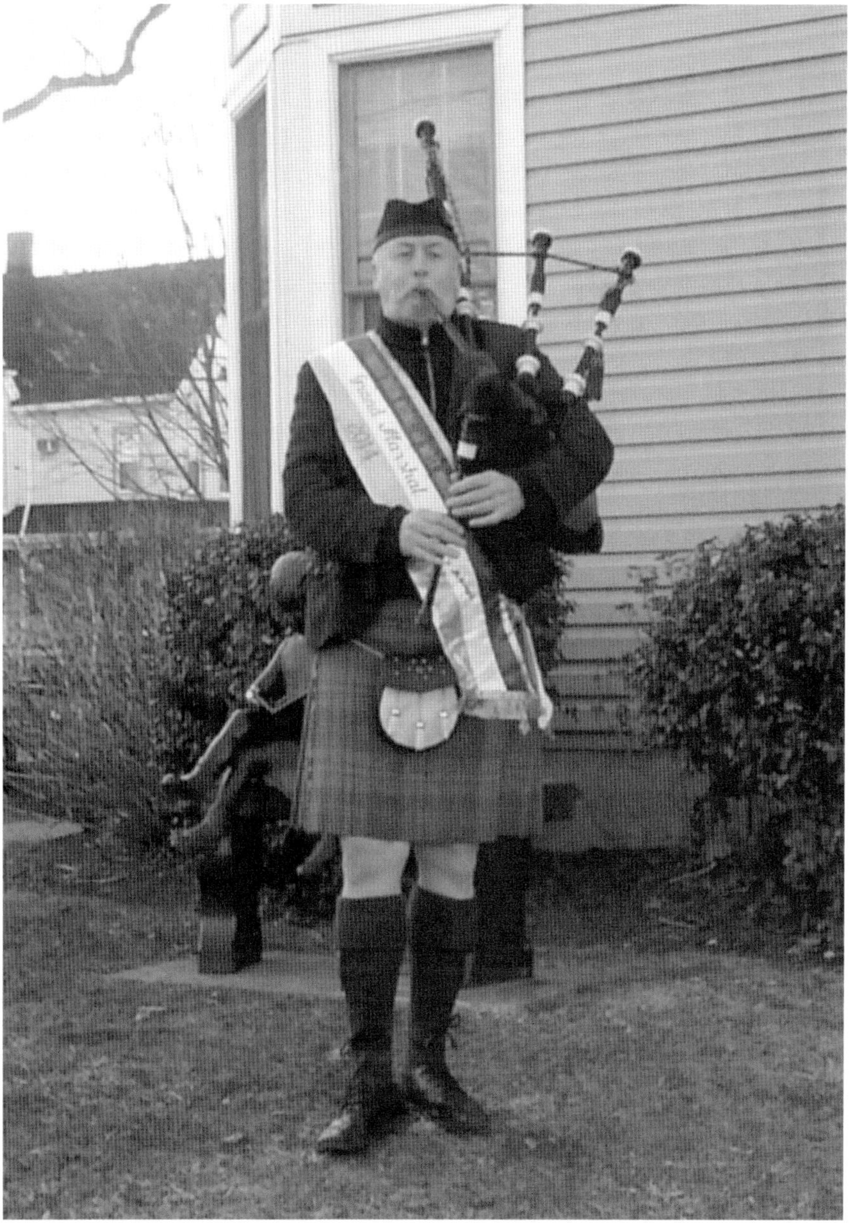

The McGonigal Clan

The name McGonigal has long been associated with Kearny and with piping. Sean McGonigal, born in Glasgow, Scotland, immigrated with his brother and cousin to the United States in 1929 at age 18. He settled in Kearny and opened a sign-painting business. His cousin taught him the pipes. In 1949, McGonigal founded the St. Columcille United Gaelic Pipe Band. During the Kearny Memorial Day Parade in 1965, while leading a junior pipe band (with grandsons Joe and Mike in the first row), McGonigal collapsed and was later pronounced dead at West Hudson Hospital. McGonigal's son J. Patrick took up the duty of pipe major and was a piper for more than 60 years. His children—Joe, Sean, Kevin, Mike, and Maura—have all been involved in piping. Joe is shown here as the 2014 grand marshal of the United Irish Parade. (Courtesy of Carol Hearn Manley.)

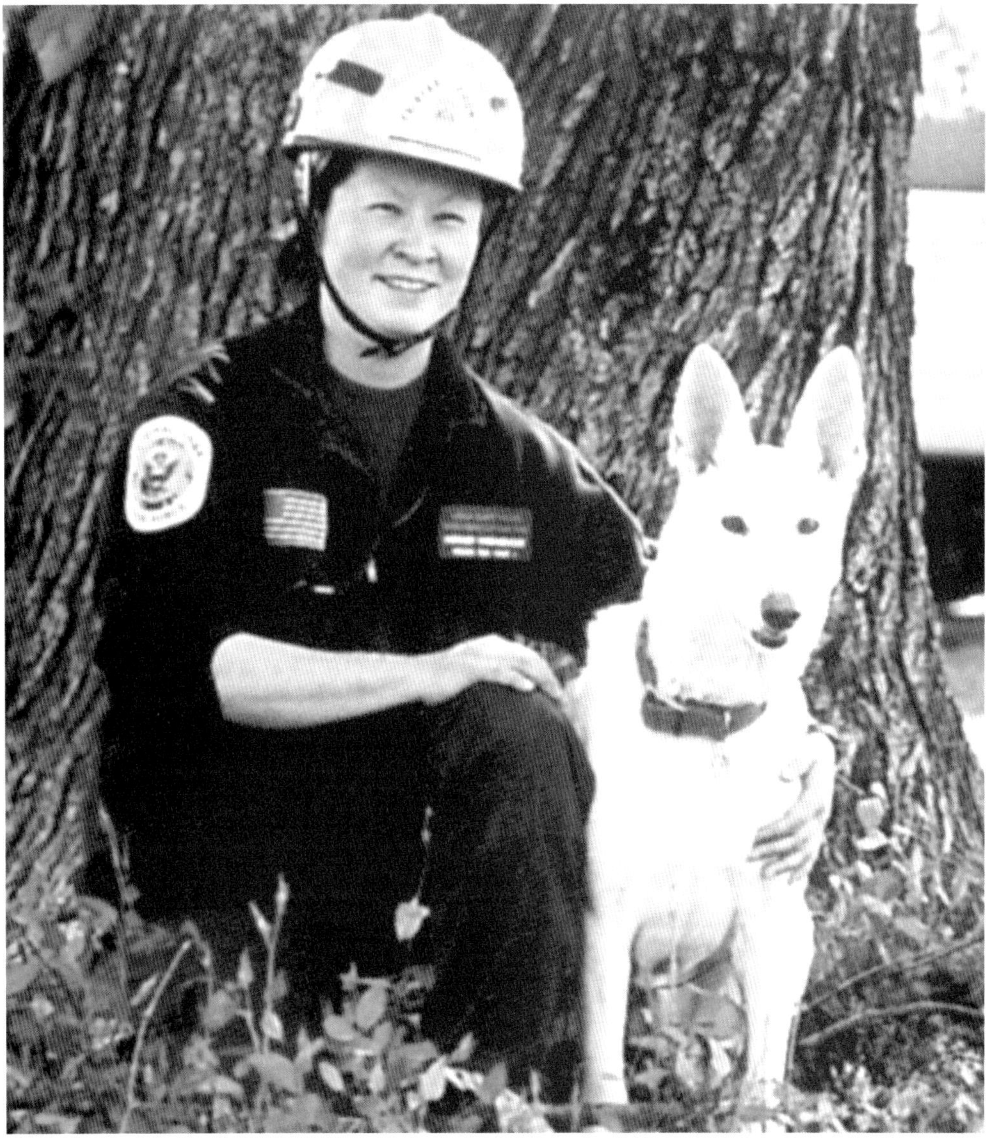

Hideko "Heidi" Yamaguchi, High Standards for Herself and Her Dogs

Heidi Yamaguchi attended Roosevelt School and Lincoln School before graduating from Kearny High School in the class of 1975. She attended the College of William & Mary in Virginia. She found a passion for community service through canine search and rescue. She died of a sudden terminal illness in 2003. Here, she is shown with Fuyu, one of her many dogs. The duo of Yamaguchi and Fuyu was the first certified FEMA team on the East Coast. Her service with Urban Search & Rescue (USAR) began in 1986 with deployment to El Salvador. She also responded to the Oklahoma City bombing, African Embassy bombing, Turkey and Taiwan earthquakes, 9/11 Pentagon attack, and Space Shuttle mission. The Kearny High School class of 1975 established an annual memorial scholarship to be given to a graduating senior with outstanding community service. (Courtesy of the Yamaguchi family.)

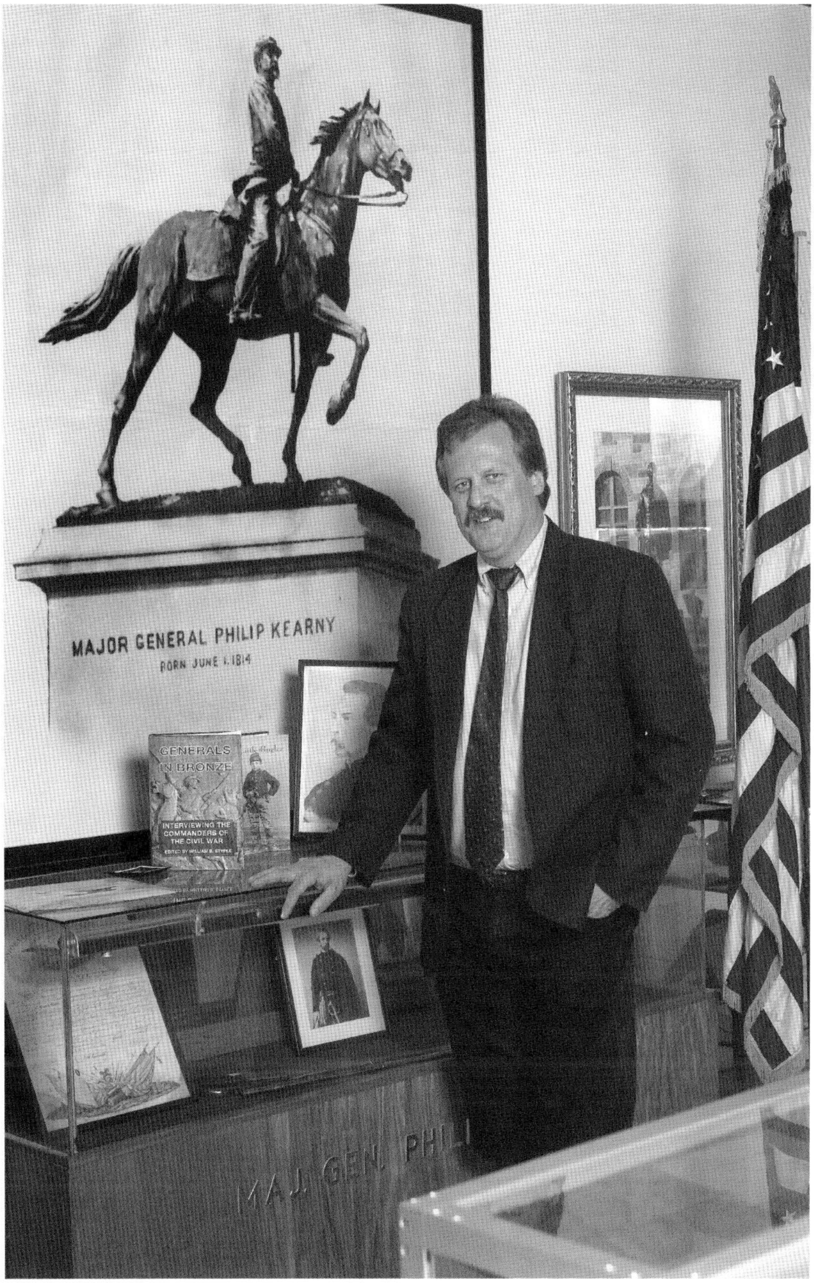

William Styple, the Expert on Phil Kearny

There was good reason for Kearny native Bill Styple to speak at Maj. Gen. Phil Kearny's 200th birthday celebration on June 1, 2015. He is the leading expert on the Town of Kearny's namesake. No stranger to archives and deep research, Styple is the author of more than 20 books about the Civil War, including the award-winning *The Little Bugler.* He graduated from Kearny High School and Catawba College and operates the Belle Grove Publishing Company, named for Kearny's brick chateau. This former town historian is currently at work on a biography of Phil Kearny. He also performs as a Civil War reenactor. (Courtesy of Kearny UEZ.)

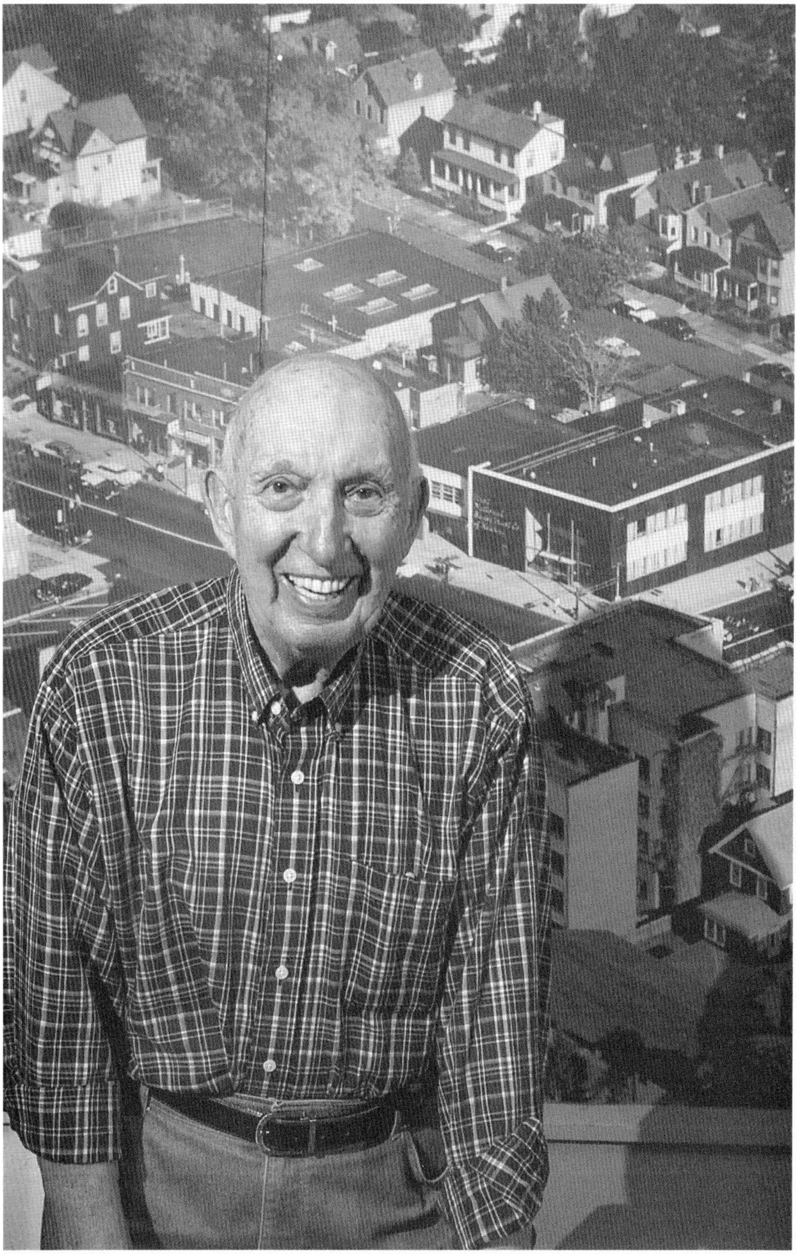

George Rogers, a Town of Kearny Role Model

George Rogers led a long and storied life in Kearny. Born in 1921, he attended McKinley School. In the mid-1940s, he played soccer on the Scots American team. He served as a firefighter and continued his civic service with the Kearny Museum. But his influence was felt beyond the town's history. As a Pioneer Boy leader, he helped hundreds of scouts. Many in the town, both young and old, looked to him for friendship and leadership. Over the course of several months in 2005, he shared his valuable town knowledge with fellow museum committee member Sandra McCleaster. His oral history is available from the Kearny Museum. An official town historian, his passing in 2009 left a huge gap in the town. A memorial plaque in the museum honors his contributions. (Courtesy of Kearny UEZ.)

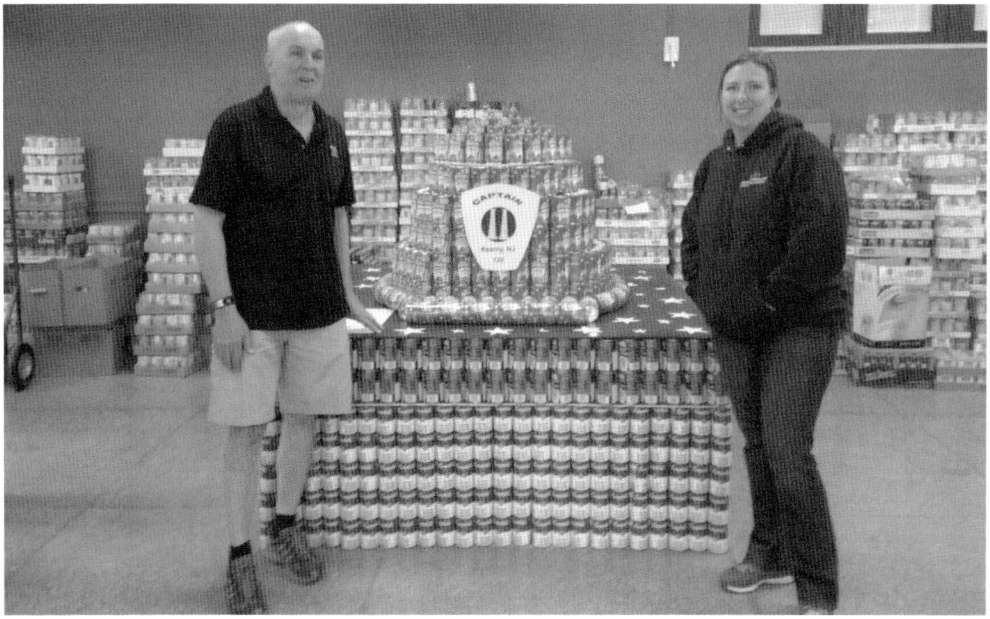

Paul Rogers and His Can-Do Attitude

Paul Rogers followed in father George Rogers's footsteps. After graduating from Kearny High School in 1977, he joined the town's firefighters. Like his father, he saw opportunities to give back to the community. After viewing a New York City exhibit, he was inspired to call Kearny High School and propose a project. His idea was for students to construct canned goods that would be donated to local food banks for distribution to community emergency feeding programs. With sponsoring by a nonprofit group called Canstruction, Rogers's proposal received a green light. The community donated nearly 20,000 cans and about $20,000, much of which was used to buy more canned goods to complete the projects. With one man's vision and a concerned call to his alma mater, Rogers was able to make his dream of feeding the hungry a reality. The year 2015 marked the fourth year of the program. Rogers received an award for his community service from the Salvation Army Kearny Corps. (Courtesy of Eileen Rogers McDonald.)

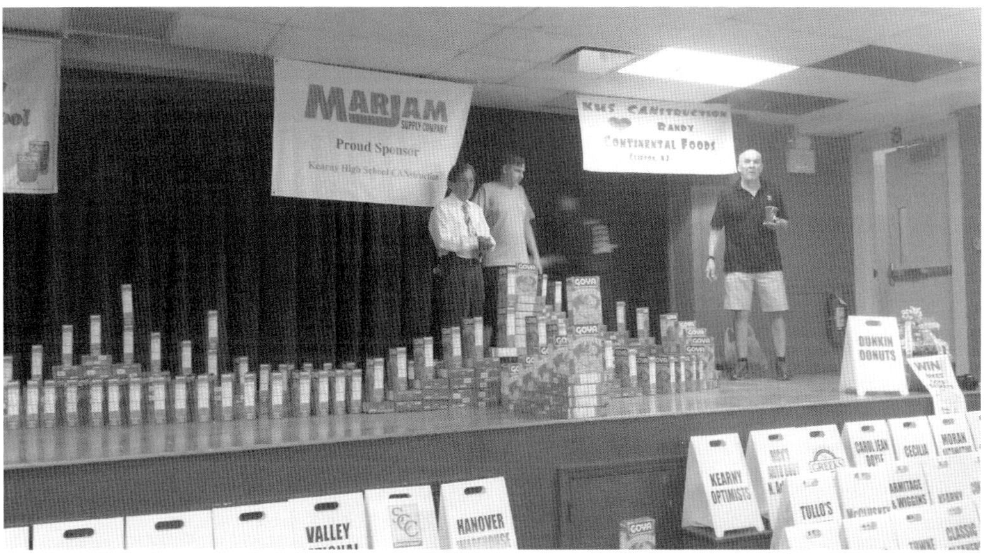

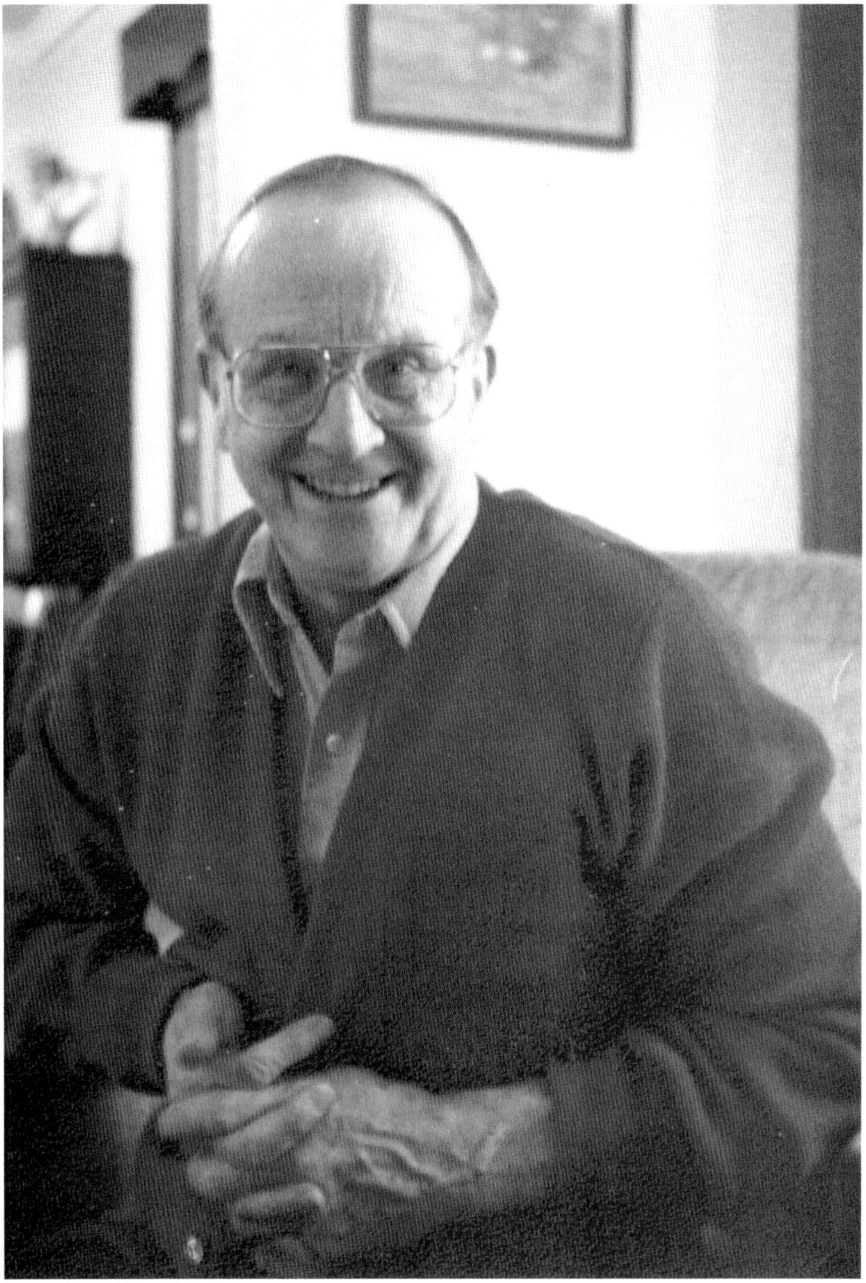

Charlie Waller, Kearny Museum Pioneer

Born in Harrison in 1914 and raised in Kearny, Charlie Waller raised his hand immediately when Jessie Hipp needed help in compiling Kearny's history in preparation for the town's centennial in 1967. Mayor Healey and the town council appointed him to the museum committee for many years. He scheduled volunteers, guided classes through the museum, and helped family historians find their roots. He also lent his own background—captain of Kearny High School's 1933 state championship soccer team and the 1935 baseball team as well as years playing semiprofessional soccer and baseball—to exhibits in the Kearny Library. He passed away in 2006. (Photograph by Susan Lignowski, courtesy of Nancy Branin Waller.)

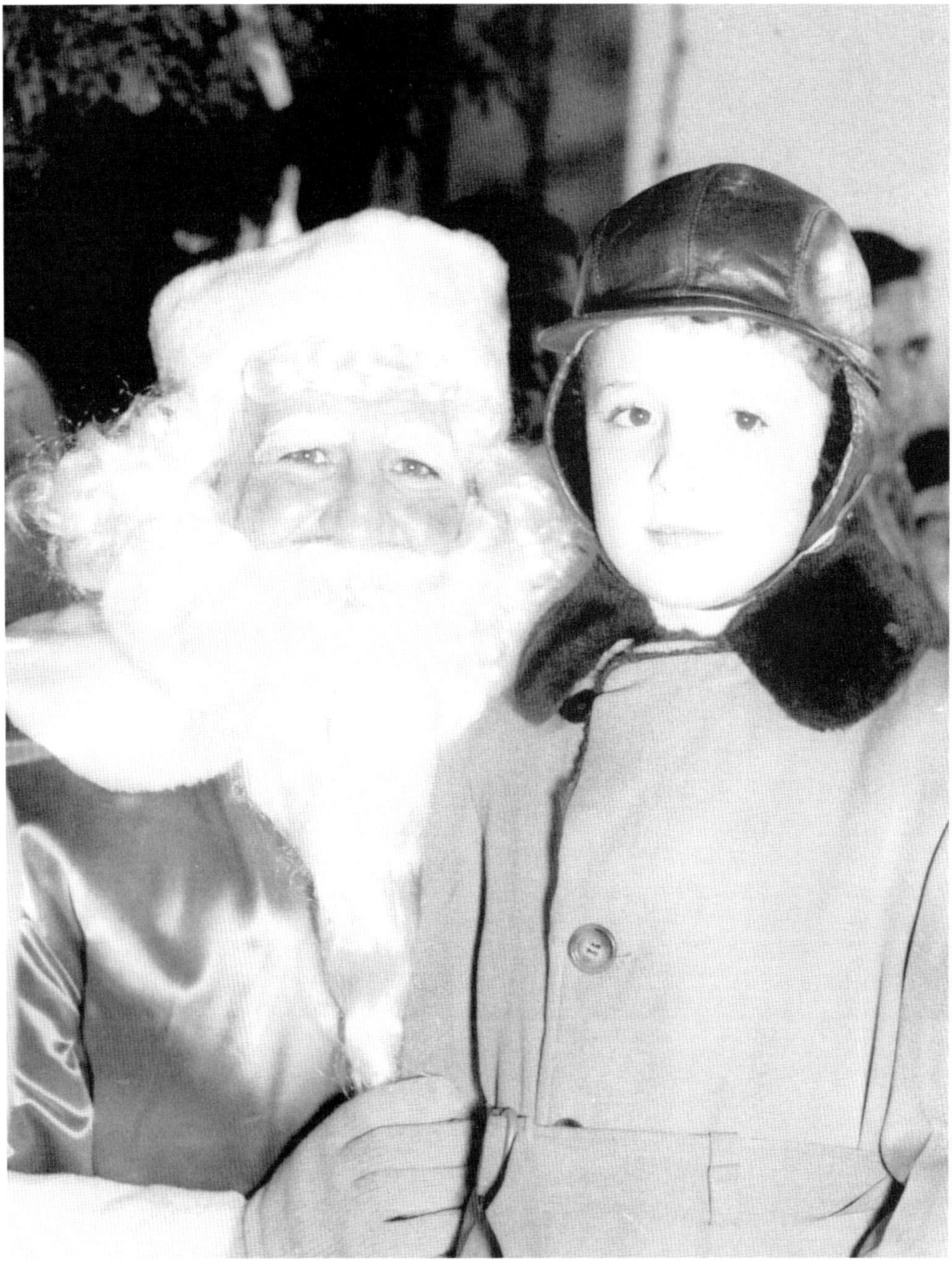

Joel Harrison, the Unlikely Santa
Insurance broker Joel Harrison was a beloved Santa Claus at Christmastime. But he made for an unlikely Santa. Harrison was the son of Jewish immigrants from Russia and England. He was a member of Mayor Healey's Kearny Civic Committee of leading businesspeople. Harrison served as Santa for many years, arriving by train at Arlington Station and then touring the town in a convertible. When he reached town hall, he distributed stockings and fruit. He is shown here with Jay Healey, one of the mayor's sons, around 1967. Born in New York in 1911, Harrison passed away in 1989. (Courtesy of Kearny Museum.)

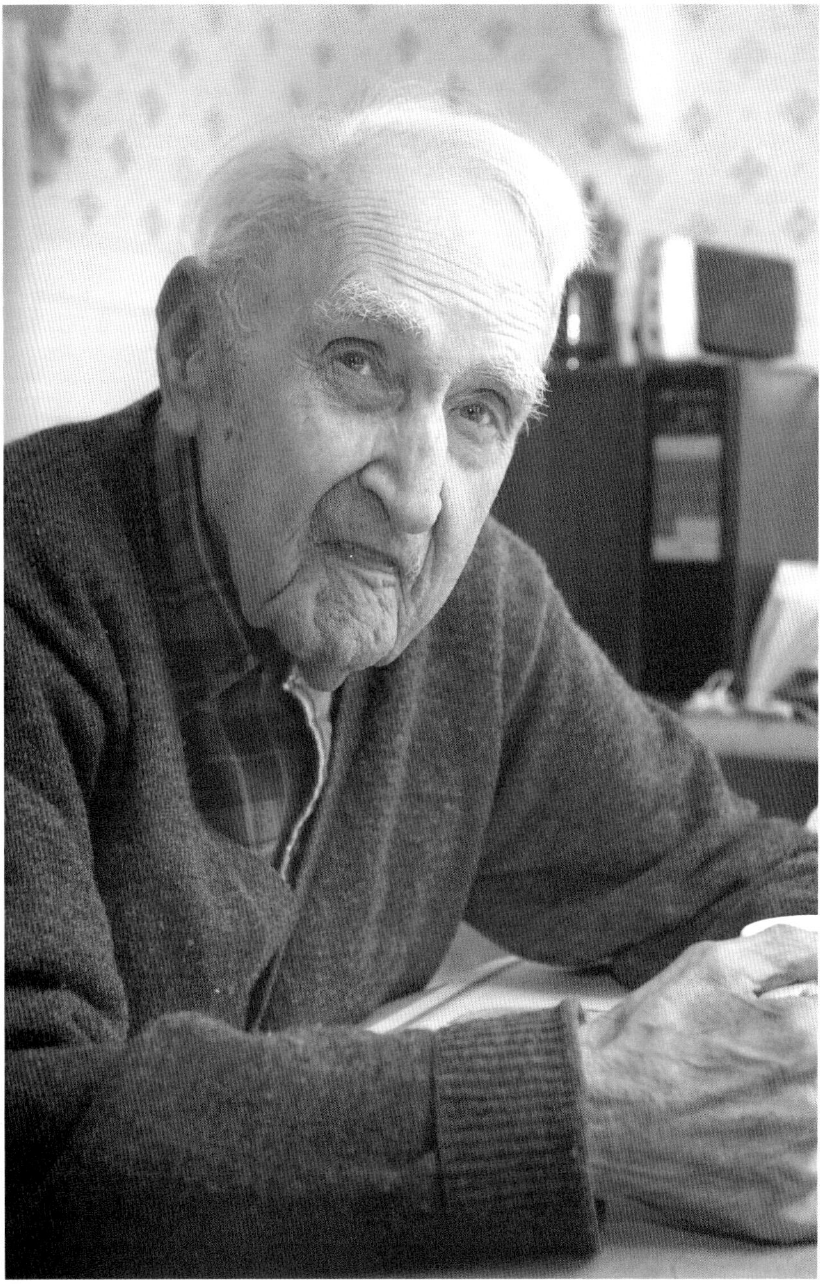

Robert Watson Built a Long Life

In 2005, Kearny resident Robert Watson turned 100. He moved to Kearny from Jersey City around 1917. He worked for his father, building homes for $1 a day, when he was 15. He owned and operated R. Watson, Mason & Builders until he was 75. He recalled that cows roamed throughout the neighborhoods where many roads were not yet paved. Watson was a building contractor and lived in the house he built until he was brought to Clara Maas in November 2008. He was involved in Trinity Church and Knox Presbyterian project and was a member of the Copestone-Ophir Lodge No. 108 of Freemasons. He passed away in December 2008 at the age of 103. (Courtesy of Kearny UEZ.)

Monsignor Carroll of St. Cecilia's

Msgr. Joseph A. Carroll was born in 1904 in Elizabeth to Irish immigrants. He graduated from Seton Hall University, entered Immaculate Conception in Darlington, and was ordained in 1931. He was appointed assistant at St. Bridget's in Jersey City, where he served until 1937. That same year, he was sent to assist the pastor at Our Lady of the Valley in Orange and four years later to St. Catherine in Hillside. He then arrived as pastor at St. Cecilia's in 1956. During his time at St. Cecilia's, he saw to the upkeep of the church, the elementary school, the high school, the rectory, and the convent. He passed away in 1996. Irish Heritage Park, a section of Riverbank Park, is dedicated to his memory. (Courtesy of St. Cecilia's Church.)

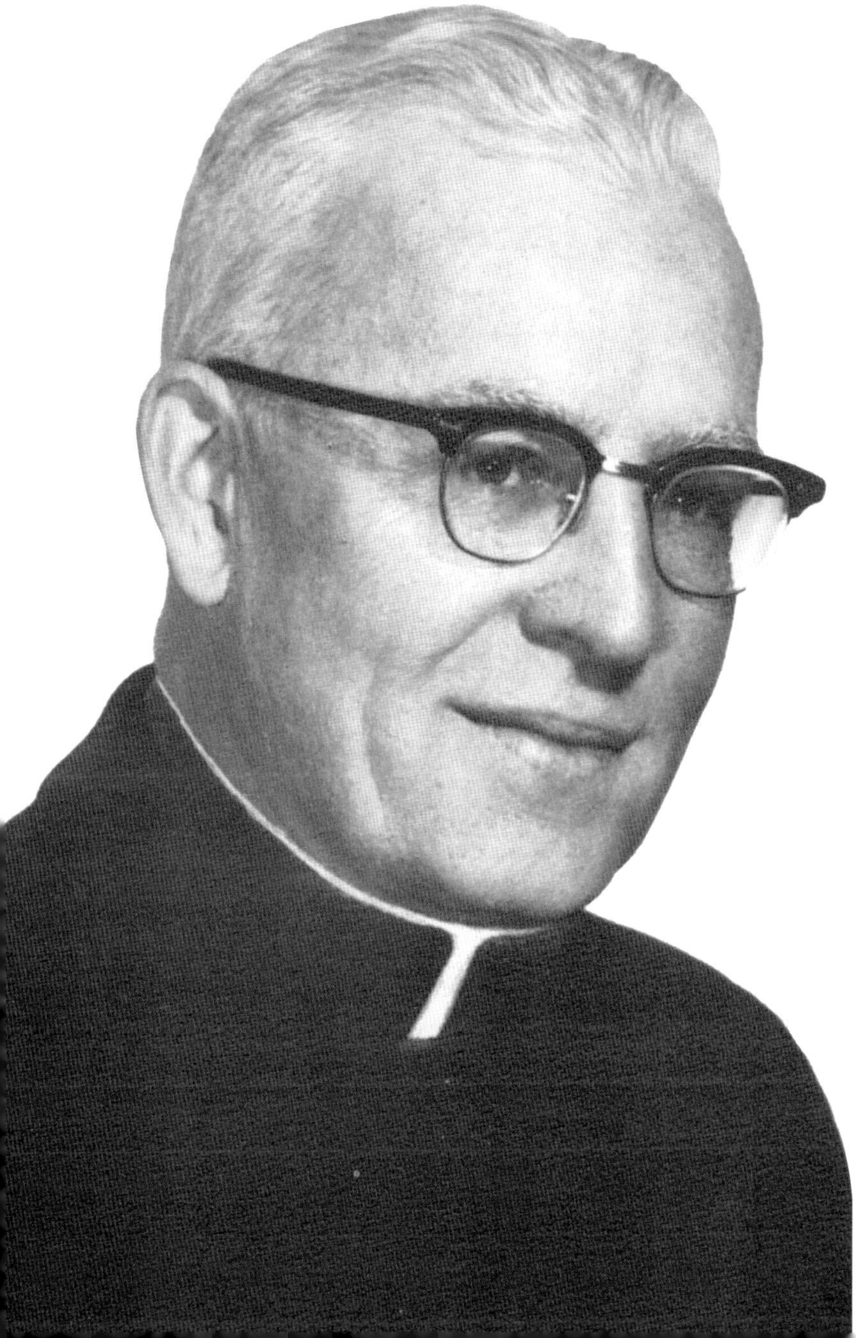

Rabbi Sidney Bogner of Congregation B'nai Israel

Sidney M. Bogner served as the spiritual leader of Congregation B'nai Israel, serving Kearny and North Arlington from 1958 to 1974. He was born in 1909 in New York to an Austrian rabbinical family. During World War II, he served as chaplain at Fort Jay on Governor's Island. Before coming to Kearny, Rabbi Bogner served congregations in Daytona Beach and New York City from 1938 to 1958. He was active in many organizations, including the New Jersey Board of Rabbis. He was one of the Kearny clergy, along with Rev. Blackwell and Msgr. Carroll at the first citywide ecumenical service at St. Cecilia's. He served as chaplain for the fire and police departments, the Civil Air Patrol, and several hospitals. In retirement, he taught at Essex County College as an adjunct professor of history, philosophy, and religion. He died in 1986. (Courtesy of Jewish Historical Society of New Jersey.)

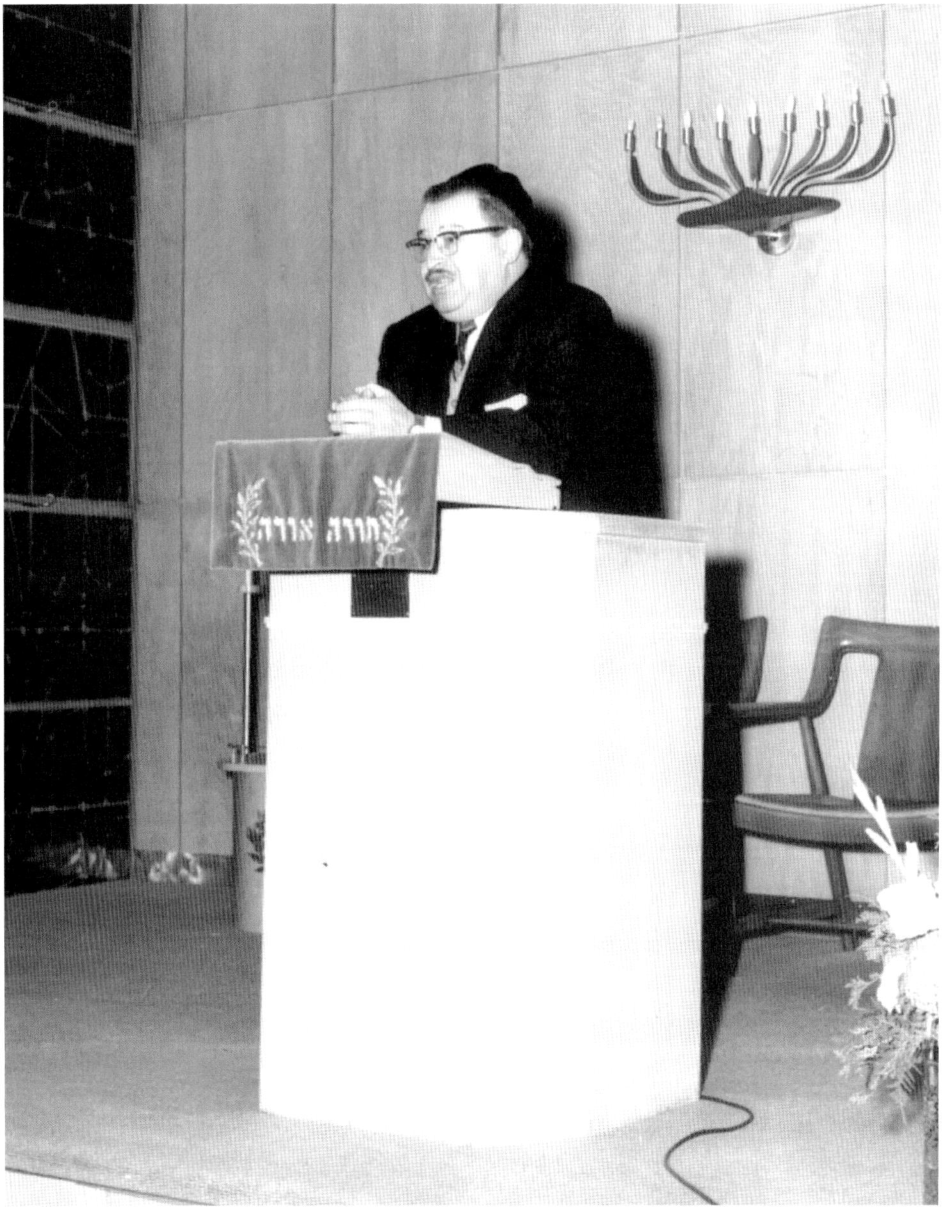

Rev. Robert L. Blackwell of First Presbyterian Church

Rev. Robert L. Blackwell served as minister of the First Presbyterian Church for 33 years. He was born in Scranton, Pennsylvania, in 1929. After graduating from Lafayette College in 1951 with majors in English literature and Greek, he enrolled at Princeton Theological Seminary, earning first a bachelor of divinity degree in 1954 and ultimately master of theology degree in 1962. In between, he was ordained in 1954 as a minister of the Presbyterian Church. While no members of his family were ministers, Blackwell grew up in an environment of active Presbyterian church involvement. His list of accomplishments is long and varied, inside and outside the church. Some include serving as chaplain for the Scots American Club, the Irish American Club, the Ulster Club, and the Kearny Fire Department. He put innovative programs in place at First Presbyterian. He retired in 1997. (Courtesy of Robert L. Blackwell.)

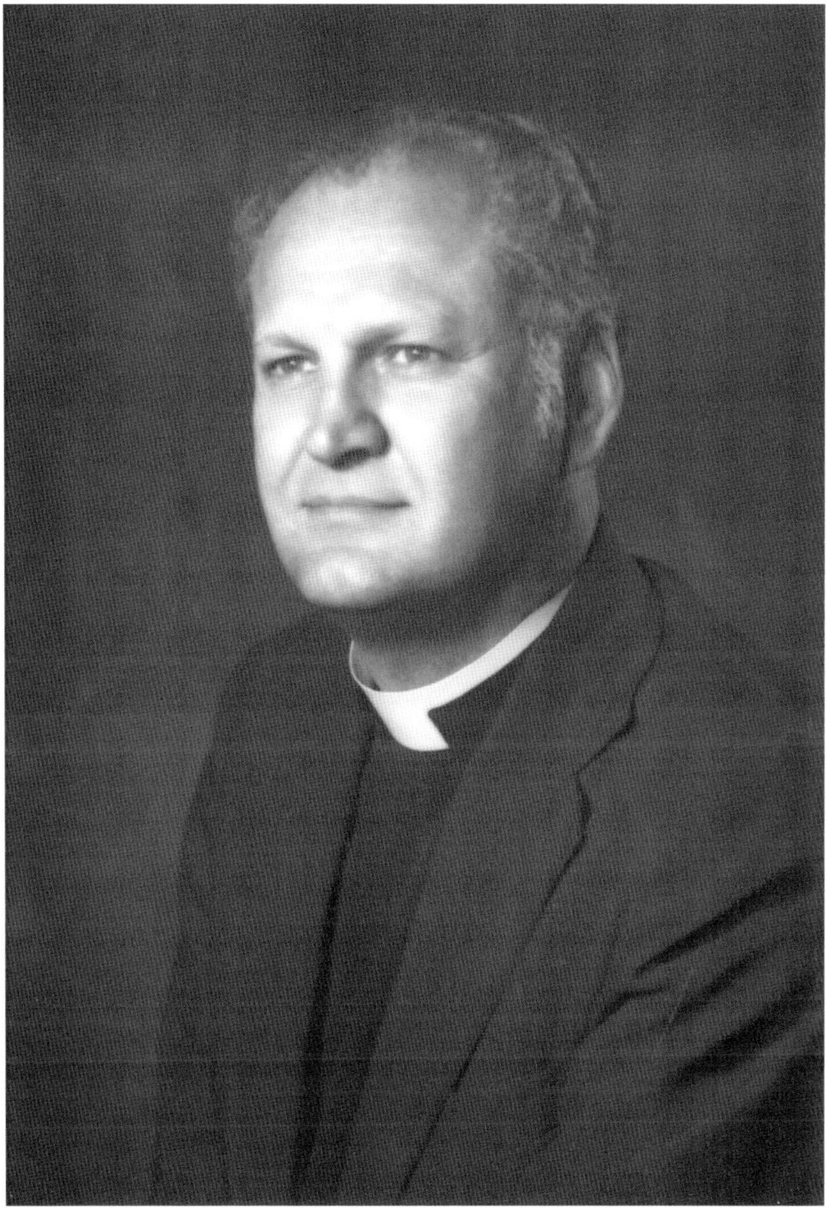

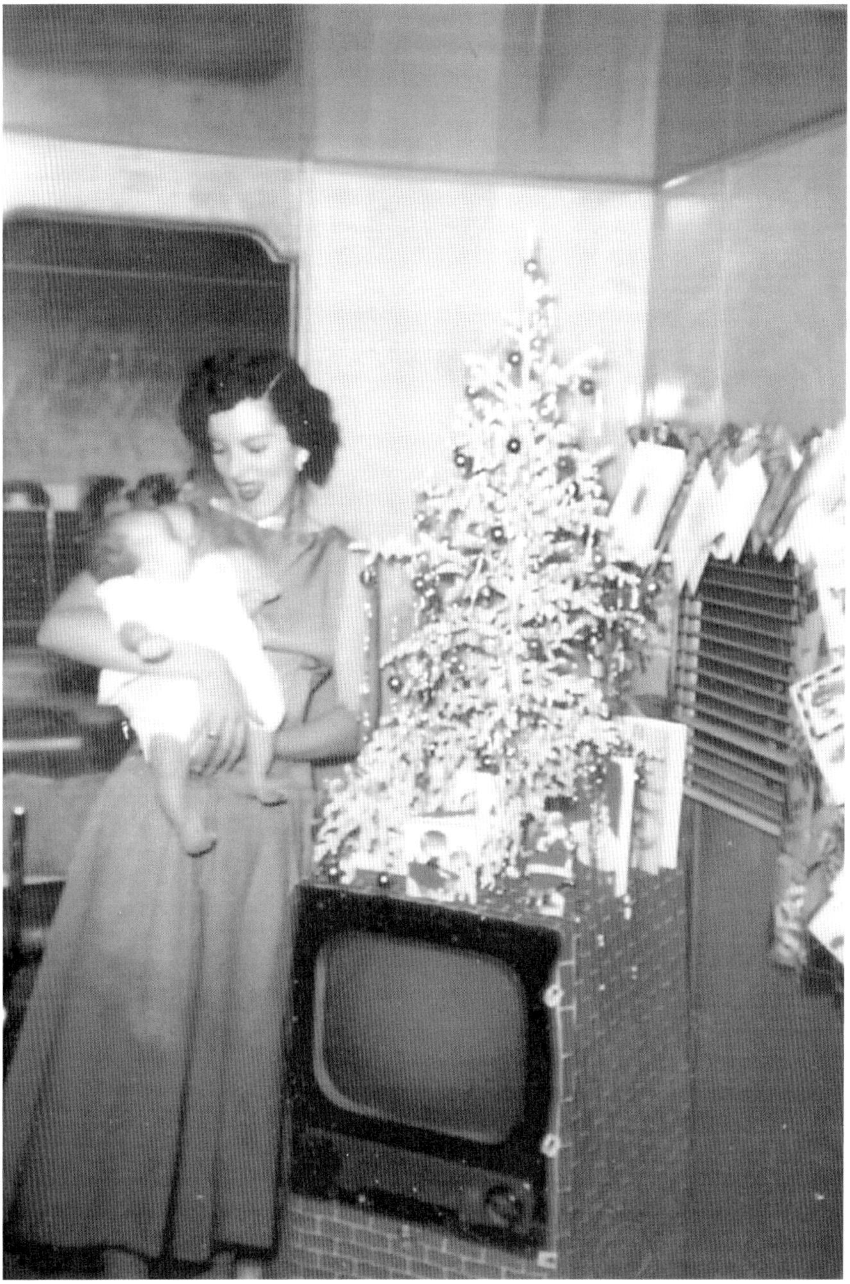

Eleanor Flavell, a Well-Loved Loving Woman

Eleanor Meikle Flavell was born in 1934 at West Hudson Hospital. She met her husband, Herb, by chance in 1953 during a traffic jam on Route 3 in Rutherford. They married the following year. The Flavells had three daughters and lost four boys to miscarriage. Eleanor opened her home as a foster mother for the state of New Jersey from 1965 until the mid-1970s, when the Flavells adopted two mentally-impaired sons in 1973 and 1976, to whom Eleanor devoted her time. She was a proud president of the New Jersey State Auxiliary of the National Association of Letter Carriers. She passed away in 2012 and is sorely missed. (Courtesy of Herbert Flavell.)

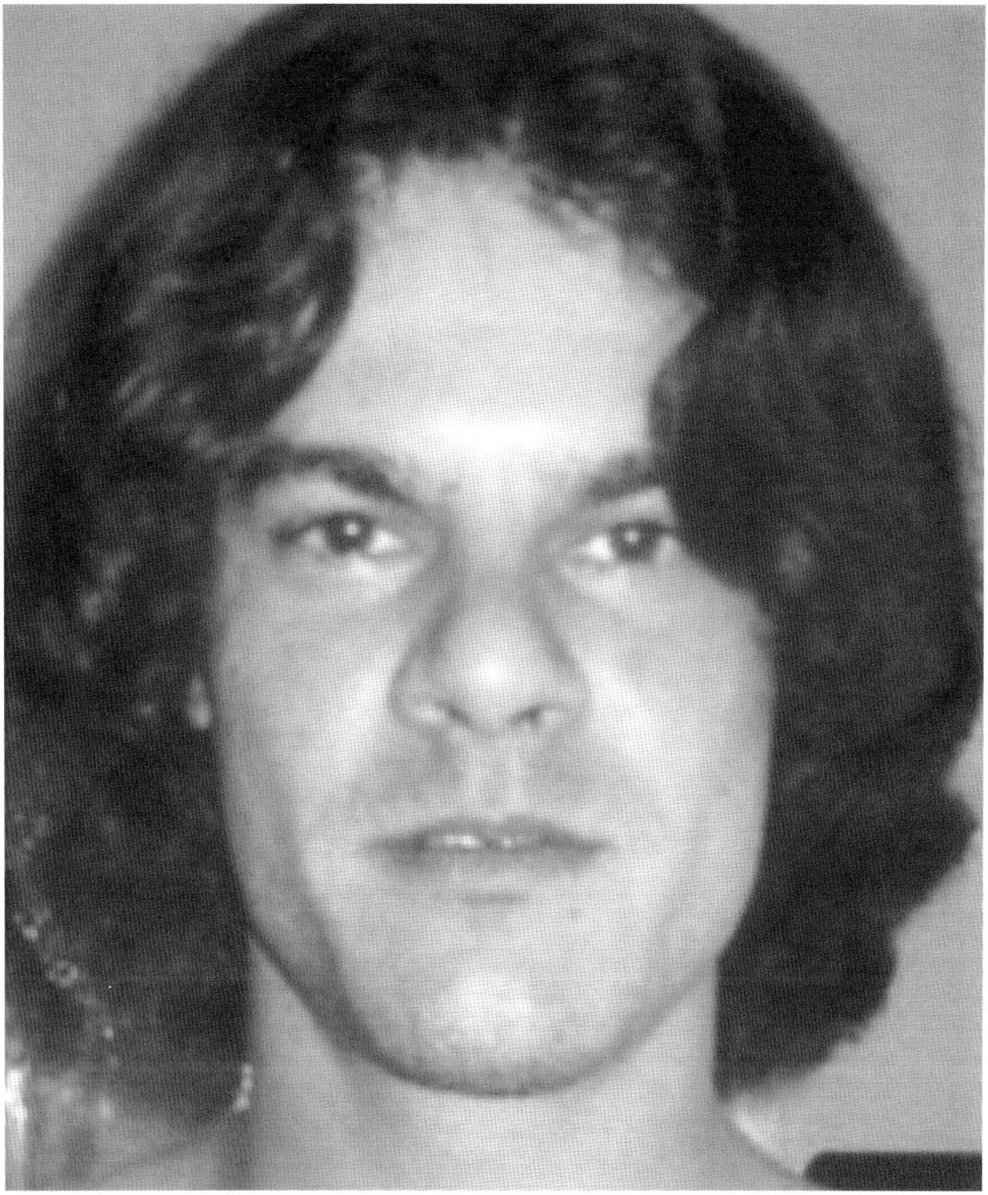

Albert Gonzalez, Master Hacker

In 2010, Albert Gonzalez was convicted and sentenced to 20 years in federal prison for leading a group of cyber thieves in stealing more than 90 million credit card numbers from retailers. Born in 1981 in Cuba, he lived in Florida and New York before moving to Kearny in 2000. Even at age 14, he was able to hack into NASA computers. While in Kearny, he was accused of masterminding a group of hackers who trafficked in credit card numbers. He has been called the "most cunning cyber crook in American history" by CNBC's *American Greed.* He moved seamlessly between fraud and innocence. He hacked into a New Jersey–based Internet company and then persuaded that company to hire him as security. He became an informant for the Secret Service. But, in the end, he deluded them all until his arrest. (Courtesy of SIPA.)

Alexandrina "Rena" Webster

The mother of football greats Alex and James Webster, Alexandrina Webster worked at Congoleum Nairn, the linoleum company. She was originally from Glasgow, Scotland, born in 1902, and immigrated in 1910 aboard the SS *California* with her sisters and parents. She married fellow Glaswegian James Webster in 1929 in Kearny. She is shown below around 1928 in a group photograph of company workers and on the next page in a family photograph from 1927. From left to right are (first row) Tom Glen and Annie Glen; (second row) James Webster, Rena Webster, Annie Webster, Glen, Alexander Webster, Cissie Webster, and Annie Webster. All the adults were born in Scotland, and all the children were born in Kearny. Widowed in 1941, she passed away in 1992 in Bricktown. (Courtesy of Mark Webster.)

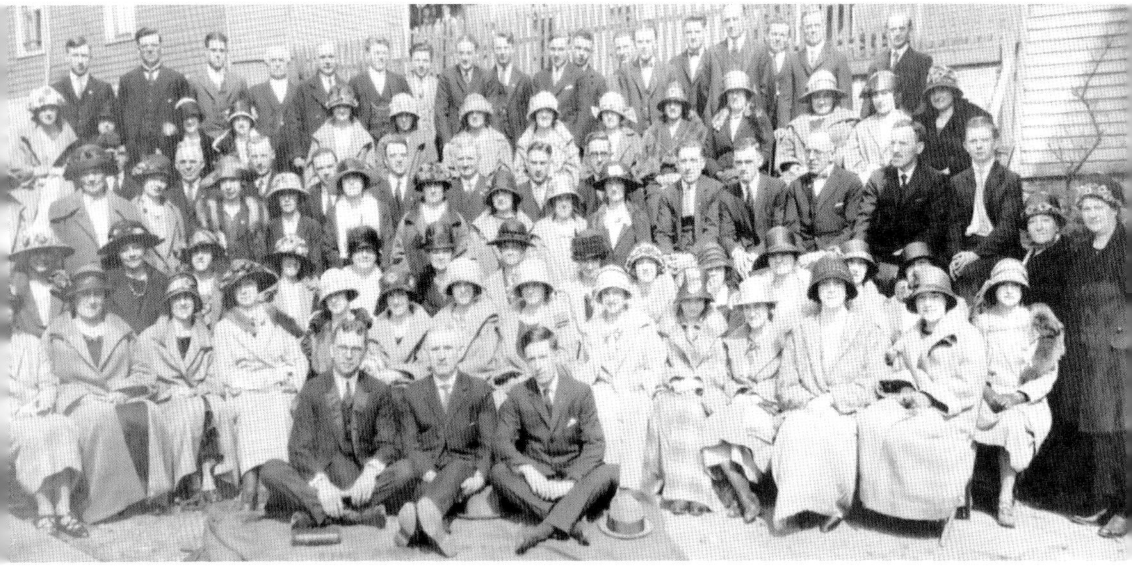

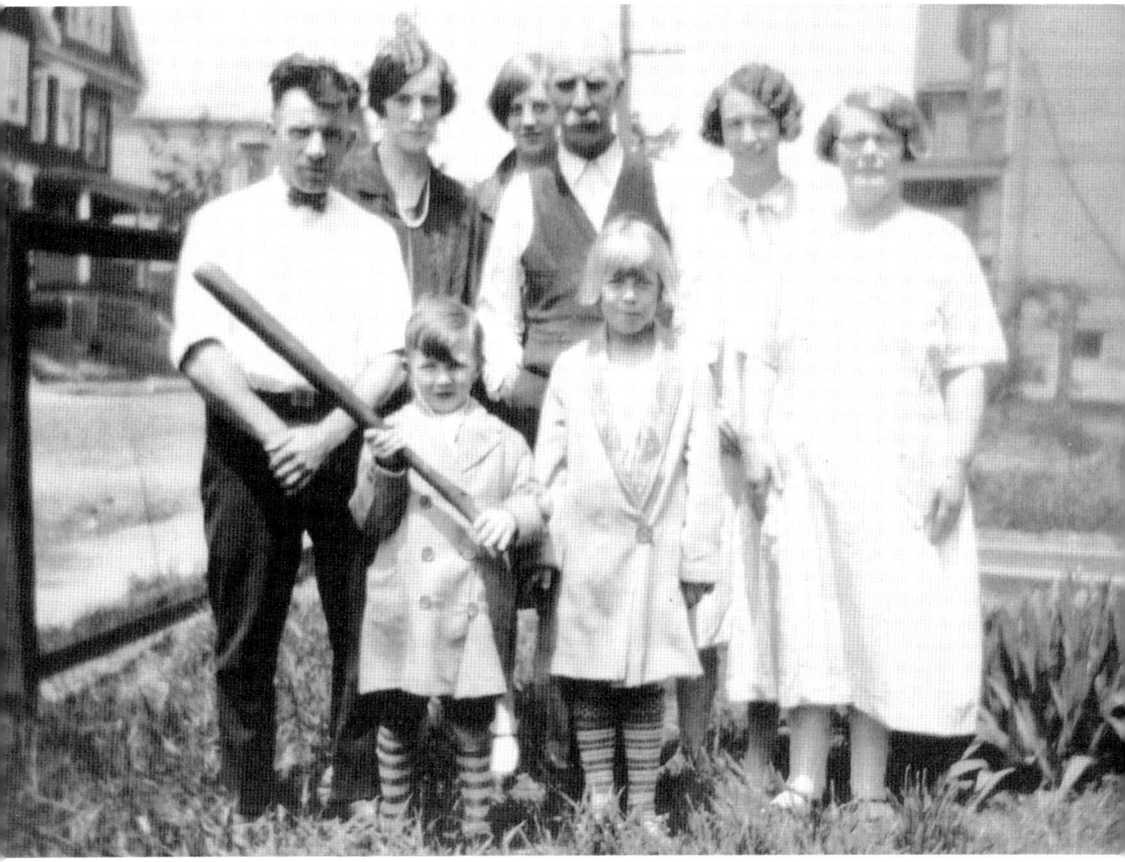

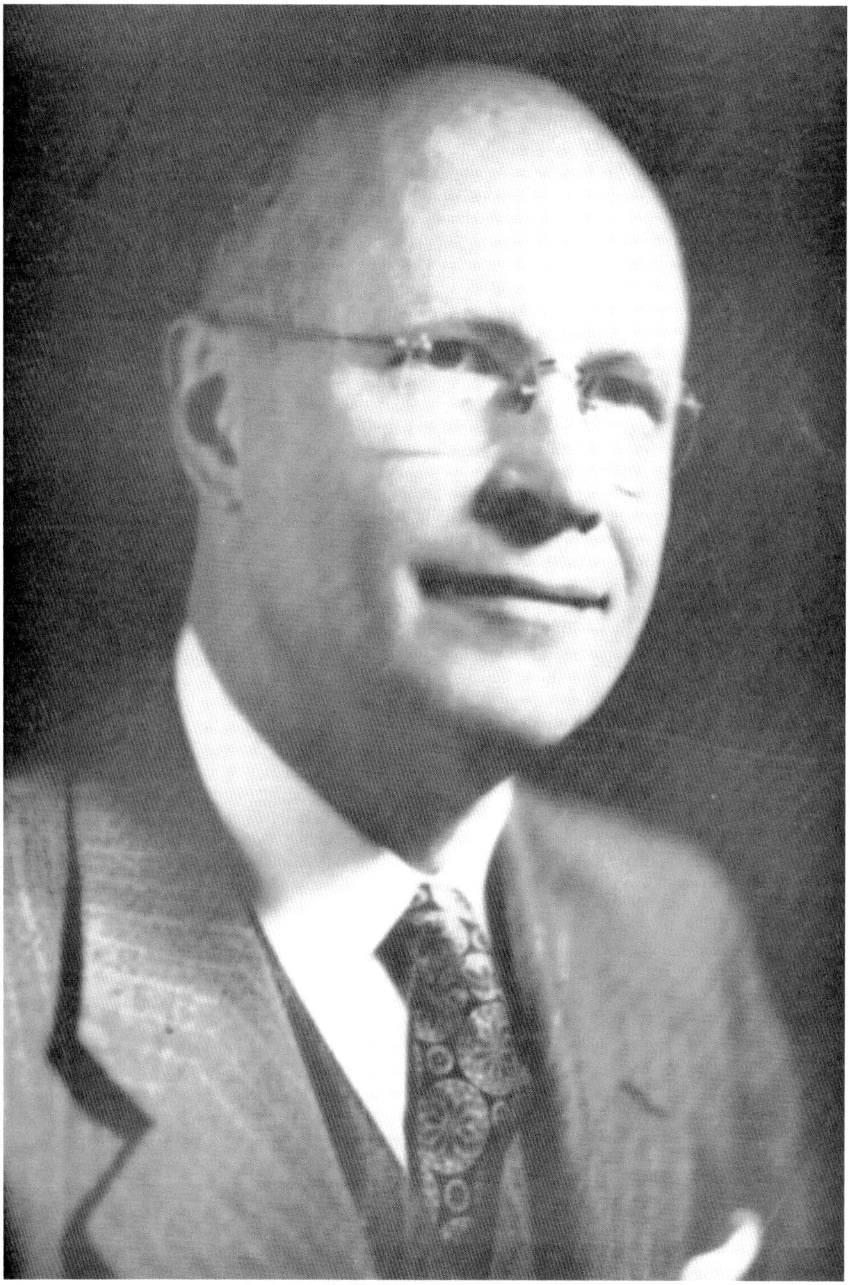

Kenneth Pfleger, Two Lives

Electrical engineer Kenneth Warner Pfleger filed 36 patents. Born in 1899, he lived on Alpine Place, and after earning his bachelor's and master's degrees in engineering at Cornell University, he worked at American Telephone and Telegraph in New York City. He is perhaps best remembered as a charter member and chairman of the Presbyterian Boys Club (PBC), founded in 1909. He served as chairman of the PBC board of directors from 1923 to 1930. He particularly enjoyed summers with the PBC at Kamp Kiamesha, where he practiced his skill for practical jokes on the boys. He had a zest for life. He passed in 1965. (Courtesy of Kearny Museum.)

Charles Joseph Dolan, Community Volunteer Extraordinaire

Chalie Dolan had it tough as a kid. His parents were divorced, and his grandmother took care of him while his mother worked hard to provide for the family. He became best friends with neighbor Jack McDonald, who at seven years old than him, would give him piggyback rides when he came home from school. Dolan had a natural ability for soccer, basketball, and baseball and held many records at St. Cecilia's High School in all three sports. He earned a Lifetime Achievement Award from the Salvation Army and was involved with West Hudson Hospital, St. Barnabas Health, and Clara Maass Medical Center. He volunteered at Kearny High School, helping with the basketball team for many years. He has been married to Jo-Ann Foster for more than 57 years. (Courtesy of Bernadette Dolan Jerry.)

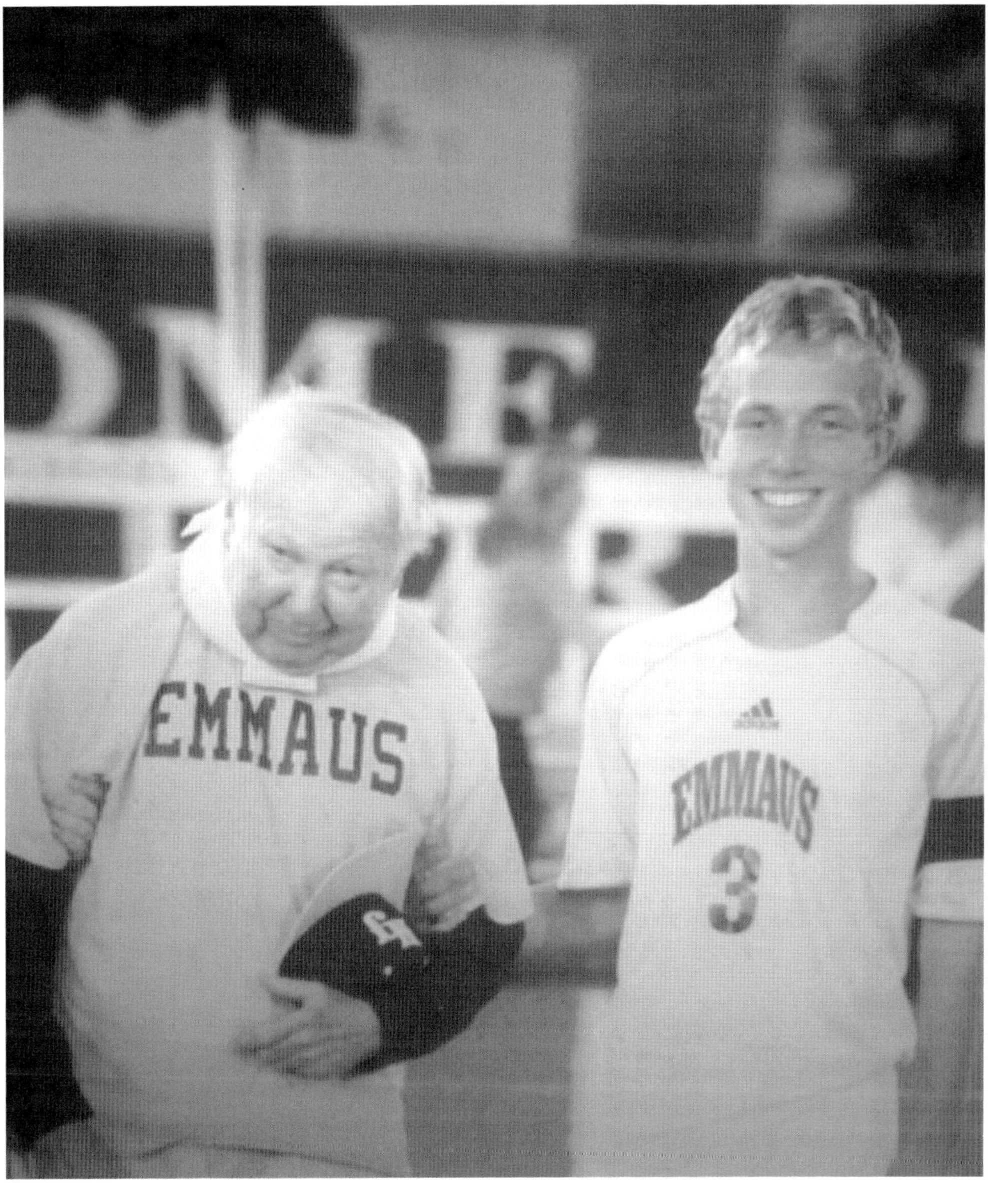

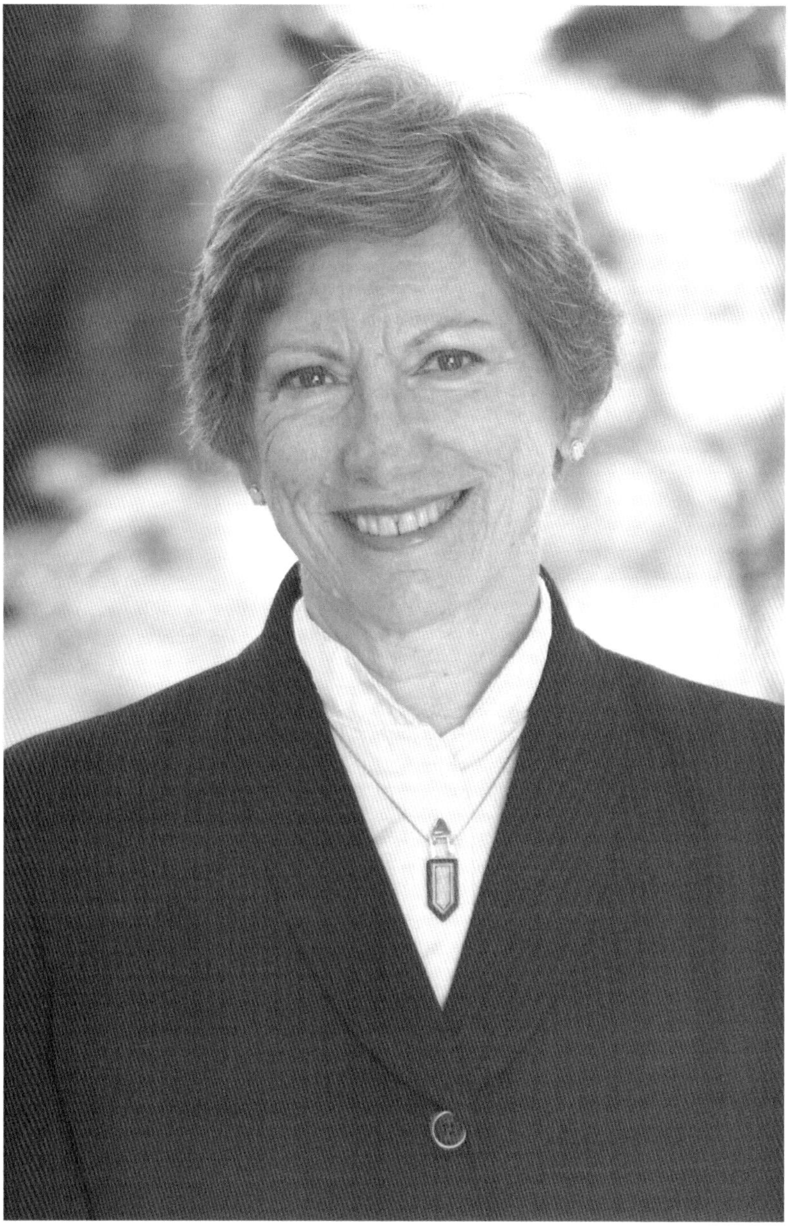

Donna Caputo Shandle, Navy Engineer
While a sophomore at Kearny High School, Donna Caputo read *Women in Engineering* for a book report. It sparked her interest. However, few universities accepted women into engineering programs in 1967. Caputo entered Douglass College, the women's college of Rutgers University. She was one of the first two women to graduate from the Department of Chemical Engineering in 1971. Caputo spent more than 38 years as a civil servant with the Department of Defense, earning the moniker "Miss Test and Evaluation." She was often the first or the only female on her assignments, which included test director of the Aberdeen Proving Ground in Maryland, project manager for emergency preparedness in eight states, service team leader to view equipment from East Germany after the fall of the Berlin Wall, and member of an Army technical team to Japan. (Courtesy of Donna Caputo Shandle.)

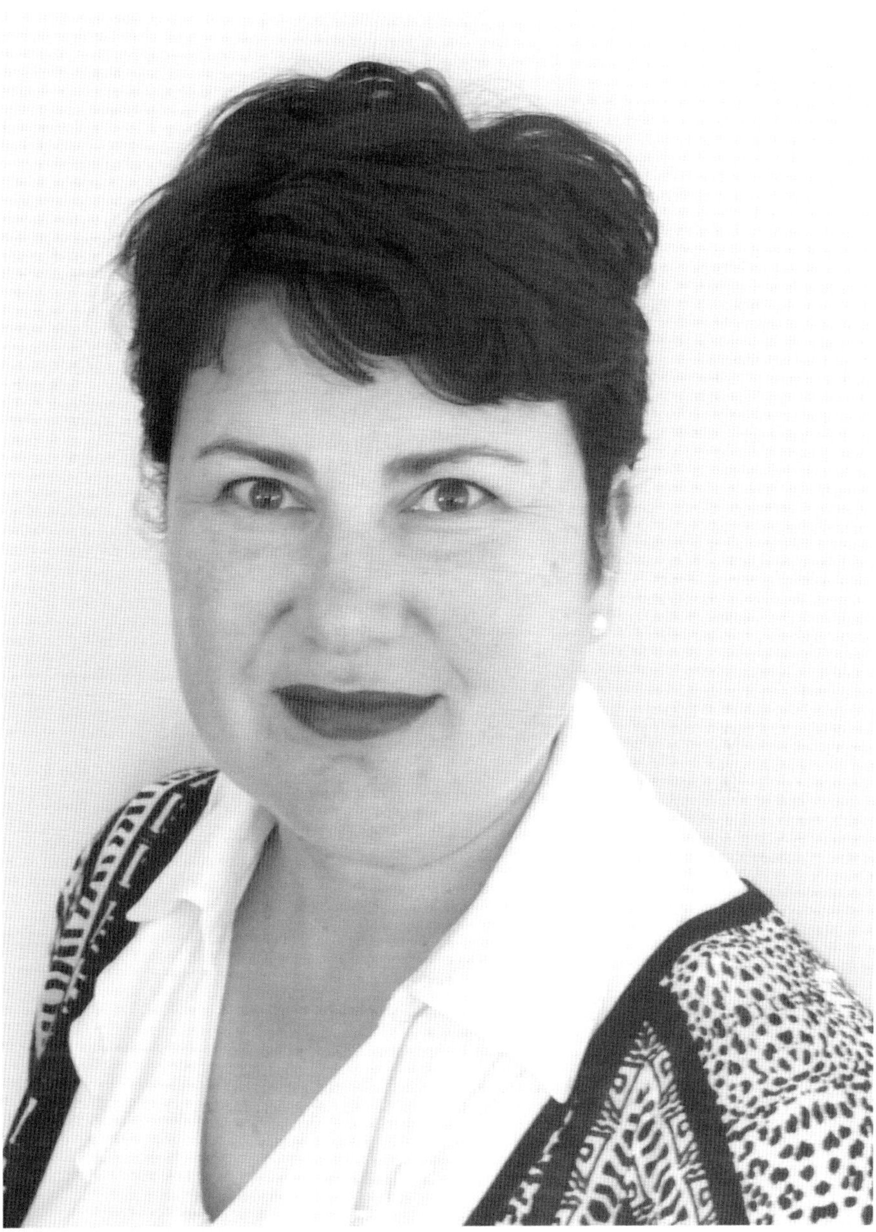

Christine Jablonski, the Consummate Volunteer
Christine Ferrie Jablonski of Belgrove Drive has been proud to call Kearny home for the last 19 years. When she moved to Kearny, Jablonski set out to become involved in the local community. In 2001, she attended her first Junior Woman's Club, following in the tradition of her husband's family. In 2008, she also became active in the Arlington Women's Club and that club's membership department. She serves as president and seeks to document the history of the club. She has represented Kearny's women's clubs at the state, national, and international levels. But Jablonski's commitment to the community does not end there. She is a board member of Friends of the Kearny Library and is active in the Boy Scouts and PTA, among other organizations. Her husband is Jeff Jablonski, a former attorney at Gillespie, Gillespie & Jablonski and now a superior court judge. (Courtesy of Christine Jablonski.)

INDEX

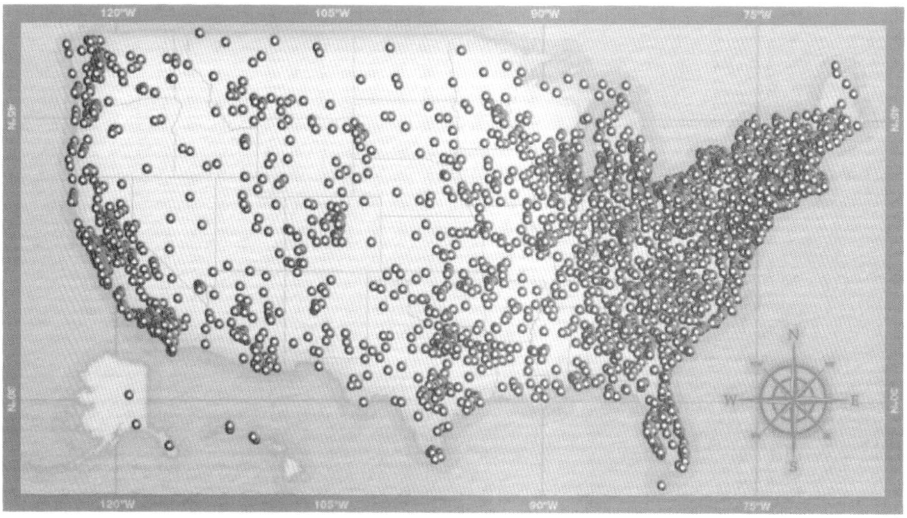

Consistent with our mission to preserve history on a local level, this book was printed in South Carolina on American-made paper and manufactured entirely in the United States. Products carrying the accredited Forest Stewardship Council (FSC) label are printed on 100 percent FSC-certified paper.

MADE IN THE USA